D0432721

SECOND CHANCE

SECOND CHANCE

THE AUTOBIOGRAPHY

MARK TODD

with Kate Green

© Mark Todd 2012

The right of Mark Todd to be identified as the author of
this work has been asserted in accordance with the
Copyright, Designs and Patents Act 1988.

First published in Great Britain in 2012 by Orion Books
An imprint of the Orion Publishing Group Ltd
Orion House, 5 Upper St Martin's Lane,
London, WC2H 9EA
An Hachette Livre Company

1 3 5 7 9 10 8 6 4 2

A CIP catalogue record for this book
is available from the British Library.

ISBN-HB 13 978 1 4091 4319 2
TPB-978 1 4091 4320 8

Designed in Sabon by Geoff Green Book Design, Cambridge

Printed in Great Britain by CPI Group (UK) Ltd, Croydon, CR0 4YY

The Orion Publishing Group's policy is to use papers that are natural, renewable
and recyclable products and made from wood grown in sustainable forests. The logging
and manufacturing processes are expected to conform to the environmental regulations
of the country of origin.

www.orionbooks.co.uk

To Lauren and James

There has never been a comeback like this. Amid scenes of universal rejoicing, Mark Todd, 55, who returned to eventing in 2007 after a seven-year 'retirement', completed a clear round with NZB Land Vision to win his fourth Badminton Horse Trials.

(Jenny MacArthur, The Times, 26th April, 2011)

All this would be wonderful enough at any time, but here is Todd doing it at 55, his competitive nerve still intact, his skills still intact, his sheer physical courage undented ... Todd has demolished every accepted truth of his sport ...

(Simon Barnes, The Times, 26th April, 2011)

Is it the greatest sporting comeback of all time? It was 1980 when Mark Todd first won Badminton. Yesterday, the New Zealand horseman nonchalantly pulled off another victory, his fourth, 31 years later, at the elegant age of 55 – making him not only the oldest champion, but one of the most remarkable masters of the sport whose governing body has named him their greatest rider of the 20th century ... There is something doubly triumphant about a sportsman who brushes aside the years to show himself still at the height of his game ...

(Leader, The Times, 26th April, 2011)

Mark Todd was voted Rider of the 20th Century when he retired with a bronze medal at the Sydney Olympics, but the 55-year-old is still running rings around riders of the 21st ... Todd was tearful as the enormity of his achievement began to register. 'I was relaxed beforehand but I had always had a feeling this would be "my" Badminton,' he said.

(Pippa Cuckson, *The Daily Telegraph*, 26th April, 2011)

It was less a surprise victory, more a highly-charged emotional one, the 15,000 crowd in Badminton's hallowed arena giving him a heart-felt ovation as they paid tribute to the master at work.

(Julie Harding, *Eventing* magazine, May 2011)

When Mark announced his comeback in 2008, aged 52, there were many of us worried that he was just an old genius raging at the dying of the light. At Badminton, we were watching nothing less than a rekindling of the lamp.

(Brough Scott, *Horse & Hound*, 28th April, 2011)

As much as he is a naturally brilliant rider, the truly impressive thing about Mark's comeback is that he still has the desire and enthusiasm to work as hard as any top eventer must. He didn't return to the pinnacle of the game in one shot from the pistol; the sport had moved on and he had to adapt and strive to regain his place.

(Catherine Austen, *Horse & Hound*, 28th April, 2011)

Your success on NZB Land Vision was reported in the *Waikato Times* as the 'stuff of dreams'. In order to attract further awareness of your achievements, I moved a Notice of Motion congratulating you in Parliament.

(Letter from Tim Macindoe, MP for Hamilton West, 12th May, 2011)

Tim Macindoe to move, That this House congratulates New Zealand's outstanding equestrian competitor, Mark Todd, for winning the sport's most prestigious annual title for the fourth time ...

(*Order Paper*, 12th May, 2011)

SECOND CHANCE

CHAPTER
ONE

I T I S A M Y S T E R Y how my fixation with horses started. There was nothing about my childhood in 1960s New Zealand that ever suggested I would make a career out of riding and, looking back, it seems inexplicable that I have. Yet, from a very young age all I ever wanted to do was ride; it was all I thought or read about. I wrote to Santa Claus every year requesting a pony and would rush out on Christmas morning to see if one had arrived. It never did – I got books about horses instead.

So I read avidly, drinking in the glamorous exploits of show jumping's heroes of the day: Pat Smythe, the d'Inzeo brothers, David Broome and Marion Coakes. The sport of eventing – or horse trials – was very much at embryo stage in New Zealand then, and the international scene was completely off the radar for a little kid there, but a picture in one of my books stuck in my mind. It was captioned: 'Badminton winners Anneli Drummond-Hay and Merely-a-Monarch jumping into the Quarry'. It seemed so dramatic, and my imagination was fired from that moment. Her horse was still a hero to me when I eventually met Anneli in 1999, by which time I'd won Badminton three times myself.

I was brought up in a country town, Cambridge. It is a major bloodstock centre, but my home life was totally unconnected with that culture. My father, Norman, had a successful business in farm machinery – something in which I've never had the slightest interest. Neither he, nor my mother Lenore, was remotely horsey, and by New Zealand standards it was a fairly suburban upbringing. As a small child, the nearest I ever got to a horse was a crazy, mean-tempered Thoroughbred mare that my maternal grandfather, Pop, had on his farm. My older sister Kerryn and I were terrified of her because she would chase us out of her paddock.

Pop was a natural countryman, a born stockman who had an affinity for animals that combined empathy with pragmatism in equal measure. I was his first grandson (my brother, Martyn, arrived four years later) and I think he viewed me as the son he never had. I spent a lot of time with my grandparents, accompanying them to market, going racing or just drifting around on their sheep farm. This overlooked a property owned by Kenny Browne, who was something of a legend in New Zealand sport. I'm not the sort of person who particularly goes in for hero worship but Kenny was – and still is – the sort of person I look up to, and from an early stage I wanted to be like him. Along with Pop, he remains the greatest influence on my life.

Kenny was primarily a racing man but also represented New Zealand in polo. His wife Ann, who still trains racehorses today, was an accomplished horsewoman, mainly in showing and show jumping, and when I watched her schooling horses down in the fields below I was completely fixated. Kenny and Anne had an old pony called Shamrock who had taught loads of kids to ride, and I was allowed to borrow her. I don't remember any process of learning to ride – I think I just scrambled on, hoping for the best and getting regularly bucked off or scraped off under trees. Certainly Pop's old mare wasn't suitable for lead-rein duties; instead, he would take me down towards Kenny's on a dead-end road with big grass verges either side and we'd have races back up it.

Pop's farm was surrounded by steep hills and, although I didn't have a clue then, I now realise that learning how to stick with whatever Shamrock did was the best start I could have had. I was soon riding around the farm with Pop, which I loved, especially at shearing time when I would get up at 5am to accompany him. I was his shadow.

Pop kindly bought me a pony, Hunter. He was only three but, recklessly, Pop decided he would break him in for me. This came to an abrupt end when his flapping coat startled the pony which bucked him off, breaking his ribs. The next purchase, Rusty, didn't last much longer. He bucked me straight off into the garage, where I landed on my head, and gave Pop another set of broken ribs. After that, Pop was more circumspect, and the far more sensible Nugget arrived. He proved third-time lucky so that, finally, the thrilling prospect of Pony Club – and being a real rider – was in sight.

By this stage my parents realised I ought to have a hard hat and borrowed a policeman's helmet from a friend. I think that if I'd have fallen on my head with that on, I'd have broken my neck. My mother also bought me a second-hand saddle and, bless her, gave it a clean – with brown boot polish, up to a high sheen. This had the effect of making it as slippery as glass and, obviously, the polish came off all over me.

My equestrian fixation made me a demanding brat and I would pester my mother to drive me to Pop's farm, as there were no buses. Once she got so exasperated with me for dawdling that she made me walk home. Although I wasn't considered old enough to bicycle to the farm, strangely it was all right for me to ride five miles to a Pony Club rally on my own.

For this milestone, I had new jodhpurs, a new bridle with a white browband and, I hope, a vaguely acceptable hat. I thought I was pretty cool at riding, so was mortified to be put in the bottom ride. But the trotting round in circles didn't last long, and soon I loved it, doing bending races and similar high jinks with like-minded children. I had found my metier.

* * *

Riding took over, to the detriment of school, but I must have been bright enough to survive. I was quite good at English, terrible at maths, and could have been successful at athletics if I wasn't so obsessed with horses. I did the minimum to get by and although my parents set a strict home routine, which involved the odd belting from my father when I was particularly irritating, they were probably resigned to the fact that when I was in my room I was more likely to be reading horsey books instead of doing homework. In those days, few people made careers out of horses, so my parents looked upon my enthusiasm benignly and hoped I'd grow out of it. Anyway, they knew that my ambition was to be a farmer.

Occasionally, I wished for knowledgeable, horsey parents but the upside was that they weren't embarrassingly competitive and interfering either, and their tolerant attitude made me independent which, I am convinced, was better for me in the long run. I quickly learned how to patch bits of money together to do what I wanted, and with holiday jobs on farms I managed to fund the riding more or less by myself.

My parents paid the rent on a nearby field, which I shared with a school friend, Anne Wrigglesworth. She and I would ride for miles, looking for cross-country fences to jump. We mostly over-faced our ponies and they'd stop, but we'd persevere. We'd also gallop down the middle of roads – the ponies must have had amazing legs – and one day mine shied and I fell off. I complained to my mother that my arm hurt, but she told me not to make a fuss. Eventually, we went to the doctor and, sure enough, it was broken. On another occasion, we decided to jump out of a field onto the road; Anne's pony turned so sharply she flew off and wrapped herself round a letter-box.

I sold Nugget and, with the proceeds, bought Little Man whom I saw advertised in the *Waikato Times*. He was a five-year-old, part Arab, part stock pony, ugly with a long back and he cost me $70. I would never buy a three-quarter Arab now but I thought he was amazing. Little Man was a brilliant jumper, but he did have drawbacks. He was spooky and naughty and hated men; when Pop tried to catch him, Little Man jumped straight out of the cattle yard, over the rails. Another time, when he was tied to a gate, he saw Pop coming, took fright and took off, wrenching the gate off its hinges.

Another snag was that he wouldn't go in an enclosed horse-box, so I was either restricted to going to shows that I could hack to, or else Mum and Dad would hire a cattle truck with no roof. He wouldn't go up a steep loading ramp either, so you always had to find a bank to put it on. I saved up to buy a single trailer with no roof, which wasn't great when it rained, but Little Man didn't mind, and after I passed my driving test at 15, I'd borrow my parents' car, hook up and go.

Little Man gave me my first taste of winning rosettes, and the confidence that went with it, but he also gave me my first and possibly worst ever crashing fall. My mother was always too terrified to watch me going cross-country but, unfortunately, she was there at a Pony Club training session to witness this.

Little Man spooked and stopped at a jump made out of oil drums, so at the second attempt, I hit him, which made him take off miles out. He landed on the jump, flipped over and squashed me. The next thing I knew, I was waking up in the car with broken ribs, a broken jaw and bruised lungs. After that, it did occur to me that it wasn't a great idea to make the pony take off quite so far back.

My teens coincided with a particularly good era in the Cambridge Pony Club and, looking back, we were a pretty enterprising group of kids. We did all sorts of fund-raising activities, like making sandwiches at the flea market in Cambridge, and we found the sponsorship to run a night-time show jumping competition with floodlights, which attracted some of the best jumpers in the country.

By now, my riding ambitions were more defined. I was massively in awe of the senior Pony Club riders who were jumping Grade A courses, and I wanted to compete in the eventing at the Pony Club championships. Senior horse trials were few and far between in New Zealand then and the international scene was out of reach, but I knew from my avid reading of *Horse & Pony* magazine that these things existed and I wanted to do them.

I never did make the Pony Club championships, and I failed my Pony Club B test, possibly because my bandaging was weak. It's an omission that still rankles. But, in truth, my riding was still some way behind my peer group: the likes of John Nicholson (older brother of my team-mate Andrew, and now a renowned course-designer), Joanne Bridgeman (now a prolific seller to international riders) and Nicoli Fife (a judge at the highest, four-star, level). By comparison, I was a latecomer, and they were certainly better than I at that stage.

* * *

My 'light bulb moment' came when I attended a clinic given by an Englishman called Ted Harrison, who had become one of New Zealand's leading instructors. He had been abroad for classical training, and he brought a whole new perspective back to the country. Suddenly, I realised that riding wasn't just about hooning around and sticking on any-old-how; you had to train your horse and sit correctly. It opened up a whole new life for me. I've always been the sort of person who feels that if you're going to do something, you might as well do it well, and it dawned on me that I needed to get a grip of some real technique if I was going to be any good.

Despite this broadening of the mind, however, I was still set on a farming career. I left home and school at 17 – I wanted to leave at 16 but failed my university entrance exam – and got a job on a dairy farm outside Cambridge owned by Barry and Betty Harvey, with whose daughter, Bronwen, I'd been at school. Their neighbours were the Keyte family of international polo fame, who are still good friends.

Here, I had my first involvement with racing. The Harveys' son Bruce and I went to a sale and bought a racehorse called Mr Papagopolous for $200. He'd won a couple of races and we were extremely chuffed with ourselves. We asked a jockey who had ridden the horse what he thought. He answered: 'He's not worth a c**t-full of cold water' – devastating information to a couple of aspiring trainers, but too late.

Mr Papagopolous's first run, an amateur steeplechase at Rotorua with Bruce in the saddle, was something of a comedy moment. Bruce made the mistake of going to the front; at the first fence, the horse shied, ran-out and deposited his hapless jockey. He then took off and, with everyone cursing him and trying to catch him, did his best to bring down the entire field. He cut across the track and, as we watched helplessly, galloped head on into the middle of the oncoming field. Eventually, he finished over the line in front, with his ears pricked, and we didn't know whether to die of laughing or of embarrassment.

Alongside our comical attempts to be racehorse trainers, I was also competing a horse called Killarney, bought from a guy called, believe it or not, Tom Cruise. I evented Killarney in a small way but mainly show jumped him, as I was very much in with the show jumping crowd. Ted Harrison helped me a bit but essentially I was doing my own thing – the idea that one might actually have regular riding lessons hadn't really caught on then.

Tom and another friend, Ian Campbell, were my great mates on the show jumping circuit and, after a somewhat sheltered home life, I loved my new social life. Practical jokes were a major part of it – during a picnic at Hastings Show Tom filled the ham sandwiches with condoms, which we thought was hysterically funny.

Another 'joke' very nearly killed me. We were at Gisborne Show and, as usual, there had been a bit of a party. I went to bed, vaguely aware that there was another prank in the offing, with me as victim, so I pulled down all the zips on my tent so that no one could get in. It turned out that my friends had put a smoke-bomb, of the variety used to smoke out woodworm, in the tent. I woke up with a start, coughing my lungs out on the toxic fumes and thrashed about in panic trying to find the zip. At first, everyone thought it was hilarious, but fortunately Ian realised it was serious, ripped the tent and dragged me out. I spent the night in hospital, which made me a bit late for my jumping class next day. No one batted an eyelid.

Unlike most normal New Zealand teenagers, all my holidays and days off were spent going to horse shows and in between I'd make up the time by doing extra work milking. I had no thoughts of travelling; I was on a farm cadet scheme, a practical training in farming linked to a college course, and the idea was to end up with a diploma in agriculture. I envisaged my future as a New Zealand farmer who rode a bit. Subtly, though, the horses began to intrude.

One of my farm placements was with David and Anne Goodin at Te Kauwhata. David was a successful show jumper and their son Bruce was a past mainstay of the New Zealand team. It was here that I had my first encounter with a horse called Charisma. Then owned by David Murdoch, he came as a three-year-old to be turned out on the hills. He was a very good-looking colt, black and striking. I thought what a smart little horse he was, just such a shame he wouldn't be big enough.

* * *

The horse that held my attention then was Top Hunter, whom I'd bought from Lyall Keyte. He was a Thoroughbred that had been raced and was now Lyall's hunter, and he lent him to me in the summer of 1976 for one last try at the Pony Club championship (for which I was reserve, yet again).

Top Hunter was a good-looking horse who moved well and had tons of scope; he jumped to Grade A level but he wasn't good enough to be a top show jumper. He was, though, an ideal type for eventing. However, it was still a minority sport at our end of the world and my main aim was to win money, so he had to be an all-rounder – I even showed him and did dressage. Getting a horse to Grade A level in jumping was part and parcel of producing an eventer in New Zealand in those days because there weren't enough horse trials to keep you occupied. Looking back, it was a pretty good method and I now think I should do more show jumping – it's good for an event horse. The show jumping phase is very important now. I was jumping 1.50m; so when you have to jump 1.30m in eventing it seems so much easier.

I didn't do my first three-day event until 1977, aged 21. It was at Taupo, and I finished third behind Ted Harrison's

wife Carol, who won on Topic. There were only a dozen or
so of us in the field, and it was pretty wild and woolly – a few
ramshackle trucks and the horses all turned out in paddocks
divided by electric fences. It was also freezing cold, but we
all had warm sleeping bags and it was a good excuse for yet
another party. As it turned out, though, Taupo was more significant than that. It was the catalyst for New Zealand's first
ever attempt at an international championship, the notorious
1978 World Championships in Kentucky, USA, which will go
down as the toughest competition in history.

It was Lockie Richards, a New Zealander who had trained
in England and taught in America, who planted the idea. He
was at Taupo giving a clinic and said to a group of us – myself,
Carol, Joanne Bridgeman, Mary Hamilton (now Derby) and
Nicoli Fife: 'With training, you guys are good enough to go to
Kentucky.' We were thrilled.

The first thing that happened was that all prospective team
horses were vetted by the New Zealand federation, and not
one of them passed because the vet was used to looking at
Thoroughbred racehorses, not a bunch of less refined eventers,
some with less than perfect legs. As a result, the New Zealand
Federation refused to back our championship bid, which had
serious financial ramifications. They told us we were not considered a serious team but if we proved ourselves, we might
get future funding. So we had to fund the trip to the USA ourselves, which meant raising around $21,000 each, a huge sum
in those days.

I left the Goodins to return home to live with my parents
and concentrate on earning more money. I did shift work in
the local dairy factory, packing milk powder, I took in horses
for breaking and did the night watch at a local stud. We held
fund-raising events and staged raffles, and I sold my car, but
it was hard to raise the publicity because the New Zealand

newspapers had no idea what eventing was. I still had to borrow $7,000 from my parents. Raising that amount of money in seven months was a big ask, but it was a good exercise.

* * *

We left New Zealand in early 1978 for our big adventure. Mary Hamilton's father lent us the money to buy a truck to get around in and Lockie Richards arranged for us to stay with a friend, Elizabeth Streeter, at Chester Springs in Pennsylvania. My main role was team farrier; despite having no training, I'd been shoeing my own horses for years, and that would save us a bit more money.

Considering our claustrophobic conditions – poor Carol and Joanne had to share a room with me – the five of us got on remarkably well. It was hot and humid; there were ticks galore in the long grass – every day we had to pick them off the horses and, even worse, off each other. We lived squashed together with no privacy in a two-room flat where we shared the cooking. I don't remember any arguments though, probably because we were all united in our mission.

We were also so excited by this thrilling new culture of discos, bars and ten-pin bowling. The social possibilities suddenly seemed endless and I, at least, took full advantage. The Americans found us a bit of a novelty – they probably felt sorry for us, as we were young, poor and rather ill-equipped – and they were so kind and welcoming. They couldn't do enough for us.

We did some competitions, which was also thrilling, even though we had to travel miles. Suddenly, there were all these big names: Jeremy Beale, a British rider who had won Burghley in 1965, had an equestrian centre down the road; Bruce Davidson, the reigning world champion, was nearby, and there were revered names like Tad Coffin, the 1976 Olympic gold medallist, and his team-mates Mike Plumb and Denny Emerson, plus the likes of Beth and Bea Perkins, Derek di Grazia and Torrance Watkins (later Fleischman). We felt like country hicks, but it was stimulating to be part of such a sophisticated competition scene. Lockie had told us we wouldn't be out of our depth and, amazingly, we weren't; we got placed at one-day events and dressage competitions and it made us realise that despite our limited experience, we weren't that far behind.

Lockie did his best to get us physically fit, but Carol and I would run down the road, disappear behind a tree for a smoke and come back again. Lockie was disgusted with us, so I challenged him to a race. We went five miles round the block and I beat him, but I couldn't walk for days afterwards. He also banned us from having sex the night before a competition because he said it would make our legs wobble, not that I took any notice of that one!

Sally O'Connor, who was well known as a trainer and writer on the American scene, and for taking her two young sons Brian and David on an epic ride across the States, was a good friend of Lockie's. She acted as our guardian angel and arranged for her boys to be our grooms. Jan Mossman, a New Zealander who was working in racing in New York, also got in touch and ended up being my groom. She was brilliant because she was used to dealing with injuries to racehorses' legs, which was to prove very useful.

* * *

Next stop, Kentucky. I picked up my parents from the airport and, keen to show off my skill at negotiating an American highway, set off round Lexington's one-way system the wrong way. Never mind, I thought, I'll cut across the central reservation. Unfortunately, this had a big dip and we got stuck, so I ended up being ignominiously pushed out by my parents.

The whole Lexington area – Blue Grass country – is a Thoroughbred paradise of big studs, endless grass and white railings. The Kentucky horse park, a shrine to Thoroughbred names like Man O' War and Seabiscuit, was built specially for the world championships with the most luxurious stables we'd ever seen. There were glamorous parties and accents I'd never heard before – the Germans, who took their running rather seriously, made a particular impression. It was all quite an eye-opener for a country boy like me.

Then the British arrived. There was the legendary Richard Meade, the 1972 Olympic gold medallist and the pin-up boy of his day, Jane Holderness-Roddam, and team Olympic gold medallist and dual Badminton winner, Jane Starkey, who many years later was to own horses with me, and Lucinda Prior-Palmer, who'd already won Badminton three times and two European titles. 'There's Lucinda!' we'd whisper, in awe. I also had my first introduction to the flamboyant Lizzie Boone (later Purbrick). They were all to become close friends.

All the British girls wore headscarves, the men tweed – a bit of a contrast to my flared trousers and open-necked shirt at the first horse inspection – and there was a huge army of hearty flag-waving supporters, who rallied round on cross-country day to 'fence-spot' and relayed back information with military precision. The whole set-up seemed so professional in its organisation that we shamelessly eavesdropped on their meetings in the hope that some of it would rub off on us, not that we had the resources to replicate it.

In the end, the British didn't actually fare any better than us. No one, even the event organisers and leading officials in the sport, had given a second thought to the fact that the humidity in Kentucky in summer is dangerously energy-sapping and debilitating. Nowadays, the cross-country would be reduced in distance, and cooling stations and vets monitoring the horses' temperatures and heart rates would be everywhere. But in 1978 we were faced with full-scale roads and tracks phases, a five-and-a-half minute steeplechase course (in later years, this was rarely more than four minutes) and then a massive cross-country course, all at faster speeds. The temperature was 90 degrees, with 100 per cent humidity, and no one had a clue about the consequences.

I borrowed a top hat and tails from the tallest British team member, Chris Collins, and was rather pleased with my dressage test on Top Hunter, which had us in 10th place individually, but the style of dressage riding was quite different then – all long reins and horses with their necks out.

Carol was first to go for the team and went brilliantly across country, recording the third fastest round at that stage, despite a run-out – she eventually finished sixth. Nicoli's horse, Never Dwell, went lame and didn't start, and Joanne completed despite a fall on Bandolier. Mary rode as an individual. You have to watch old footage of Kentucky 1978 to take in just how bad it was, for I hope there will never be another competition like it. People talk about tough conditions now but this was something extreme and the only good thing about it was that the sport realised it must never happen again. Even so, it left a negative legacy in the States where for years there was political pressure from the Humane Society for the sport to put its house in order.

There was some appalling, terrifying riding and horrendous sights, with exhausted horses diving and crashing over fences yet being kicked on again. Back at the stables, horses were flaked out everywhere, including the eventual winner, Bruce Davidson's Might Tango, who had to be propped up on the way back and revived with oxygen. He was never quite the same again, and he wasn't the only one. Cambridge Blue, the horse ridden by Irishman John Watson to win the silver medal, and Topper Too, who finished seventh with Jane Starkey, were two of very few horses that didn't need oxygen.

The British team, except for Richard Meade who always delivered the goods no matter what, was eliminated, and the Canadians won team gold because they'd sensibly adopted a strategy of hacking round. In those days, it was all about 'for the sake of the team' – three out of four members had to complete for a team result – and if your horse was still upright, and you hadn't actually lost a limb, you were expected to keep going.

There was such carnage that by the time I went, all I had to do was complete the course for New Zealand to have a chance of a medal, but poor Top Hunter had probably broken down on the steeplechase by then. I'd gone like a maniac, clocking the second fastest time behind the speedy Lizzie Boone on Felday Farmer, and he'd landed badly on the lip of the water fence. Top Hunter wasn't lame at the start of the cross-country, but by the time we got to Fort Lexington, a huge bank, he'd had enough, and refused three times at the little rail on top of the bank. He didn't feel exhausted, but he felt as though he just didn't want to do it any more.

I returned, crushed, to the stables, feeling totally deflated, especially as Top Hunter was supposed to be the form horse of the team, but when I took the bandages off and saw his swollen tendons I felt terrible. They had slipped down and created a pressure point halfway down the leg. I've never used bandages since for cross-country. Typically, though, it didn't take me long to see the bright side of the experience. I worked out that if I'd got round the cross-country, and then show jumped clear, I could have won! Instead of being put off, I was spurred on. I can do this, I thought. And, 30 years later, finishing 18th at the 2008 Olympics in Hong Kong was to have exactly the same effect.

CHAPTER
TWO

AFTER KENTUCKY, none of us could afford to do anything without selling our horses, so there was a nerve-racking period of waiting to see who would strike lucky first. I played a trick on Joanne, phoning her up and putting on a posh British accent, pretending to be interested in Bandolier. Joanne came running into the room, shouting 'Guess what! I've sold my horse.' She had the last laugh though. He was sold to Lucinda Prior-Palmer and renamed Mairangi Bay, going on to great success later with Lucinda and her husband David. Joanne has since built up a brilliant reputation for supplying event horses.

Thanks to Jan Mossman's expertise at putting Top Hunter back together after his ordeal, I was able to get a good price for him, too. He was bought by Jurg Zindel, a Swiss dealer who used to buy a lot for the Italians, and I got a job offer and enough money to pay back my parents and buy another horse.

On returning to New Zealand, Lockie recommended that I should to go South Island to see a horse called Jocasta, who was owned by Diane Guy. Jocasta was a chestnut, part Hackney, and had a rather hot temperament. In hindsight, he wasn't a good buy and, deep down, I never really liked him but he was the horse I took with me to England in 1979 to try my luck. Jurg had offered me a job riding young horses at his base at Chieveley in Berkshire, and Andrew Scott, another young Kiwi eventer, came with me as a student.

That September of 1979 was the beginning of my love affair with Burghley. I was thrilled to be at such a historic event and instantly loved the parkland, with its beautiful trees and autumnal light, and the majesty of the house and its extraordinary roof, like something out of a fairytale. It's always been a professional yet friendly event, and in those days foreign riders, being rather more few and far between, were put up at The George, the smartest hotel in nearby Stamford.

Jocasta and I got round the cross-country with two stops. I can't remember being terrified by the course, even though it was huge, because the prevailing attitude then was just 'well, I've got to do it'. I was used to speed because I'd schooled racehorses and to being accurate over show jumps and being faced with big fences – if you're accustomed to 1.60m then 1.30m doesn't look so scary, even if there's a massive ditch underneath. I wasn't complacent but I certainly wasn't freaked by it all, a typically casually confident young male rider, in fact.

I was soon stuck into the social side, too, drinking whisky in the caravan park with the late Tom Hudson, who was the commentator and a legendary *bon viveur*. We were told to shut up by Lizzie Purbrick's husband, Reggie; I thought he sounded an awful twit, his British army officer's voice barking in the dark, but he has ended up being a good friend, too.

I also met the Irish rider, Brendan Corscadden, who was to become my best man and a very loyal friend – we got so plastered that we spent ages looking in the grass for a contact lens which was actually still in his eye – and Clissy Strachan (now married to the former Dutch event rider Edward Bleekman), who was to become another great mate. One of our first encounters was when Jocasta had a loose shoe and I needed a hammer. I asked Clissy: 'Have you got a himmer?' This met with a blank look. The New Zealand accent was a novelty then – the only foreigners around were Irish or Australian, – with Andrew Hoy, an Australian farmer, winning Burghley that year on Davey – and none of us were big into tweed, so we rather stuck out next to the well-groomed likes of Richard Meade and Captain Mark Phillips.

The lack of a tie – and Clissy's lack of a skirt – nearly prevented us getting into a Stamford nightclub, but I found a stock in my car to serve as a tie and Clissy borrowed a big jumper from me which just about came past her knickers.

After that initiation into the European eventing circuit the big end-of-season party was the three-day event at Boekelo in Holland the following month, and Clissy invited me to go with her. We set off with a packed Bedford TK lorry for a marathon journey – you had to be vet-checked at every border, which took hours. Now, it takes about four hours once you've crossed the Channel and is considered one of the more accessible events.

Boekelo has become my favourite three-star level event; it's not pretty like a British three-day but it is hospitable and relaxed and the atmosphere is fantastic. That year, in the old indoor school, there was a bar with free drinks. The Russians were drinking their own vodka. Riders of all nationalities were getting tanked up on whatever drink they could lay their hands on – I've never been able to face genever since – and dancing all night. The concept of getting a good night's sleep before riding cross-country didn't come into it but somehow Jocasta and I managed to finish seventh. I was thrilled with my placing; I felt I was on my way.

* * *

Eventing could hardly be called a profession then; it was a sport, and basically an amateur one at that. Lucinda was really the only rider who could have been considered truly professional, as she was the only one with a title sponsor. I now count her as a close friend but at that stage, when she was at the height of her career, although she was always polite and kind she was distinctly on a mission compared to the rest of us.

There was a totally different mentality in the sport. Course-designers weren't under any pressure to get a balanced result, and if your horse fell, it was jolly bad luck. None of the accidents seemed to be serious and you were expected to turn up for show jumping next day even if you'd been concussed. You went to a three-day event for a bit of a crack, and you certainly didn't worry about its impact on your livelihood, or get obsessed with qualifying for anything. My big goal was to ride at the Moscow Olympics in 1980, but it was very much in the Corinthian spirit and I certainly never imagined then that eventing would become my life; it was something to do while I was young before I went home and got a proper job. I was living the dream while I could.

Representing New Zealand at an Olympic Games was a childhood ambition, although then I had envisaged it being in the high jump, rather than eventing. Now I felt it was on the horizon. It didn't matter about being qualified then – or even if your horse was a novice – because you practised at Badminton. However, although Jocasta had gone well at Boekelo I still felt I ought to look for some more ammunition for the big one.

I still had some money left over from Top Hunter's sale and returned to New Zealand at the end of 1979 to look for another horse. I'd heard about one called Southern Comfort, owned by Shirley Woods. He had hunted, show jumped to Grade B level, done quite a lot of eventing and had a reputation for being very reliable, if not brilliant, and a good jumper.

Southern Comfort – Monty – wasn't full Thoroughbred, but he was Thoroughbred-type, a handsome 16.2hh horse with a lovely bold head.

Heading back to England with him in 1980, the plane touched down in Sydney and this surfer-type guy got on. He introduced himself as David Green and announced to me and my fellow traveller, Andrew Nicholson, who was coming over to work for a racehorse trainer, that he was going to marry Lucinda Prior-Palmer. 'Oh yeah,' we said. 'Pull the other one.' Astonishingly, it turned out to be true. He'd met her when she was teaching in Australia and she'd invited him back to England.

As well as horses, the plane transported rams, which we dropped off in Buenos Aires, frozen live eels and cattle that gave birth on the flight. It was like Noah's Ark. The flight took two-and-a-half days, by which time Andrew and I stank, thanks to the smell of ammonia from the sheep.

I was met at the airport by my new hostess (I'd had a minor falling out with Jurg, though he and I are good friends nowadays and sometimes ski together). She was Baroness (Penelope) Barth von Wehrenalp, who lived at Harwood Lodge in Wootton Hill near Newbury, and rented some funny old stables up the road at a dark old mansion owned by a gun dealer.

Penny also introduced me to my next landlady, Bobby Neville, who owned a butterfly sanctuary at a property that had previously belonged to Mark Phillips's aunt, Flavia. Bobby had five stunning daughters, one of whom, Cassie, is now Lady Derby and a major owner of racehorses and dressage horses. Another, Hetty, was tragically killed in an accident on the road that summer. Unlikely as it may sound, I acted as the girls' sort-of nanny and taught them all to ride.

I spent the spring becoming thoroughly integrated in the

British eventing scene. There were parties with Penny and her husband Uwe, and in between I tried to get serious about my riding. I had flatwork lessons with Bridget Nicholls, who trained Lucinda, and went for cross-country schooling at Wylye, the Wiltshire home of Lord and Lady Hugh Russell, a Mecca for British riders. Lady Hugh was an extraordinarily charismatic woman who had a massive influence on my generation. She had been paralysed by a riding accident, but had such presence and personality and was so uncomplaining that you forgot that element of her life. She went round events in her 'mini-moke', an adapted mini car that always had riders hanging off it, desperate for her advice. Everyone respected her because she had an amazing ability to observe where you needed help – even riders at the top of the tree like Lucinda Green and Richard Meade continued to go to her for advice in a way that most of today's senior riders wouldn't think about.

I got on very well with the Russells and used to be invited down for dinner, which I loved, as it was a magical place. To a lone New Zealander it felt like a family set-up and I loved the feeling of being integrated into the British system. Lady Hugh could be terrifying but I used to get off quite lightly because I think she had a soft spot for me. Many years later, when she was dying, I was touched that she asked to speak to me on the telephone from New Zealand.

The fences at Wylye were huge but Lady Hugh would tell you to sit up, put your leg on and don't be such a pussy. An added hazard was that her dogs would chase you, so you had to think quickly. There weren't the variety of fences as at today's principal schooling grounds, such as Aston-le-Walls in Northampton, which is run by my former riding contemporaries Nigel and Anne-Marie Taylor, or Russ Hardy's Boomerang in Wiltshire, but they were decent.

Lady Hugh was a stickler for keeping a rhythm, being

accurate and having the right canter pace. There was a particularly terrifying coffin fence with vertical rails at the top of a slope, and if you didn't organise yourself with the correct canter you soon knew about it. It certainly instilled the correct principles of cross-country riding, and if that didn't, the courses designed by the then Badminton director Frank Weldon would.

I don't care what people say about changing course-design; in my view, the courses of the 1970s and 1980s were bigger and more difficult than most of what you see today. It's true that what you needed then was essentially a brave horse, and now you need one which will jump narrow fences accurately, and the training for that takes time. But there was still a huge variety of obstacle at Badminton, and many of them were pretty 'technical' – Frank was very keen on S- and W-shaped fences, big open corners, and bounces through apexes of corners, as well as the 'rider-frighteners' like the Normandy Bank, which produced the most amazing pictures of horses leaping into outer space and made the sport look extremely glamorous and daring.

* * *

After the books and dreams of my childhood, Badminton was like the Holy Grail for me, and everyone rallied round for my first ride there. We travelled there in a funny old ancient lorry of Penny's, which looked like a hearse, and camped in the caravan park. I only had one pair of breeches, so after my dressage the people at the village shop kindly washed them. To press them, I put them under the bed in the caravan and slept on them.

I was used to grooming for myself but Andrew Nicholson came as a gesture of friendship and helped me – the first time he'd been to Badminton as well. We overslept on the morning of my dressage and so plaiting was a hilariously rushed affair, with one of us starting at Monty's head and the other at the wither. I still hadn't acquired a top hat and tails, so Chris Collins kindly lent me his again and I pinned the New Zealand silver fern over the Union Flag.

Although Monty was a better horse than Jocasta, his dressage wasn't that brilliant, and we were midfield after that phase. Although he'd gone well at the spring advanced events, an eighth place at Brigstock was about the highlight, and we were a long way from being favourites. All the attention was on Richard, and on Mark and Lucinda who had already won Badminton three and four times respectively.

On cross-country day, the roads and tracks phases (phases A and C, which ran either side of the steeplechase, phase B) seemed to take for ever, so I was blissfully unaware of what was going on in the competition, which was probably just as well. I later discovered that the cross-country course was causing chaos – Lorna Sutherland (now Clark) broke her leg at the Footbridge, Sue Hatherly (now Benson) fell into a bed of nettles beside it, Mark Phillips pulled up the Queen's horse Columbus at the Luckington Lane, and all my companions on the previous night's serious whisky-drinking session in the caravan bit the dust, too. By the time I went, only about three people had got round.

Sally O'Connor, who was bringing over a tour from the US, had agreed to help me in the 10-minute box (the waiting area before cross-country). She was in a dilemma as to what to say, as she could hardly report that the course I was about to ride for the first time was causing carnage. So she just said: 'It's fine – go out and ride as you planned.' So that's what I did; ignorance was bliss.

I'm not sure to what extent you can really enjoy a course

like that; it was more a case of survival. I had a hairy moment at the Footbridge myself, coming in too deep to it. But Monty was a good jumper and his hunting background in New Zealand came in useful, because he got himself out of it, although he landed on the lip of the ditch, went down on his knees and slid along the ground. Somehow, though, he picked himself up and flew on over the next fence, the huge Irish bank.

The course ran clockwise that year, with Huntsman's Close on the way home. There was a gap you had to go through to get out of the wood, but I just sliced the corner and jumped a set of rails. I must have felt very confident in him, and on the video of our round we do look assured.

Still, I had no idea when I got to the finish what an achievement it was. It wasn't until I looked at the scoreboard that I realised that mine was one of only three rounds clear inside the time and I'd moved up to third behind the previous year's winners, Lucinda on Killaire, and Helen Butler and Merganser, who were in the lead. This was beyond my wildest dreams and there was euphoria all round.

That evening, I decided to cook my brilliant horse some barley on the barley boiler. As I went to light it, I stupidly peered in and the flash of flame took off my eyelashes and eyebrows. Going to the first-aid tent didn't seem an option, though.

Monty felt a little jarred after cross-country, as the ground was firm that year and there were a lot of drops. Andrew set to poulticing the horse and the vet, Peter Scott-Dunn, gave him 20cc of bute, a painkiller. Later, bute was to be completely banned in the sport, even a small, aspirin-like amount, but the view then was that as long as the bute wasn't masking anything serious – and it wasn't with Monty – it was much the kindest thing to do for a horse. He felt like a two-year-old on Sunday morning.

Monty show jumped clear and I was hopeful of going up

a place as I knew that, sadly, Merganser might be good for a couple of rails, which he was. No one expected Lucinda to make a mistake, but Killaire put a foot in the water jump and got four faults which caught everyone so much by surprise that Dorian Williams, who was commentating for BBC television, announced: 'It's another win for Lucinda. Oh no, it's not! It's that Mark Todd from New Zealand!'

Sally escorted me through the chaos to the press tent, where I rang my astonished parents. It was three in the morning for them and they were asleep when I woke them to say: 'Guess what? I won!' Mum was in tears and so was I, as the enormity of it all began to sink in. Life would never be the same again.

CHAPTER
THREE

M Y BADMINTON WIN was the first time eventing received any recognition in New Zealand. It was big news: I'd beaten the Queen's son-in-law, I was presented with my trophy *by* the Queen and the papers wanted to know what she'd said. (I can't remember, but I do know that she was very nice to talk to.) There was a cartoon of Prince Philip saying 'Mark who?' Another depicted a sheep farmer coming in from mustering and his wife saying 'Tea won't be ready until you've done another hour's dressage.' For a small country that was into royalty, horses and sport – even though it was a sport no one knew anything about – this was a huge deal.

Considering that Lucinda was the queen of British eventing, the Whitbread Trophy had been in British hands for fifteen years since Eddie Boylan won it for Ireland in 1965 and I was a complete unknown, I got an extraordinarily welcoming reception in England, too. People seemed genuinely thrilled for me, both during Badminton and afterwards, when I received lots of letters. One of the nicest was from Sue Benson, who was one of the most fiercely competitive riders around, and I was particularly pleased to get a poem from Ginny Holgate, someone who had been piquing my interest for a while.

The roll continued when I took Jocasta to Punchestown a couple of weeks later and finished second behind one of Ireland's leading riders, David Foster on his European team gold medallist Inis Mean. Punchestown was another meaty track and the weekend was an excuse to let my hair down with my new Irish friends after the formality and tension of Badminton. I spent some of my Badminton prize-money – £3,000 which, as I owned the horse myself, I didn't have to share – on a car, a little steel-grey Mazda, and I thought I was the bee's knees.

It couldn't last. By now, my Olympic goal was obviously realistic, but Monty developed a niggling little lameness and was off the road, which meant it would be down to Jocasta – not ideal. And then forces beyond my control in the real world took over when the news came that New Zealand was boycotting the Moscow Olympics in protest at Russia invading Afghanistan. At 24 I understood the politics of it but it was a deep disappointment. I couldn't know then that I'd be going to another six Olympics, and I thought my one big chance had been swept away.

Other leading eventing nations, such as France, Ireland, Britain and America, also boycotted Moscow, so an 'alternative Olympics' was hastily assembled at Fontainebleau in France. As the sole New Zealander, I was adopted by the Irish – particularly Eric Horgan, Helen Cantillon and the inimitable Van der Vater, one of the most colourful characters in the sport. We got lost on the way and none of us could speak a word of French, so it was pretty tortuous, but we all had the same fairly relaxed attitude. It was just another big adventure.

The cross-country course was like a cat's cradle, weaving in and out of woodland, which didn't fill one with confidence. Van, who deserves a book of his own because there are so many great stories about him, was clearly not looking forward to it all and he found a brilliant ruse for getting out of it. He returned from Phase C, announcing his bit had broken and he wouldn't be able to hold the horse on the cross-country – later, he admitted he'd thrown it into the bushes.

I was well placed after dressage and fairly upbeat about my chances, given how I'd shot up the leader board at Badminton, but it was to be a second fruitless championship. Jocasta gave himself a fright at a log on top of a ramp, sailing through the air and landing heavily at the bottom, so that when we came to a much smaller version near the end of the course he refused three times and we were eliminated.

It's a cliché, but 1980 could certainly be considered a year of highs and lows: I won the greatest prize in the sport at my first attempt, missed the chance of my first Olympics and bombed out of the alternative – but I acquired my first serious girlfriend.

* * *

Ginny's poem was the trigger. I'd been intrigued by her for a while and, with a bit of courage on my part and some helpful advice from Clissy, who knew Ginny from when she was living in Devon, we started going out. Things were greatly helped by the fact that I was now living with the Nevilles in Great Somerford, a stone's throw from the Holgates at Acton Turville, near Badminton, but I'm not sure Ginny's mother, Heather, was too thrilled. I think she feared that I didn't take my career seriously enough then – she was probably right there – and would be too much of a distraction to the more serious business of her daughter's.

Ginny was the next big thing in eventing. She'd won the Junior European title, she was doing well in senior competition, and she was very pretty and charismatic and attracted a lot of attention. The 1980s was to be her decade – three consecutive

European titles, a world title, Olympic medals and Badminton and Burghley victories – and when we started going out, she was on the brink of this phenomenal success.

The winning combination was Heather's good eye for a horse, the precise training system organised by her and Dot Willis, Ginny's long-time resident trainer, which in terms of its professionalism was ahead of its time, and the very talented rider they had to work on. Ginny was good on the flat, brilliantly accurate over fences and very brave. She made me much more accurate in my riding and I'd like to think I helped her to ride more naturally and faster. I went with Heather to buy Master Craftsman, the horse on which Ginny subsequently won the 1989 European Championships, a lovely horse I wouldn't have minded owning myself. I helped Ginny to get him galloping better. In turn, she sorted out my problem with jumping corners, which I went through a phase of avoiding if I possibly could.

There were, of course, differences in our approach, and when we all walked courses together there was sometimes far too much information for me. I'd say, 'Well, I'll just gallop down here,' and Ginny would say: 'No, I'm going to steady up here and aim for this spot.' Even now, I can still visualise her coming down to the Vicarage Vee at Badminton on Priceless in this lovely balance – boom, boom, jump.

I returned to Badminton in 1981 to defend my title, mostly because I felt I should try, and it was deeply unsuccessful. My parents came over to watch, staying in my flat at Great Somerford, and my poor mother's worst fears were all confirmed. Jocasta, who had never recovered from his fright at Fontainebleau, had fallen three times at spring events and then hit the deck again at the Elephant Trap fence at Badminton. I got back on but he jacked it in at the next fence, the Quarry, so I retired him from the course.

My finances were in a pretty dire state by now, and while everyone was kind and supportive it was clear that I had to do something about it. We'd managed to get to the bottom of Monty's endless lameness – a piece of gravel in the hoof – so I sold him to the American rider Torrance Fleischman for £45,000 – a profit of £40,000. The Americans were one of the few nations then prepared to pay good money for horses, and he was, after all, a Badminton winner. The next season he was America's leading horse and Torrance took him to the World Championships in Luhmünlen, Germany. Jocasta had to go too – a slightly harder task – and I sold him for £3,000 'hunter money' to the prolific Dutch rider Eddy Stibbe. Jocasta was never heard of again but, fortunately, Eddy and I have remained good friends!

Word got around about my teaching the Neville sisters, and I was sent more pupils as a result. One of them was Mimi May, whom I met with her husband Tom at a drinks party at the Nevilles' and who was to be a key figure in my continuing with the sport. She also helped me out by lending me her Range Rover and trailer, and I rode a novice horse for her called Felix Too. That had to be on a non fee-paying arrangement, as I'd have lost my amateur status by being paid and I didn't want this to happen because in the back of my mind was the vague notion of riding at the 1984 Olympics; in those days you couldn't compete at an Olympics if you held professional status.

In 1981, all the top riders were aiming for the 1982 world championships, but it was pretty obvious I wouldn't be one of them. Felix Too would be too inexperienced and a horse I'd been generously offered for Burghley, David Lloyd-Thomas's Milton Tyson, had a back problem. There were two New Zealand riders in Luhmühlen, Mary Hamilton and Ross Renwick, who had been on the British circuit for a while, but it was sad that we couldn't get a team together after all our efforts to go to Kentucky and it felt like a backward step.

* * *

By now, I had the strong feeling that I'd had my fun and it was time to return to New Zealand. I'd been away for three years and the guy share-milking on Pop's farm was retiring, so this was a good opportunity for me to have my own farming business. It didn't feel like an agonising decision, just an inevitable one. I held a farewell party in the village hall near Great Somerford for all my eventing friends and the locals who had been so kind to me. We had a disco and I mixed a punch, but I'd rather forgotten about food, so everyone got pretty merry.

The money I'd made from Monty and Jocasta enabled me to buy Pop's herd of 120 Jersey-Friesians and I took over his farm, splitting the milk money 50-50 with him. This meant Pop was getting an income from his land, and I felt I was paying my way and running my own business, and it was an arrangement that worked well.

Ginny came over to stay and it was one of the happiest times in our relationship, but it was pretty obvious that this wasn't the time for her to become a farmer's wife in New Zealand – she had too much to go back to and I couldn't expect her to give it up. Her departure made me momentarily unsettled, thinking wistfully about the 1982 British eventing season about to start but, actually, I was content. I was making a good living from milking and horse-dealing, and I'd settled back into my old social life, often going straight from partying into the milking parlour in the small hours of the morning, sometimes with friends to help me.

Thanks to winning Badminton, I was getting quite a bit of teaching. A group of ladies came for a joint lesson every

Wednesday. They were great fun and used to bring me cakes, and it was a hilarious time. One of them was Judy Hall who, with her husband Bill, was to play a major role in my life. I had horses to compete: Beaumont, a very strong, part Cleveland bay, on which I finished second at Taupo, and Snowstorm, a Grade A jumper owned by Kenny and Ann Browne – he was previously ridden by their son, Roger, who was tragically killed playing polo in Australia. I slipped happily back into my old life, travelling to shows in my truck and catching up with old mates. The New Zealand Horse Society approved my entry for the World Championships on Beaumont, but I decided it wasn't worth bothering about.

My seemingly settled life came to an abrupt end when, at the start of 1983, Mimi May rang up. Angela Tucker, who had taken over the ride on Felix Too, had broken her leg. Would I like to ride the horse at Badminton? I said: 'I'll have to think about that. I'll call you back.' Two minutes later, I was back on the phone, saying: 'Yes, I'll do it.' Badminton 1983 was another 'light bulb' moment. I loved being back there and finished ninth on Felix Too, Angela, now a senior judge, having done a brilliant job on his flatwork. My friends were all on at me to come back to England and I thought: 'What am I doing? I don't want to be milking cows for the rest of my life.'

Pop was understandably disappointed and I think he thought I was slightly mad, but he let it happen because he understood that this was what I wanted to do. I think my parents were just relieved not to have to milk any more cows while I was away at shows.

The only slight snag was that I didn't have any horses to ride. The only lead was a phone call while I was away at Badminton from Virginia Caro – her father, Boy Caro, had done a huge amount to develop eventing in New Zealand – asking me if I'd like to ride Charisma. This was the cute little black horse

I'd seen running wild while I was working for the Goodins and had dismissed for being too small.

***

Charisma was born at Peter and Daphne Williams's Mamaku Stud on 30th October, 1972 to their brilliant little jumping mare, Planet. She was only 15hh, with a dash of Percheron blood, and, ridden by Sheryl Douglas, she was the first mare in New Zealand to jump her own height. After injury, she returned to stud with the Williamses and was put to the Thoroughbred stallion Tara Mink. Charisma was the result.

Daphne called the little black foal Stroppy, though by all accounts he was a laid-back, charming character who loved his food. He also had immense presence and radiated intelligence which is what attracted him to David Murdoch, who bought him as a yearling. On his first morning with David, Stroppy, ever motivated by greed, jumped out over a four-foot wire fence because he fancied the nicer looking green grass outside the pen.

David got him gelded and broke him in as a four-year-old, finding him to be a quick learner and a powerful jumper, and sold him for $3,500 to Sharon Dearden, one of his working pupils. It was Sharon who named him Charisma. I remember seeing him at the Pony Club Championships when I was training the local Waikato team. He became quite well-known for his flashy movement and for his antics. Sharon would have won the Pony Club Championships if he hadn't shied and missed the finish flags. On another occasion, she won a maiden hack class but, just as she was receiving the rosette, Charisma bucked her off and performed the victory lap on his own. Sharon did a good job on Charisma and they were long-listed for the Los Angeles Olympics, but her teaching career was beckoning and she reluctantly sold him.

Sharon turned down some significant offers for Charisma because she adored him and wanted him to have a family home. He was bought by Fran Clark, a mother who was interested in getting back into dressage and jumping. When this didn't work out, she lent the horse to Jennifer Stobart, who had taken over from Lockie Richards at the National Equestrian Centre. Jennifer also loved Charisma and got him up to Prix St Georges level in dressage, at which point I came into the equation.

Despite all I'd heard, I still wasn't convinced. It was a snowy two-hour drive down to Taupo, and when I got out of the car there was this very hairy, rather plain-looking little horse. I wondered what on earth I was doing, but I thought if I'd come all this way, I might as well sit on him. He felt amazing: he moved beautifully, he had a brilliant canter, a huge stride, jumped really well, and although I couldn't know he'd be a superstar, he was certainly a nice prospect for the forthcoming season in New Zealand. It all went perfectly: we had five starts, including the national one-day championships and the national three-day-event at Taupo, and he won them all, leading from the start at Taupo and finishing on his dressage mark. I absolutely loved him.

Taupo was made even more special by the fact that Ginny came over for it, our complicated, long-distance relationship having been given a boost by my decision to return to England. I found her a horse to ride, Casino, on whom she led the intermediate dressage before having a stop near the end of the cross-country.

Despite Charisma's obvious talent, there was work to be done, though. For a start, he was a little porker, which was how he earned his enduring nickname, Podge. My friend Greg Keyte helped me divide up the barn so I could control his diet and I bedded him on newspaper strips because it was the only thing he wouldn't eat. I also took him up Kenny Browne's gallops, which had a long uphill pull, every other day, and with his toughness, soundness and endless reserves of energy, he soon hardened up. He was highly trained on the flat, but not in the outline I wanted – he tended to float along with his head in the air and above the bit – and here we did have a few battles. Charisma would stamp his feet and go red-eyed with rage and we'd both be steaming and dripping with sweat.

In December, the chairman of the FEI, Vicomte Jurien de la Graviere of France, came out to New Zealand to give certificates of capability to Olympic hopefuls, which was the only way New Zealand-based riders could qualify for Los Angeles. Charisma easily won the selection trial – and the Vicomte's heart. 'Petit cheval – très, très bon èquilibre. Peut progresser en dressage. Cavalier superbe,' he wrote in his notes, adding: 'I am glad and proud to have met that marvellous horse before he came to Europe.' Despite this vote of confidence, there were quite a few people who wondered why on earth I was taking a Pony Club horse to the Olympics. Fortunately, Bill Hall wasn't one of them, as my next task was to gather up some finance. Fran was keen for Charisma to go to Los Angeles, provided she didn't have to pay the expenses.

* * *

The lucky break came when Judy Hall, one of my lady pupils, tipped me off that her husband Bill might sponsor me through his company, Woolrest, which made sheepskin under-blankets. Bill was a brilliant guy whose kindness was a significant influence in my success in the 1980s. Woolrest leased Charisma and, with no preamble, fuss or even a contract, Bill generously handed over $35,000. My first task was to appear in some advertisements for Woolrest: one for Bell Tea and a television advertisement with Miss World, who was a New Zealander. Bill also bought my other horse, Carlsburg (later rechristened Nightlife), a small brown horse by the same sire as Charisma, Tara Mink, and out of Planet's half-sister.

Before I left New Zealand, I couldn't resist one last dabble in the bloodstock world, and I'd done well on the sale of the cows for $500 a head. I went to the yearling sales in January 1984 and, on the advice of Patrick Hogan, one of New Zealand's leading stud men, bought a filly to race and breed from. I had a budget of $60,000, and found Sounds Like Fun, by Sound Reason, a relatively young but successful sire, for $32,000. I decided that I might as well go to the best trainer, so I sent her to Jim Gibbs, one of the leading trainers and known to be especially good with fillies. Sounds Like Fun became one of the best mares of her generation, winning more than half a million dollars in stakes; she won 11 races, of which seven were Group races, and was second in the New Zealand Oaks in 1986. I gave my parents a half share and, although they had no interest in racing, they got an enormous amount of pleasure out of following her. I kept her to breed from and her bloodlines became the foundation for several horses I had to race some 20 years later but, sadly, she never produced anything anywhere near as good as herself. She's still alive in retirement.

I arrived back in England in February 1984, just before my 28th birthday on 1st March, and, after so much preparation and expectation, everything felt very flat. I'd arranged to rent some stables, but the flat there was damp and cold with no heating. I got a stinking cold and spent my birthday on my own, feeling miserable.

Things looked up when some friends, Charlie and Sarah Cottenham, who had given up eventing by then, let me have their yard at Priory Manor in Kington St Michael near Chip-

penham, and I rented a cottage which rejoiced in the marvellous name of Honeyknob Hill. The horses arrived soon after,
and so did Helen Gilbert, who was to be Charisma's devoted
groom for the next four years. She is English – though she is
now married to a New Zealander and lives in South Island
– and I'd met her when she was working for Toby and Gail
Sturgis in Great Somerford.

* * *

Things got off to a slow start and we nearly didn't go to Badminton. Charisma had caught a bug on the plane which was to
affect his sinuses for the rest of his career, though it certainly
didn't affect his appetite. I also hadn't bargained for the fact
that he'd never experienced soft English mud, and he didn't
like it. He was a very tough, sound horse and he liked the
going to be as hard as a road. He was hopeless at show jumping in mud, and that's why we never won a British three-day
event. Bert also caught a fever on the plane, so it was all down
to Charisma, and after a run-out at Aldon and a fall at Rush-
all, things were not looking good for Badminton. However, he
coped remarkably with it.

I'd started having dressage lessons with Bill Noble, the guru
of his day. He was just down the road, so I could hack there
for lessons, with his partner Trish Gardiner, a leading light
in British dressage. Bill was a good progression for me from
Lockie Richards and Ted Harrison; his thing was working on
the basic principles and I got on well with him. He did a great
job for me. At Badminton, Charisma and I were sixth after
dressage – me in my own tailcoat at last – six penalties behind
Lucinda Green on Beagle Bay, so well in touch. The steeplechase phase was less smooth. After a near miss, when I fell
asleep in the caravan and left myself just seven minutes to get

to the start of Phase A, Charisma found the chase fences rather confusing and thought he had to clear them by miles instead of brushing over them. This was not only rather terrifying, but I was worried that he would take too much out of himself, so when we got to the next roads and tracks, Phase C, I jumped off and led him for the last mile.

The cross-country was not quite the survival test of 1980, but it was big enough for an inexperienced horse. Charisma grew in confidence all the way round, flying Horsens Bridge, a replica of the unfinished bridge over a gaping ditch seen at the recent European Championships, and galloping home strongly to move us up to second place behind Lucinda. It was too much to hope that she'd make a mistake in the jumping again, and of course she didn't, but second place felt thrilling because it seemed to confirm that my instincts were right and we were genuine Olympic contenders.

Ian Stark, a hitherto unsung rider from Scotland, was third on Oxford Blue, which gave him his big break, and Ginny was placed on Priceless. Andrew Nicholson got two horses round at his first attempt, Rubin and Kahlua. The latter was clear and sound, and on that basis Andrew was selected for the Olympics – that's pretty much all you needed to get into a New Zealand team in those days. The other two team-members were Mary Hamilton on Whist and Andrew Bennie, who had yet to come over from New Zealand, on an eight-year-old, Jade.

* * *

New Zealand's Los Angeles bid was a far more concentrated effort than Kentucky six years earlier. This time, we had a vet, Wally Neiderer, a trainer, Bill Noble, and a *chef d'équipe*, Peter Herrick, whose daughter Sarah Harris is now our performance manager and very good at her job. In another circle of coincidence my working pupil then, Erik Duvander from Sweden, is now our *chef d'équipe*.

Los Angeles was amazing. Immediately we had the 'Wow, we're at the Olympics' feeling. Andrew and I went mad: we were down on the athletic track, running and training over the hurdles, we had massages, saunas, everything that was on offer. We ate constantly because the food was brilliant and free, and we had a delightful team liaison officer, Davida, who would come and see us every morning and ask, in her broad Californian accent, 'Wanna go shoppin';' wanna go fishin'?' The slight downside was the stables were an hour away at Santa Anita Racecourse and we had to get up at 6am, but even this had its moments, as we loved it when the bus driver would say: 'Morning, athletes!'

The wonderful thing was feeling a part of it all, along with great athletes like Carl Lewis, tiny Russian gymnasts, tall Chinese basketball players, African-American women runners who walked like panthers and the Kiwi wrestlers and boxers with whom Andrew and I were sharing an apartment and who complained about my smoking. The diversity was endless, and here we were, a bunch of event riders straight off the farm in New Zealand. Los Angeles still rates as the most fun and the friendliest of all the Games I've been to.

As far as our prospects went, I was the only one with realistic form. However, together we made up a useful team and we had a chance of a medal if we all got round. I didn't consider myself to be an individual medal contender, even after my second place at Badminton because, I reasoned, Badminton was only for British riders and all the other big names would be here: Bruce Davidson, his fellow American Mike Plumb, Hansueli Schmutz from Switzerland, and European champion Nils Haagensen from Denmark. The only thing that did seem to be in my favour was everything felt right; in fact it seemed to be going almost too well.

* * *

I was fourth after dressage, behind Hansueli on Oran, Bruce on JJ Babu, and his team-mate Karen Stives on a lovely grey, Ben Arthur. There were discrepancies in the judging – nothing is new in this sport – as although the American judge had put me first on 173, the Swiss and French judges gave me 147 and 142. As we circled the arena before going in for our test, I did a few flying changes and some extended trot, just to give the judges a preview, even though there weren't any changes in the test. Podge had an amazing extended trot and would flick his toes, which made the American crowd go wild. They burst into applause, not realising they should wait until after the test, and Podge flew forward and we nearly blew the whole thing. Fortunately, he had a great mental attitude and I was able to get him back and settle him.

The team order, after much discussion, had been decided as Andrew first, because Kahlua was not full Thoroughbred and needed to go across country in the coolest part of the day, Andrew and Jade second, Mary and Whist third and me as anchorman.

The cross-country was a further hour away, on a golf course at Del Mar, San Diego, at the former home of the Hollywood stars Douglas Fairbanks Jnr and Mary Pickford. Hence Fairbanks Bounce, one of the signature fences on the course and one that has been much copied since, including by Frank Weldon at Badminton the next year. It was beautifully designed by Neil Ayer and had an American theme – there was a rattlesnake at the 13th and a western town at the 14th – but the obstacle that held our attention was a water complex which involved jumping up through two waterfalls; the spray from the first meant you couldn't see what you were doing at the second.

I remember feeling pretty upbeat; I thought the course, which was twisty, would suit Charisma and I was in a good position. We had a day off, in which to settle the horses, and we were buoyed at finding ourselves by the coast and able to have a few drinks at a bar, our first for a few days, although I did, on this occasion, actually go to bed early.

Andrew Nicholson got the team off to a great start, saving Kahlua in the early part of the course and then stepping on it for the last quarter. In a brilliantly judged round, he finished with just one time-penalty – the first of the many trailblazing cross-country rides for which he has become, rightly, so famous. Andrew Bennie didn't have as much luck on Jade, incurring 80 penalties for a stop and fall when he was unseated as the horse swerved at the Golfer's Bench fence. Mary was then under pressure to complete a slow clear, which she did, with 24 time-penalties.

We were clearly out of it as a team, so I was allowed to go for it as an individual. I hadn't been able to hold one side of Podge in training, and now he fairly flew. Pat Daly, a British-based Irish trainer who was helping at the steeplechase phase, said: 'Christ, that horse should be going round Cheltenham.' Podge pulled like anything. He would tuck his head in like a bull and charge, and there was little one could do except pray he wouldn't make a mistake. Unsurprisingly, he had the fastest cross-country round of the day and, despite the boiling temperatures, finished easily inside the time.

There was huge excitement in the New Zealand camp. I was now in second place, behind only Karen Stives. There had been all sorts of excitements. Ginny had gone brilliantly on Priceless for the British team, but her team-mate Tiny Clapham had fallen off quite spectacularly in the water and Bruce had also unexpectedly fallen.

I still wasn't that confident of a medal, though, as show jumping wasn't Podge's strongest point. At home he was as cute as a button and you couldn't catch him out, but when you got him in the ring he either wanted to jump or he didn't. One factor in our favour was that the surface at Santa Anita was very good, and I knew he would like that. My other trump card was that I had Ted Edgar, one of the great names of British show jumping, to help me. I'd been going for help with him in England and he was out in Los Angeles helping the Australian jumping team. Ted was known for being quite frightening – he didn't suffer fools gladly – and there was no messing around, but he gave me confidence. He walked the course with me and, after that, I felt better because I had a plan.

There was a lot of galloping on the show jumping course, with long runs between fences, and Ted advised me to let the horse roll along and then to get him together before the jump instead of holding him up all the way round. Podge had a tendency to tap his way around, which was quite nerve-racking, but in his own funny way he would make an effort. He had good action behind; it was the front end you had to look after.

The last combination on the course, two from home, was like a mass of coloured poles when you turned towards it and I thought if he was going to have something down, it would be that. But he tried his heart out and when he jumped that last fence clear, I thought: 'My God, we've won a silver medal.'

I'd been warming up at the same time as Karen and Ben Arthur, who had been well tuned and was hitting the roof. I thought there was no way he would have a fence down. While she was in the ring someone gave me a cigarette, so I was puffing away, standing on my own, unable to watch. Karen's round seemed to be going on for ever, so I walked up the chute

to have look and, as I did so, she came into that last combination and had part of it down. I just put my hands to my face
and gasped. It was very hard to take in, the fact that I'd won
an Olympic gold medal and, even now, sometimes I have to
remind myself that it actually happened. Everything becomes
a blur, with people crowding in on you, hugging you and offering congratulations. It's euphoric, but bewildering.

* * *

The medal ceremony was one for the record books. It was
New Zealand's first medal of the Games, the first one ever in
equestrianism, and the two either side of me on the podium,
Karen and Ginny, who had the bronze, were making history
as the first women to win individual eventing medals. Extraordinarily, 28 years later, there is still no female individual gold
medallist.

In the first of what was to become a tradition, there was a
huge British-New Zealand party at the stables. I hid my gold
medal in the fridge, as I could see it was going to get messy,
stripped off to my underpants and started a water fight. No
doubt Ian Stark, who was to become a bit of a soul mate on
these occasions, was something to do with it. Ginny and Tiny
both ended up soaked and, in what was to become another
tradition, I dunked Joan Gilchrist, the always jolly editor of
NZ Horse & Pony, in the water trough.

It was all great fun but eventually it all became too much
for me and, to everyone's apparent fury, I purposely went missing the next day. I asked a Californian friend, Nina Patterson,
whom I'd met back in 1978, to rescue me and we spent the day
at the beach where, in the days before mobile phones, I was
oblivious to the frantic search for me. My name was on top
of the New Zealand medals board in the Olympic village, and

the press were going mad. Looking back, it seems naïve but, unpractised in receiving gold medals, I simply didn't realise how much it would mean to everyone.

CHAPTER
FOUR

THE AFTERMATH OF the Los Angeles Olympics was a wonderful time, once I got myself together. There was champagne on the plane home, mainly thanks to Andrew tipping off the airline staff. The Cottenhams and Tom and Mimi May had decorated my cottage with a banner proclaiming 'Well done Toddy' – actually the nickname my father was known as at home, and now mine in Britain – and, of course, there was a party.

It had been New Zealand's best Olympics by far, with eight gold medals – amusingly, all for 'sitting down' sports like sailing, rowing, cycling and riding. So when I eventually got home there was a hero's welcome, even at the airport, and a huge reception in Cambridge where I was given a gold bar on a chain representing the freedom of the town. There was massive media interest – one newspaper described me as New Zealand's most eligible bachelor – and everyone was very excited by the fact that I had kissed Ginny on the podium. The reality was that they were a little slow; we'd had fun in Los Angeles and it was thrilling that we both did so well but, ironically, our four-year on-off relationship was nearly at an end and we knew it.

New Zealand suddenly became the new epicentre of eventing and several international riders were invited out to Pukekohe for the December three-day event. Ian Stark (Scotty), Andrew Hoy, Mark Phillips, Ginny, Mike Plumb, Torrance and Karen Stives all came and competed on borrowed horses. NZBC used the opportunity to broadcast the first ever *This is Your Life* programme in New Zealand, with me as the subject, and even flew out the Baroness. You could have knocked me down with a feather.

The only person who didn't seem too pleased at the turn of events was Charisma's owner, Fran Clark. I think, perhaps, after the heady few months when I was winning everything on her horse in New Zealand in 1983 she felt a bit distanced from events, but she had agreed to lease the horse to Woolrest and it was her decision not to come out to Los Angeles.

Charisma was turned out for the winter with Mel O'Brien (now Duff) near Swindon while I was back in New Zealand for Christmas. Nothing stays a secret in eventing for long and I eventually discovered that Fran had actually been trying to sell the horse for some time – apparently to anyone but me. But she hadn't bargained for the fact that event riders are, generally, a loyal bunch and, though the temptation of buying an Olympic gold medallist must have been great, no one wanted to be the rider that split up what was evidently such a special partnership. The first I knew was a kindly tip-off from the American rider Karen Lende (who later married David O'Connor), who had been contacted about the horse. Then Sally O'Connor got in touch to say that she'd been asked to be the selling agent in the States, and what was the story?

At this stage, Fran and I were still communicating, albeit a bit frostily, but the price she was quoting me – $250,000 – was ridiculous and way beyond my scope. She kept changing her mind about whether she wanted Charisma at home in her paddock or whether she wanted to sell him, most of which I gathered through the New Zealand press but, ultimately, I was made aware that I wasn't part of any deal. The greatest friend in this debacle was Lizzie Purbrick. She was a tremendous wheeler-dealer – many a drinks party would be punctuated by Lizzie manically shouting into a phone about selling shares – and she had no fear of confrontation. She is also fiercely loyal and had become a close friend by now.

Having met Fran at Badminton and scooped her up for a drink, Lizzie too received the call asking her if she was interested in the horse. Reggie managed to stall the deal, saying cautiously that the horse would make a wonderful birthday present to Lizzie, but what Fran didn't know was that Lizzie was pregnant and not looking for any more horses. I was so desperate not to be parted from Charisma that I eventually asked Lizzie if she would buy him and sell him straight to Woolrest. It was a tall order but Lizzie loves a challenge, and the two women agreed to meet at the Cavalry Club in London to discuss the details of the sale.

I felt much more confident after we'd formulated this daring plan but there was potential for an awful lot to go wrong. Fran asked Lizzie lots of searching questions about her plans for the horse and was insistent that she try him. This was the last thing Lizzie wanted to do, being in the early stages of pregnancy, but a lucky snowstorm blocked the M4 and Fran left England before the weather cleared. Then the timing was tight on wiring the money – agreed at $50,000 – from Woolrest into Lizzie's account, so that it could then be transferred to Fran, all in a couple of days. I felt completely helpless in all this, so the relief when I heard the plan had come off was overwhelming. Really special horses only come along once in a lifetime – I fully understand how the show jumper John Whitaker must have felt about the thought of anyone else riding Milton, or the devastation the Dutch dressage rider Edward Gal must have felt when world champion Totilas was sold from under him.

My horse was Charisma both by name and by nature, and I adored him. We were such an unlikely combination – he was cute and small and I was tall and lanky. It was such a good story – a little horse just doing Pony Club in New Zealand travels across the world and wins the Olympics – that we captured everyone's imagination. The thought that I might have lost him was – and still is – unbearable. He was far more than just another event horse to me.

* * *

Los Angeles had been the point of such sustained focus that when it actually came off I almost didn't know what to do with myself, and found it hard to re-focus on my career, which was not helped by a fall at Burghley 1984 on Nightlife. But now Charisma was actually mine, life could go forward at last.

We had a great 1985 season, with three one-day event wins in the spring before second place – again – at Badminton. The great sadness is that Charisma never won a three-day event in Britain, but the show jumping phase was always the weakest link. We lost Badminton in that phase. We'd been second after dressage to Torrance on Finvarra, swapping places after cross-country despite being nearly blinded by a snowstorm while we were on the steeplechase. Ginny was in third place after cross-country on Priceless and both Torrance and I had to go clear in the show jumping to stay ahead of her – neither of us did, and so, amid great fanfare, Ginny notched up the first of her three Badminton wins.

The 21st-century idea of saving a horse for a championship hadn't entirely caught on then, mainly because the major events were few and far between and riders had fewer chances and fewer horses. But Charisma was 13, an age when a lot of horses' careers tended to peter out after season after season of marathon three-day events – roads and tracks alone was 14 miles at top level. My next big goal was to win the World Championships in Gawler, Australia in 1986, the last time it was staged as a stand-alone event. So I gave him a lighter autumn, and he won four out of his five one-day events, including the British Open at Gatcombe in torrential rain. A lot of people withdrew, but I had the benefit of an earlier ride on Michaelmas Day and knew that Charisma would be able to gallop through the sloppy conditions.

Gatcombe is always a great competition, with the cross-country run in reverse order of merit up and down the steep slopes of the Princess Royal's park, and if you're in the lead after dressage and show jumping, it's a nerve-racking wait. I was in the joint lead with Jonquil Sainsbury (now Hemming) on Hassan, and she went last, maintaining suspense right to the last minute as she finished just one second slower than me.

I moved yards that season, as the Cottenhams wanted to convert their stables into flats. After a brief spell in a yard at Mere, Wiltshire, where Erik lived in a mobile home and kept an eye on the horses by night, I moved to the equestrian centre at Cholderton, near Salisbury, after hearing about it from Moysie Barton, whose children I taught. The yard, which had been previously occupied by Sue Benson and then Richard Meade, had 19 boxes, which seemed an alarming amount, but it's funny how horses arrived to fill them. I'd sold Nightlife to Germany, and his replacement was Susan and Michael Welman's Michaelmas Day, who became a favourite. We won our first three-day together at Rotherfield Park and afterwards 'Mick' was always there or thereabouts in the prizes, and was a good second string to Charisma.

I had one of the most dramatic cross-country moments of my life on Mick at Boekelo. We were going at high speed, Mick's preferred pace, on the way to the first fence, which involved going over a bridge. I'd already been warned by an official that the right-hand side of it, which was taped off, was beginning to give way, and as we flew across it Mick went straight through. I came off, with the bizarre feeling that my horse had simply disappeared from underneath me, and he then galloped off, but I was blowed if I was going to give up at such an early point on the course and chased after him. When I eventually caught him, the reins and breastplate were broken but, in typical Boekelo fashion, the officials insisted that I was allowed to regroup and start again, something I can't imagine happening now. Mick, who could easily have broken his leg, was quite unfazed and we finished third.

* * *

The next year, 1986, was momentous in many ways. It started with a fantastic trip to a show jumping competition on snow at Koessen, Austria, to which I'd been invited with Clissy and Mel, plus the British show jumping comedy act of Graham Fletcher and Geoff Billington. There was never a dull moment and I decided it was the place to celebrate my 30th birthday six weeks later. Clissy, of course, came for that one too, plus the German rider Bettina Overesch (now Hoy), British rider Bryn Powell and his wife Sue and Rodney Powell (no relation).

There are few sports in which a nation would be so ready to embrace a competitor from another country, especially if there was the possibility that they might beat you at the championships, but it's one of the reasons why I still love this sport so much. Charisma was allowed to join the British team horses in quarantine for Gawler at Wylye. I shared a room with Andy

Griffiths, reserve with a horse called Hullabaloo (Andy is now an FEI technical delegate, involved in developing the sport in Eastern Europe), and was invited to join the riders for formal dinner with the Russells every night – unlike the Germans, who also had their horses there!

The Russells were remarkably tolerant, because it goes without saying that a group of event riders confined to barracks with only one horse apiece to ride will inevitably start messing around. Or, at least, they did in the days long before world-class performance plans and government targets in sport. We used to fill Lord Hugh's gin bottles with water and one day we organised a lethal bareback puissance in the indoor school at Cholderton.

Clissy and Scotty both had other horses stabled with me at Cholderton while the world championship horses were in quarantine, and there were lots of laughs, the *pièce de résistance* being a somewhat disgraceful occasion when Scotty and I ended up in prison. We'd been to Dynes Hall, a good advanced event that used to be run by the Hunnable family in Essex, and Scotty won a magnum of champagne. It poured with rain and the lorry park became gridlocked, waiting for the one tractor to pull everyone out, so, while we were waiting it seemed only sensible to have a couple of drinks. We then set off, and after about 10 miles we decided we were in such fine form that another gin and tonic might be in order, so we stopped in a pub. Ian then mentioned that he felt a bit pissed, to which I said carelessly: 'Oh, I feel fine,' and got behind the steering wheel of his car.

By the time we were on the M25, it seemed a really great idea to tap into the champagne. The next thing I knew, there was a blue flashing light behind me. I pulled up and got out of the car, trying to look together for the benefit of the policeman who coldly informed me that I was doing 100mph in thick fog

– I was wondering why I couldn't see very well. He gestured to Scotty and said, 'You're coming with us – he can drive the car,' at which point I felt compelled to point out that my passenger was in a worse state than me. When we got to the police station, I promptly fell asleep in my cell and Scotty stomped around ranting until they got fed up and threw him out into the car park.

Twenty-five years later, this is not an episode that I look back on with any pride, but it shows what an appallingly relaxed attitude we all had to drinking and driving in the 1980s. I pleaded in court that, as a fit sportsman, I wasn't used to drinking and, as a result, was lucky to only lose my licence for a year. I was also lucky to have such a lovely chauffeur to rescue me, for by now Carolyn Berry had entered my life.

I first noticed her in 1982 when we were introduced, through a mutual friend, Martin Dobson, at a show in Hawkes Bay, New Zealand, and she was wearing a notably brief pair of shorts. Then her father, Keith, published a book that I wrote with Sally O'Connor, *Todd's Ride*, and I signed a copy for her, which gave me the excuse to chat her up a week later at a party given by Cindy Mitchenor in Wellington. Carolyn subsequently wrote to me to ask if she could base herself with me to do her British Horse Society AI (Assistant Instructors) exam with me but, paperwork not being my strong suit, I failed to reply. At our next meeting, she presented me with a box of pens and, with what I was to discover was typical feistiness, suggested that lack of a writing implement had obviously prevented me from replying to her.

Carolyn was not only strikingly gorgeous, with lovely wild white-blonde hair and a beautiful face, but she was also funny, gutsy and combative and, right from the start, we always talked very naturally together. I enjoyed her company hugely and I think I always knew that our relationship was going to

With Shamrock on Pop's farm – with Kenny Browne's in the background

Me aged nine, and Nugget, on Pop's farm – wearing the policeman's helmet that doubled as a hard hat

Pop, the man who probably started the whole thing, and my old terrier, Dazzle

Surprise winners of Badminton, 1980. Monty and me with the beautiful Whitbread trophy

Innocence is bliss: Monty flies the terrifying Normandy Bank en route to winning Badminton in 1980

The Gawler World Championships, before disaster struck. Note the huge fence and flimsy timber, typical of 1980s-style cross-country

This was a proper cross-country fence – Any Chance at the awesome ski jump at Badminton, 1986

With Michael Welman, one of the most loyal early owners, at Thirlestane Castle, 1986

A hug from Carolyn after a clear round at Burghley in 1987

Podge (right) is thoroughly annoyed at being second to Wilton Fair at Burghley 1987

Perfect partners, even if we're not seeing eye to eye here. Charisma at Stockholm, 1987

Charisma was the fittest of them all in Seoul

You know you've done well when the equestrian press surround you. Joan Gilchrist is on my right (Seoul Olympics, 1988)

At the Seoul Olympics in 1988 with my two great mates Scotty and Ginny – but I'm on the highest podium!

With Carolyn in Seoul

I didn't quite do the double in Seoul – Bago tries his heart out in the show jumping

With Scotty in one of our many mad moments – Oxford Blue and I have the advantage over him and Sir Wattie around the Cheltenham fences

Carolyn on Dun for Fun (Banana) at Everdon in 1989

Mr Todd gave me a nerve-racking ride over Bechers in the Eventers v. Jockeys challenge (1989)

Podge takes centre stage again – the only horse to open a Commonwealth Games
(Auckland, 1990)

Fairytales do come true – winning Badminton on Horton Point for the Bevan sisters in 1994

My face says it all – doing the Badminton lake on Bertie Blunt with one stirrup is not ideal (1995)

At last – Bertie Blunt gets the win he deserves at Badminton in 1996

be far more than working pupil and trainer, not least because she didn't mind arguing with me. She didn't take long to pass her AI in the spring of 1986 but, to my relief, she agreed to stay on and look after Cholderton while I was away in Australia at Gawler.

The New Zealand squad for Gawler was me, Trudy Boyce on Mossman, Tinks Pottinger on Volunteer, Merran Hain on a six-year-old Chief, and Blyth Tait on Rata. Blyth had come from the similar background in racing and show jumping as Andrew Nicholson and me. This was his first major event and he didn't really know anyone, but he was soon to discover the friendly nature of the sport after a terrible incident when Rata dropped dead of a heart attack while cantering and everyone, especially the British camp, rallied round to try and cheer him up.

We were all stuck out in Australia with not enough to do for far too long, something that would never happen now with riders fretting about getting back to their businesses, but it was brilliant fun, everyone got on and the Australian hospitality was superb. After the novelties of wine-tasting – Australian wine was a new thing in Britain then – and barbecues started to wear off, we went in search of more high-octane stuff. A group of us – Lorna Clarke, who was on the British team, Scotty, Tinks, Mel Duff and I – went water-skiing on the Murray River. We were allowed to drive our own boat and, naturally, I volunteered, and, for the second time that year, nearly did Scotty serious injury.

It was obvious that he was far from expert in water-skiing, but he is a renowned daredevil – he's a fearless skier and now flies his own plane – and was soon upright. He then got a bit cocky and started ordering me to drive the boat faster. With the others' encouragement, I got the boat on a tight turn which had Scotty going wider and wider and faster and faster until he had to let go of the rope and spun off like a pebble across the water. In hindsight, this was another ill-advised prank, but we got away with it.

We were put up in an agricultural college and Charisma was stabled next to the German horse Fair Lady, ridden by Claus Erhorn, and they became inseparable. Podge found quarantine boring but he also had a great sense of occasion, liked attention and was working brilliantly. We were second to Torrance and Finvarra after dressage – again – but this was to be the last time Podge was beaten in the dressage phase of a three-day event.

The cross-country terrain was hilly, the going was slippery – Scotty had a fall with Sir Wattie when the horse slipped – and the fences were an erratic mix of massive and tiny. The water complex, Dead Man's Pass, was controversial – a bounce stride in water, which is never an exact science, to a rail in the water. There was no nice way of achieving the distance on the direct route – Tinks was the only person who did it well, on Volunteer. Torrance's horse bashed his nose on the rail, which made it bleed, so she went slowly after that and accrued time-penalties; Clissy, a member of the British team, fell on Delphy Dazzle, and Ginny cleverly managed to fiddle a route through on the adjustable Priceless, one of the cleverest cross-country horses around.

If I'd taken some advice from the British camp who, despite being thousands of miles from home, still had a mass army of volunteer spotters, things might have been different, but my information was that Volunteer had done the left-hand route brilliantly and that was my best plan. The trouble was that Volunteer was a rangy 17hh; poor little Podge, at 15.2hh, tried his best but the bounce distance was too far, he bellied the rail and was spectacularly submerged.

Podge had water in his ears and my boots were full of it; it was totally demotivating. I was slipping around in the saddle, and furious with myself for blowing my chance of a world title, but I had to keep going for the sake of the team result. I knew that Merran had had two falls on Chief who, in truth, should never have been put under that sort of pressure. Nowadays you would never ride a six-year-old in a championship; not only would they not be qualified, but you'd be considered mad.

The good news on my return was that the New Zealand team was, unbelievably, in gold medal position and Tinks was in the individual lead. The bad news, however, was that Volunteer had developed a big knee after walloping a fence, so celebrations were muted. Next morning, Volunteer was visibly not quite right – although it wasn't a tendon problem and a round of show jumping probably wouldn't have hurt him – but the ground jury president, our old friend Vicomte Jurien de la Graviere, pronounced him 'laming dead' and that was it.

The Brits easily won team gold, Ginny took the individual title, later sportingly heaping her sash and medals onto poor Tinks, and Trudy deservedly got the individual silver medal ahead of Lorna Clarke in bronze with Myross. In the circumstances, there was nothing left to do except invade the British camp's surprisingly sober party, and I was soon drowning my sorrows and dancing on tables with Scotty and Mark Phillips, who was later seen climbing a flagpole.

* * *

Back at Cholderton, things looked up on several fronts. First, I was approached by the investment bankers Merrill Lynch offering me sponsorship. The mid-1980s were boom time and, as sponsorships so often depended on the enthusiasms of the chairman, I was lucky that Stanny Yassicovich, managing director of Merrill Lynch Europe, liked riding. He took over my faithful Woolrest lorry, which Bill Hall had let me keep when the sponsorship ended, repainting it with Merrill Lynch logos, and gave me £60,000 a year to spend on the horses in the run-up to the 1988 Seoul Olympics. It felt like riches beyond belief.

Things were also looking up on the romantic side. Carolyn may have ostensibly been the chauffeur but I was secretly keen to know what all my friends thought about her. Needless to say, she got an overwhelming seal of approval, and I invited her to come down to an event in Spain, at La Granja. This was where the relationship really took off, my being spurred into action by Clissy's Australian friend Shaun, who was taking rather too much interest in Carolyn for my liking.

I won La Granja, on a horse appropriately called Larking About, which obviously helped the merriment of the occasion, but it would have been a hilarious weekend on any count. The dressage judges sat underneath beach umbrellas, the steeple-chase phase went within 10 metres of the front of the stables, the roads and tracks went up a mountain and the cross-country fences were made of concrete blocks. I can't begin to imagine the level of complaint there would be nowadays, but then we considered these offbeat events the most fun to go to. Often, the smaller continental events would pay riders to attend, and the hospitality could be incredibly generous.

A group of us went, on that basis, to Avenches in Switzerland. We were all given Range Rovers to drive and, on the evening of the cocktail party in a tent in a field, Anna Cassagrande, a wild Italian rider, drove hers full bore across the field, lights blazing. She drove straight into the tent and pinned the ground jury against the bar. On the same trip, Clissy managed to drive hers at speed over a railway crossing, took off into space and came down heavily, bending the axle. No wonder today's events are more sober affairs. I always enjoyed having a good time, though I have never ever let partying be to the detriment of my performance at any level of competition. I do, though, concede that I may be blessed with the knack of being able to ride well with a hangover!

La Granja was followed by a holiday in Marbella, when a group of us – myself and Carolyn, Rodney Powell, British team rider Rachel Hunt and an Australian rider, Scott Keach – stayed on a boat owned by friends of Bryn and Sue Powell. It was an incredibly happy week, Carolyn and I were head over heels in love and, by now, our romance was public knowledge.

Charisma had come out of his Gawler trip in incredibly good shape, even emerging unscathed after the plane landed so badly at Luton Airport that horses and humans were swept off their feet. He seemed so fit and keen that I decided to take him to the three-day event at Luhmühlen. There was considerable muttering about the wisdom of taking a horse to another three-day event so soon, but Charisma soon silenced the critics. He produced a dressage score of 29.2, including three tens, put his bad experience in the water at Gawler behind him with a bold cross-country performance, and won, beating Bettina Overesch (now Hoy) and Lucinda Green. I was also on a winning team for the first time, as a member of the 'Commonwealth' quartet with Lucinda and Scotty. We beat Italy and Germany by more than 100 points and, as a result, Luhmühlen banned composite teams!

On the evening after Podge's wonderful dressage test, I asked Carolyn to marry me. She said yes straight away and next day we started broadcasting our good news, making such a noise that people started 'shushing' us because they were trying to concentrate on the dressage. My mother was so startled when I told her I was engaged, she said: 'Who to?' This was a reasonable question, seeing as Carolyn and I had really only been going out for two months and the last time I'd had a discussion with my mother about my romantic life, my girlfriend was a British event rider, Jane Swallow.

The wedding was on 29th November in Wellington Cathedral, a nerve-racking occasion but a very happy one. A good crowd of my eventing friends came over. Brendan Corscadden was best man, a bit of a shock to his system. Clissy, Mel and Mick Duff, Rodney, Jane Starkey and Dot Love, a Danish rider who lived in Ireland, came out. I arranged for them to ride borrowed horses at Pukekohe.

As they'd all come so far, it seemed rude not to invite them to share our honeymoon, the first part of which was spent in Pop's house on the beach at Mt Maungnamui. Carolyn and I were supposed to return to England via the Maldives, but this idea got dropped in favour of watching my filly, Sounds Like Fun, finish second in the New Zealand Oaks. It did dawn on me, even at this early stage, what a tolerant wife I had.

* * *

Our first marital home was Chauffeur's Cottage, part of the Wilbury Park estate owned by Lady St Just who, it turned out, was the latest of my mildly eccentric landladies. Maria St Just, a widow, was a White Russian and a former ballet dancer and actress. She soon ticked off Carolyn, whom she called 'Dizzy' for her blonde hair, for saying to her general help Toogood, 'Do call me Carolyn.'

'Dizzy, darling, you cannot have staff calling you by your first name,' Maria said firmly. 'You are Mrs Todd.'

Maria was well connected. The former inmate of Chauffeur's Cottage was the Greek socialite and journalist Taki, and Maria was an executor for the writer Tennessee Williams. Her dinner guests ranged from film-makers James Ivory and Ismail

Merchant to rock star Bryan Ferry and the Duke of Beaufort. We loved living there.

The cancellation of Badminton in the spring of 1987, due to wet ground, remains one of the greatest disappointments of my career. I was convinced it was Charisma's year. If ever a horse should have been on Badminton's roll of honour, he was the one, and I knew that it was his last chance if he was to get to Seoul the following year. I managed to find an enjoyable distraction that weekend though, in the form of a point-to-point ride. I had a horse that I'd bred in New Zealand, called I'm Bad, and, as his name suggests, he had been nothing but trouble. He'd been turned out for a year with a cracked pastern and was a complete pain. He ran away with Carolyn and tried to scrape me off on the wall of the indoor school.

I sent him to Moysie Barton to sell and she reported that he'd been enjoying running with her point-to-pointers, so why didn't we qualify him for the local Tidworth point-to-point? My experience in this field was limited to say the least – one hurdle ride as a teenager in New Zealand and two falls out of two rides on point-to-pointers owned by a friend of Bobbie Neville's. However, I'm Bad went really well at Tidworth and we decided to put him into training. Mick Duff and Alfie Buller, who runs Scarvagh Stud in Northern Ireland, took shares with Carolyn and me, and we sent him to be trained by David Elsworth of Desert Orchid fame. His first run was a smart novice hurdle at Cheltenham, in which he got beaten by a neck. We were offered £50,000 for him, but turned it down as we were quite excited about him. This was unfortunate as he only raced twice more. He was difficult to train – christened 'I'm Mad' by stable staff – and eventually had to be put down after another horse galloped into him and sliced through a tendon in his hind leg.

On the eventing front, Charisma won Saumur, France's pre-

mier event and now a three-star, and finished sixth in Stockholm, where he didn't like the soggy ground and hit four show
jumps. I entered him for Burghley, our last chance to win a
British four-star event.

My other Burghley ride that year was Wilton Fair – known
unflatteringly at home as Big Red Willy – which I had upgraded
from intermediate after his owner, Lucy Robinson, decided she
didn't want to do any more with him. Despite his inexperience
he went very well around Burghley and after cross-country I
was in the lead on Podge, who had been as enthusiastic as ever,
and second on Will. If only we'd stayed in that order.

Will, a really genuine horse, show jumped clear; Podge,
showing his usual disdain for the coloured poles, hit two
fences. I was still first and second, which was a new Burghley record, and I should have been pleased but it felt like the
wrong way round. Inside, I was so disappointed not to have
won on Podge, and he obviously sensed it, because as I led him
into the arena for prize-giving alongside Will, he sulked and
put his ears back.

I got four other new rides in 1987: Jued Lad, an intermediate produced by Jackie Wright, Pedro the Cruel, on loan from
Lizzie – she liked calling her horses after insane kings – Peppermint Park, a handsome, Irish-bred grey whom I bought
from Penny and Martin Podmore, and Bahlua, who had been
sent over from New Zealand by John Nicholson for Andrew
to sell. We also got Done For Fun for Carolyn, an attractive
dun with a bit of Connemara blood who turned out to be
exceptionally naughty.

Bahlua was ninth at Breda in Holland, and Pedro the Cruel
and Peppermint Park, who hadn't been evented before, were
first and third. We also had Santiago de la Rocha's horses at
Cholderton. Santi was a Spanish airline pilot with Iberia whom
I'd met at La Granja. He wasn't a very experienced rider but

he had ambitions to event at top level and asked me to find him a horse. We got him Mr Todd, who had been successful with Irish rider John Watson and was now hunting in Ireland with Erica Jewitt. Mr Todd was a brilliant schoolmaster whose honesty made up for Santi's lack of accuracy, and after a clear round at Windsor, which was only two-star level, they were suddenly qualified to represent Spain in the European Championship at Luhmühlen.

I travelled out to Germany as Santi's trainer and advised him not to take the direct route through the water on the cross-country, but he took absolutely no notice of me and Mr Todd popped through like a pro. Only one other rider took that route all day and Santi moved up to eventual 12th place, at what was only his second three-day event, so I didn't really have the heart to criticise.

Carolyn and I then returned to New Zealand in time for our first wedding anniversary. We had double cause for celebration: she was pregnant and I was given a chance to make history by competing in two disciplines at the Seoul Olympics in Korea.

* * *

Flushed with the rising prominence of New Zealand eventers, the New Zealand Horse Society decided they'd like to send a show jumping team to Seoul. Merran Hain, my team-mate in Gawler and a very good all-round horsewoman, had a horse called Bago, bred in New Zealand by the part-Hanoverian stallion Winnebago, and she was prepared to fly him to England for me to compete.

What Bago lacked in technique, he more than made up for in courage and scope. No jump was too big for him. He had been well-produced by Merran and, after we came second in a grand prix at Isola, I was thrilled by the prospect of having an extra Olympic chance.

Olympic anticipation built excitedly at Cholderton. Tinks Pottinger came to stay with her two horses, Volunteer and Graphic, and we had Santi's two horses, Mr Todd and Kinvarra, plus Bago, who arrived in May. We held a fund-raising event, as a sort of antidote to the plethora of British team fund-raising events, and called it the Alternative Olympics. Riders dressed up in fancy dress and performed dressage and jumping on hobby horses, and I remember that Robert Lemieux, the British team reserve in Los Angeles, looked particularly fetching in fishnet tights. Anyway, it was a hilarious evening which raised £2,000.

Bahlua acquitted himself well at his first major event, finishing second at Saumur in 1988, but my first choice for Seoul was always going to be Charisma, even though I was facing fierce criticism for daring to take a 16-year-old horse all the way to Korea. There was nothing wrong with Podge's fitness, though, and I almost regretted not entering him for Badminton. He peaked way too soon that spring, behaving really naughtily at Brockenhurst where he flattened the show jumps and pulled my arms out across country. His results that spring really weren't great, which made people mutter all the more, but he was way too full of himself and would play the fool at one-day events. At the final trial, at Holker Hall, he did a brilliant dressage and then ruined it by bolting in the show jumping and whacking out five fences. Most of the Brits didn't run at Gatcombe, feeling it was too close to the departure for Seoul, but I felt Podge could do with a bit of squashing. There was certainly nothing of the old horse about him that day, and he won his second British Open title.

I was also busy getting as much jumping practice as I could on Bago. We had some help from the New Zealand show jumper Jeff McVean, who was based in Britain, and we didn't disgrace ourselves although our results weren't startling. Bago never looked like stopping, but he was careless and I think the travelling probably took too much out of him. I was fascinated by the completely different feel of the jumping circuit. There is, of course, plenty of camaraderie between riders, just as there is in eventing, but it's a much more business-like, brisk atmosphere, probably because more money is at stake.

I had another chance to experience a different sport with the televised eventers versus jockeys challenge. The idea was that the jockeys, the likes of Graham McCourt, Richard Dunwoody, Steve Smith-Eccles and Simon Sherwood, would ride around Gatcombe's cross-country course on borrowed horses, which I think they found pretty terrifying in reality, and a group of eventers would jump the Aintree fences. Robert Lemieux, Rodney Powell, Ian Stark, Polly Lyon (now Williamson) and Madeleine Gurdon were among the eventers, and it was certainly exhilarating, if frightening. I rode Mr Todd, thinking he would give me an armchair ride, but he showed an alarming disdain for the steeplechase fences, whacking all of them as hard as he could except Becher's, which he jumped beautifully.

On 23rd July, Carolyn and I went to a Michael Jackson concert at Wembley with the Purbricks and the Duffs. We'd been looking forward to it for ages, and Carolyn was determined not to give birth until after the concert. She just made it – next morning, she went into hospital and our daughter Lauren was born on the Monday evening. I spent a bit of time pacing around outside with a cigarette and I can't pretend it was exactly a fun time for anyone, least of all Carolyn, obviously, but I have to say that a farming background comes in handy! We were both thrilled with our baby daughter, even if she screamed quite a lot for the first few months. Much of the burden fell to Carolyn, because I was away competing a lot, but I was still quite a hands-on father and I did my share of nappy-changing.

I set off for Seoul in early September and Carolyn followed a couple of weeks later, leaving Lauren at home with a friend's nanny. The horses' flight was reduced from 20 to 14 hours when the Russians agreed the plane could fly over Moscow, and after a 36-hour quarantine period, they arrived at Kwa-Chon racecourse in Korea.

The team – Andrew Bennie, Tinks and Marges Knighton, who had come over from New Zealand – was housed in a somewhat spartan apartment in the Olympic village. There were lots of complaints about the food, although we were promised that no cat or dog was served, but things looked up when we invented a new drink: Sustagin. This was a combination of Sustalyte, a lime-flavoured electrolyte drink which the medical team was keen that we took to prevent dehydration but we thought was a good replacement for tonic, and gin. Funnily enough, it proved quite popular with team officials, other riders and athletes when they had finished their events.

I was slightly calmer and less awe-struck by this Olympics, and didn't rush around so crazily, but this was partly due to the fact that I was dieting because I didn't want to be too heavy on Charisma's back in the heat and also because Bahlua, my second string, had kicked me in the groin when I was picking out his feet. I was also felled by a disastrous night out with the French riders to Itaewon, in the Chinatown of Seoul, where we rashly drank a skinful of rice wine and ate the local food of cooked cabbage. I only lasted half an hour in the nightclub we went on to, and had to call a taxi, mumbling 'Olympic village'. I lay in the back of the taxi with my head out of the window, throwing up, and to this day I can't cope with the smell of rice wine or cabbage

The Koreans had spared no expense in the racecourse

facilities, which were excellent, and every day we travelled there by bus, which had a police motorcycle escort and took off across red lights with no regard to the rest of the traffic. They were also very friendly and, realising they had no equestrian heritage, had made a huge effort to replicate the layout of Santa Anita with touching detail, even down to similar coloured flags.

I spent the Seoul Olympics in a strangely calm state, possessed by a sense of déjà vu, in that everything seemed to be going well, just as it had in Los Angeles. Charisma felt so fantastic and, although I was the defending champion, I felt no pressure because everyone thought it such an insane idea to bring a 16-year-old horse. No one was expecting me to replicate Los Angeles, and most of the gold medal expectations centred on the British team – Ginny, Scotty, Mark Phillips and Karen Straker (now Dixon).

Charisma confounded everyone's expectations – except mine, because I knew he would be brilliant. He produced the dressage test of his career to take the lead on 37.6, ahead of Claus Erhorn and Justin Thyme, a British horse he'd bought from Anne-Marie Taylor, an individual at Gawler, on 39.6. Ginny was third on 43.2 on Master Craftsman, who, at eight, was half Charisma's age.

In a year in which the Germans were to the fore, winning team gold across all three Olympic disciplines, it was even more to Podge's credit that the German judge Bernd Springorum gave him the best marks. The late Pegotty Henriques, then *Horse & Hound*'s dressage correspondent, wrote: 'The test they [myself and Podge] showed together was as good as you need to see at this level and probably more faultless than the Grand Prix Special that the [dressage] gold medallists Nicole Uphoff and Rembrandt performed.' The Germans led after dressage, with Britain second, but New Zealand was third, less than a fence away from the Germans, so there was great excitement.

The cross-country course-designer, Hugh Thomas, who was to succeed Frank Weldon at Badminton the following year, had his work cut out because, like Fairbanks, this was not ideal ground, and the course was hilly and twisty. He also had the heat to consider and the considerable discrepancy in ability between nations. The Brits wanted the jump into the water lowered, with which we disagreed, although the ground jury agreed and also adjusted two other fences.

The roads and tracks were certainly something different, as they passed through paddy fields and people's back yards, where we'd be waved at by women hanging out the washing. I ran beside Podge for some of the way, though he was so above himself it was a moot point who was doing the leading, and he tore around the steeplechase course, finishing 20 seconds under time.

My diet had worked and I weighed in at 11st 8lb, which meant I had to carry my saddle to weigh in at the required 11st 11lb (this minimum weights rule was dropped in the 1990s) so I was confident that I wouldn't be expecting Podge to carry more than the minimum allowed. Not that my presence on his back seemed to be bothering him in the slightest. He made the cross-country feel like a Pony Club track, taking a terrific hold right from the start, jumping immaculately and tearing up the final hill. He produced the fastest time of the day, and when I pulled him up at the finish, he showed off with a few strides of extended trot, as if to say: 'I told you so.' His heart rate recovery was the best of all the horses so to say that I felt vindicated was an understatement.

The course caused more trouble than we expected. Tinks put in a beautiful round and was one of very few inside the time; Marges had three stops and Andrew a fall, but we were still in bronze medal position behind the Germans and the Brits. The latter had had a tricky time; Mark Phillips's horse Cartier was lame and didn't start, Karen fell off in the water, and both Scotty, who was by now in silver position on Sir Wattie, and Ginny in bronze, had enough time-faults to give me three show jumps in hand.

I was hopeful that this surely had to be enough of a lee-way, even for Podge, who felt as cocky as ever on the final day. Working on the principle that he'd get less arrogant if the warm-up was kept to a minimum, I didn't do much with him beforehand, and it paid off. He had the first part of the treble down, but we managed not to hit anything else, and as the last two fences approached, I had to resist the temptation to gallop at them out of sheer relief.

We finished a whole 10 penalties clear of Scotty and Sir Wattie, a remarkable winning margin for a championship, and the elation and affection I felt for my marvellous little horse was huge. Ian and Ginny were the two leading British riders of the era, my main rivals and my close friends, so to be on the podium with them was also wonderful and appropriate, but I was delighted to be on a higher step! New Zealand's team bronze was a source of major satisfaction, too, and showed that we were on our way to being a world force. It was a proud day.

We went back to the stables to crack open the champagne and I rode Podge out in his headcollar so that he could feel part of the celebrations. He adored the attention and shoved forward to lick the champagne bottle. Joan Gilchrist got her traditional dunking, but otherwise celebrations were reasonably muted; I was still a bit under the weather from the rice wine episode and I was going straight into the show jumping contest on Bago the next day, so Carolyn and I headed off for a night of luxury – and some western food – at a five-star hotel.

* * *

My show jumping campaign got off to a rather less distinguished start. In the practice round Bago had the worst score, four fences down and a time-fault, so it looked as if I might get no further. However, he sharpened up after schooling and we were selected to join Maurice Beatson on Jefferson Junior, Harvey Wilson on Crosby and John Cottle with Ups & Downs. The latter horse was sore, though, so was replaced by Colin McIntosh on Gigolo.

Olaf Petersen, the Swedish course-designer, built a course which tested technical ability on the part of the rider as well as raw power in the horse, but it was pretty much beyond the reach of riders such as us who had little access to the big European competitions. Our team finished 12th, but my individual hopes were still alive, and Bago produced his best performance yet in the individual qualifier, just one fence down, which left us in 12th place, a satisfying result.

This meant I finally got a chance to appear in the main Olympic stadium. Historically that was the setting for the individual show jumping final, though from 1992 it took place at the specialist equestrian venue. Disappointingly, there was no bigger an audience than the sparse gathering that had attended the eventing. The course was huge, and we were somewhat outclassed. He jumped the difficult lines and big fences brilliantly but had the three easiest fences down. However, it was still a thrill and it made me determined to plan another two-pronged assault on the Olympics in 1992 in Barcelona.

CHAPTER
FIVE

CAROLYN AND I RETURNED to New Zealand that winter with two main aims: first, to show off Lauren to our families and, second, to find some more horses. Charisma and Bago had been flown back to New Zealand straight from Seoul, accompanied by Helen Gilbert. I had always had a private bargain with Charisma that whatever happened in Seoul, win, lose or draw, he would be retired straight afterwards. He was so fit that it was desperately tempting to keep him for another year, and I was dreading not having him around but, as many wise old horses do, he was starting to get cheeky and muck around when he didn't think the occasion was important enough for him, and I couldn't bear the thought of his results petering out ignominiously.

My foray into show jumping had fired me up to do more, so the first task was to find another jumper. Double Take belonged to my parents' neighbour, Penny Stevenson. He had been bred as a shepherd's horse, but Penny spotted his potential when a farm worker brought him to one of her clinics. When I tried him, I could feel that he was something special, scopey yet careful. I was also swayed by the fact that he was part trotter, and the individual gold medal in Seoul had been won by Pierre

Durand of France with a wonderful black stallion, Jappeloup, who had some trotting blood. The snag was that I couldn't really afford the horse but, once again, Bill Hall stepped in generously to rescue me.

Our other major purchase was Mayhill, a New Zealand Thoroughbred stallion who turned out to be amazing value at a mere $3,000. He came from Dorothy Johnson who was, oddly enough, my aunt's former biology teacher. She had a big herd of horses running chaotically over a large, unfenced tract of land. Mayhill was among them, a four-year-old colt with a bright, intelligent look. We liked him immediately, and the bonus was that he was well bred, by Auk, a son of racing legend Sea Bird.

We sent him for breaking with Dean Phillips, a former jockey who often worked with Kenny Browne, my childhood mentor. Mayhill had a remarkably biddable temperament and travelled well, seemingly unfazed at being caught in from the wild, broken-in and flown across the world all in the space of seven weeks.

Another feature of that winter was celebrating my second Olympic gold medal, the first back-to-back win in the history of the sport since a Dutchman, Charles Ferdinand Pahud de Mortanges, riding Marcroix, achieved it at Amsterdam in 1928 and Los Angeles in 1932. The great thing about being a successful sportsman as a New Zealander is that all your countrymen will appreciate your achievement. New Zealanders love sport, and it doesn't matter what it is. Everywhere I went, people seemed thrilled to see me, and I found myself signing autographs on all sorts of strange things, from loo paper to a pair of breasts.

We also felt a holiday was imperative, and Lizzie and Reggie Purbrick came out to celebrate with us. That, and the fact that we decided to hire a 45-foot launch to cruise the Bay of

Islands, was a cue for plenty of natural chaos. Reggie said to the owner: 'My dear chap, I assure you I used to be a Baltic sea captain.' This, of course, was nonsense; none of us had any sailing experience and Lizzie didn't even like boats, but off we headed into the open sea with our new toy. Our first mistake was when we pulled ashore in a beautiful cove to collect supplies. The fact that no one else was there should have told us something, and when we got back to the cove with our shopping the waves were so big we had no hope of launching the dinghy and had to get help. Carolyn nearly drowned getting ashore. Other disasters included Carolyn flipping the dinghy over and getting trapped underneath, a band of marauding possums pinching our supper, and getting stranded on rocks in the middle of the night, but we survived.

* * *

Back in England, Charisma's departure had left a big hole in the yard at Cholderton. I had a useful string of horses: Pedro the Cruel had won Le Lion d'Angers in France for a second time in the autumn of 1988 and Peppermint Park and Jued Lad had been second and sixth at Boekelo behind Scotty on his new ride, Murphy Himself. The Korean federation made me an offer I couldn't refuse for Peppermint Park and he was a great servant to several of their riders, going clear at the 1990 World Equestrian Games and, with Mark Choi, finishing 20th in 1992 at the Barcelona Olympics. Wilton Fair left as well, going to David O'Connor in the States, and he also went to the 1992 World Games. This left four advanced horses, Bahlua, Sue Welman's Welton Greylag, Pedro and Jued Lad. The latter was the only Badminton prospect, and he wasn't jumping particularly well.

Then, by a stroke of good luck – mine, that is – Rodney Powell broke his collarbone and offered me the ride at Badminton on his to p horse, The Irishman. Rodney came in for some flak for not offering the ride to a Brit, but the point was that he wanted to get the horse qualified for the European Championships at Burghley that September, and he felt I would do the best job at the shortest notice.

I took The Irishman, a big, honest horse who had been beautifully produced by Rodney, for a school over Debbie Kent's intermediate cross-country course at Doddington Park near Badminton. Like many riders, I'm not that keen on schooling over big fences, as if it goes wrong, it does nothing for your confidence before a major event. This is exactly what happened here, as The Irishman stopped dead at a simple chicken coop, fortunately out of Rodney's sight, and it was only the day before the horse inspection at Badminton.

Rodney and I are about the same height, so perhaps The Irishman didn't notice he had a different rider. On the cross-country, I tried not to interfere with him and to place him right at the fences, so that combined with the fact that he was very fit meant he gave me a brilliant ride, one of the best I've ever had round Badminton, and it put us into the lead. Unfortunately, The Irishman trailed a hind leg in the show jumping and we had one down, handing the Whitbread Trophy to Ginny (on Master Craftsman) yet again. We finished third, which was both frustrating, as I was beginning to wonder if I'd win Badminton again – Ginny and Scotty had won it twice apiece in the last five years – and yet it was satisfying to do so well on a strange horse. The episode certainly didn't do my reputation any harm.

Bahlua and Welton Greylag were my front-runners for the inaugural World Equestrian Games in Stockholm a year later. Bahlua – known as Baxter at home – was a similar dark colour to Charisma, but larger and plainer, although he had a noble, slightly Roman-nosed head. Apart from the time he kicked me in the groin at Seoul, he was the kindest, most genuine horse, with a heart-breaking tendency to show anxiety if he didn't get it right for you. He was the better jumper of the two horses, but he was a little stiff on the flat and didn't have Greylag's potential in the dressage arena. Greylag had a tendency to be hot, but his dressage prowess and consistent jumping meant he was favourite at that stage, a hunch that was reiterated when he won the test event in Stockholm in the summer of 1989. Bahlua, however, won Achselschwang, a three-star event in Bavaria, Germany, with Jued Lad third, and Pedro had his moment in the sun when he won Boekelo. Suddenly, I seemed to have an embarrassment of riches, which was reassuring.

The year was also notable for my first ride under National Hunt rules, at Cheltenham, no less. It was a three-mile amateur steeplechase for which I was kindly offered a ride on a New Zealand-bred horse, Robert Henry, described to me as a good jumper and an honest plodder. Sounded ideal. I was doubtful of making the weight and I wasn't sure that the owner had grasped the fact that I had little experience of judging racing pace – a completely different ball game to the steeplechase phase of a three-day event – but we finished third and it still ranks as one of the most thrilling rides of my life.

Carolyn had a great 1989 season, too. I had done a bit of straightening out of Done For Fun while she was pregnant, but he was still capable of crossing his jaw, running-out and humiliating you. She did a double clear at her first advanced class at Dynes Hall to finish seventh and, despite being a nervous wreck at Windsor, her first three-day event, she did a great job to finish 10th. She was also 10th at Waregem in Belgium and at Le Lion d'Angers in the autumn we formed a New Zealand team with Andrew Nicholson; we would have won if I hadn't had a show jumping rail down.

Carolyn nearly won Luhmühlen in 1990, but for a frustrating mix-up over her cross-country time. In my capacity as groom, I was soon in trouble for not sending her to the start in time, but when she got there, the starter was rather vague and just had her circling for ages. Eventually, I suggested to him that he might start her, and he rather casually said she could go when she liked, by which time the clock had been ticking for a minute. When we protested, Patrick Conolly-Carew, the president of the ground jury, suggested we sportingly let 'bygones be bygones' and split the time, which left her in third place.

Done For Fun suffered a minor injury after that, which clarified the fact that he wouldn't make a four-star horse. We sold him to our neighbours, the Clarkes, who had always wanted him, and he went on to win Necarne two-star event in Northern Ireland with Louisa Clarke before he was retired as a hack for Madeleine Lloyd Webber.

***

The highlight of our annual Christmas visit to New Zealand that year was when Charisma and I – and I think the invitation was probably in that order – were asked to open the Commonwealth Games in Auckland in the January of 1990. We were to share the honour with Peter Snell, the champion middle-distance runner, and our identities were kept a secret until the day. It was the first time I'd ridden Charisma in public in New Zealand since 1983, and appearing in the spotlight in the main arena, holding aloft the Commonwealth flame, ranks as one of the most emotional moments of my life. The crowd went mad with excitement and pleasure, cheering at the tops of their voices, and Podge was on his tiptoes with pride, knowing that all these people had come specially to see him. For a few minutes, we were centre of the world stage, and I was completely choked.

The ceremony had even more significance, because it was the last big thing Pop saw before he died. We had been visiting him every day in hospital, where he'd had to have his foot amputated due to gangrene, and I'd take him out in his wheelchair. He'd been active right up to that point, living on the farm on his own after my grandmother's death, and I think he had just had enough. The day after the Commonwealth ceremony, Pop went into a coma and died, surrounded by all of us around his bed. He was the man to whom I owed my career really, and I was just so glad that we'd had those few special days together to reminisce. I could easily have been thousands of miles away, but instead I'd had a chance to say a proper goodbye.

* * *

On returning to England, my hopes for the inaugural World Equestrian Games began to evaporate with alarming rapidity. Greylag pulled a hamstring at Saumur, Bahlua produced his first ever cross-country stop at an inopportune moment and, at Badminton, the faithful Michaelmas Day, back in action after a year's lameness, trod on his overreach boot and hit the deck at the Pond. Nicky McIrvine (now Coe) took everyone by surprise by skipping around on Middle Road to win, and my compatriot Blyth Tait shot to prominence when second on Messiah, a New Zealand Thoroughbred who was brilliant across country.

Our new sponsors, Kimberley Clark, were probably less than impressed. Their support was thanks to Sam Barr, breeder of Welton Greylag, because Kimberley Clark's European chairman was his brother-in-law Ron Huggins, who later became well known as a racehorse owner, most notably of Double

Trigger. The only snag to their generosity was that among the company's products were a range of sanitary towels; the back of our lorry was covered with a picture of Carolyn jumping Done For Fun, adorned by the slogan 'Simplicity Freedom'. She was less than happy about that.

Despite my own inauspicious start to the season, the good news was that New Zealand was building a serious team. We had Blyth's exciting performance on Messiah, Andrew did a masterful job to win Punchestown on Spinning Rhombus, who was once a naughty hunter sent to him to sort out by Rosemary Barlow, and Andrew Scott was back in Britain with a good horse called Umptee. In addition, Vaughn Jefferis who, like the rest of us, had started in show jumping, had bought Marges Knighton's Seoul horse Enterprise, and Vicky Latta, a property lawyer in Auckland, had bought Chief from Merran Hain and had done a great job on getting his confidence back after Gawler.

The World Equestrian Games (WEG) was the brainchild of Prince Philip during his presidency of the Fédération Equestre Internationale, the idea being to bring together all the competitive disciplines – eventing, dressage, show jumping, endurance and carriage-driving – for one extravaganza. I believe that it was first intended to be a one-off and perhaps, in hindsight, that's what should have happened, for none of the subsequent WEGs have quite lived up to that original billing. Stockholm was magnificent, beautifully laid out on the edge of a beautiful waterside city, and the Swedish welcome was terrific.

The team comprised me on Bahlua, Andrew Nicholson, Andrew Scott and Blyth. We weren't favourites to win – that was still the British, who had emphatically swept the board at the European Championships in 1989 – but we were confident, with strong team morale, and I had high hopes of another individual medal to add to my collection.

Bahlua tried his heart out in the dressage and did one of his best ever tests, which greatly pleased my new Danish trainer, Hans Eric Pederson. I was in for a major disappointment across country, though. There was an influential water complex, where I had advised the rest of the team to keep moving forwards so as to get three strides in before the bank. Bahlua landed a bit short into the water and, like an idiot, I held him for four strides instead of kicking on for three. He was then flat-footed at the bank and stopped at the rail out. It was one of the sharpest disappointments of my life, and I felt angry at myself for ages. There was so much trouble on the course that I still finished fifth overall and would clearly have won but for that stupid mistake. Another World Championship mishap!

However, I had to put aside my own feelings because from a team perspective, we were having a dream competition. Blyth and Andrew were first and third after cross-country, with Didier Seguret from France in second, the only three riders to achieve the optimum time. Three of the British team – Rodney, Karen and Ginny – had stops and Scotty's Murphy Himself, although having jumped flamboyantly, had tired towards the end due to the heat.

There was a bit of a shuffle round in the show jumping – Didier and Andrew both dropped out of the individual medals and Scotty and Bruce Davidson on Pirate Lion moved up – but Blyth deservedly won the individual title, New Zealand won a first team gold, we had three riders in the top five and, for good measure, Vicky was 11th on Chief. It was the start of a golden era for New Zealand eventing and there was justifiable national pride. Soon, the corks were popping in the New Zealand supporters' tent, which was run by a British-based Kiwi, Vicky Glynn, and it wasn't long before the Brits, Irish, Brazilians, Poles and anyone else who was passing were joining the celebrations.

* * *

When I got back to England, a brand new ride was awaiting me. Angela Davis, a New Zealander, had entered her horse Face the Music for Burghley, but realised he was too strong for her and offered me the ride. This gave me precisely one week to get to know him, and I managed to squash in an advanced run at Ickworth, where we finished third.

Face the Music was a big chestnut ex-racehorse, with a tendency to be uptight in the dressage. We were only midfield after that phase at Burghley, but he gave me a terrific fluent ride across country. That year there was a mistake with the measuring of the course and it turned out that the optimum time was a minute shorter than it should have been. No one got inside it, but Face the Music was closest and we moved up to second as a result, behind Mary Thomson (later King) on King Boris. When she had a fence down on the last day, we won, which is never quite the way you want to win a major three-day event, but it was certainly a welcome compensation for the Badmintons I'd lost in the show jumping arena.

By now, we were starting to burst out of Cholderton, at least in terms of staff accommodation. Madeleine Gurdon, who had been a successful eventer in the 1980s, had taken her friends by surprise when she started going out with – and in due course married – the composer and impresario Andrew Lloyd Webber. She persuaded him to convert a derelict farmyard at his home, Sydmonton, into stables, but he never does anything by halves and employed an architect to create a dream yard, although his fantasy about building an indoor school which could double as a theatre never materialised. The deal that we would move in was sealed with an invitation to the Australian premiere of *Phantom of the Opera* at the Sydney Opera

House, which was a great thrill, and we arrived at Sydmonton in the spring of 1991.

By now I was starting to think about my bid for a hat-trick of Olympic gold medals, and I needed to rationalise my horse-power. One of the hardest things is selling a horse that you love and is going well for the pragmatic reason that, first, you need the money and, second, it's good for your reputation to sell on a good horse. Bahlua was a horse I particularly loved, but I couldn't afford not to sell him to the Dutch rider Eddy Stibbe. Eddy, whose family money came from sports leisure wear, was a prolific rider and, by his own admission, his main aim was to go to as many of the big events and championships as possible, so he kept up a large string of advanced horses, many of which he bought ready-made from other riders. The upside to the sale was that Eddy loved Bahlua as much as I did; he was probably his most successful horse and he gave him the sole individual medal of his long career, bronze at the 1993 European Championships.

I hoped to get Greylag to Badminton in 1991, but he went lame again, and instead I got another amazing chance ride. This time the rider casualty was Robert Lemieux, who had broken his leg the week before Badminton, and kindly suggested that I take the ride on Just An Ace, a really nice horse. We finished fifth and, in a neat result, the event was won by Rodney on The Irishman, a greatly deserved outcome after he'd had to watch me ride the horse two years previously. Rodney then sold the horse to Bruce Davidson, a move that earned him some flak in British quarters but which enabled him to buy a yard and set himself up for life.

The main difference with this chance ride, though, was that, ultimately, I got to keep the horse. A year later, Robert had a disagreement with the owners, Robin Patrick and his late wife Mary, who offered me Just An Ace. It was a hideously awkward situation, but Robert, with remarkable generosity, agreed that if I didn't have the ride, someone else would and he advised me to go for it.

In the meantime, Greylag came sound and gave me a back-to-back Burghley victory in 1991, which set a new record. He was a horse that took a lot out of himself, both by fretting and by galloping heavily into the ground and this was always the bar to greater things, but on this occasion I managed to get him relaxed enough to produce the dressage test of which he was so capable. He was only beaten by David O'Connor on my 1987 winner, Wilton Fair, and when they had a stop we found ourselves in the lead. The use of a magnetic blanket overnight prevented Greylag tensing up and he jumped clear, with just a quarter of a time-fault. We won by just 1.75 of a penalty and Face the Music, who by now belonged to me, was 10th. What pleased me most was that it was such a deserved win for Greylag's owners, Michael and Susan Welman. They had been incredibly loyal supporters, and I knew that they had been given some stick by some of the more narrow-minded in the British establishment for having their horse with a foreigner.

My choice of ride for Barcelona was between Greylag and Face the Music. Greylag was the form horse but the more fragile; Face the Music was tougher and would fare better in blazing Spanish heat. I decided that he needed the mileage, so took him to Badminton in the spring of 1992, along with Madeleine's horse, Alfred the Great.

Badminton 1992 turned out to be the most disastrous in history. It was very wet and slippery and the fence we were all most worried about was an arrowhead over the Vicarage Ditch. I was one of the first on course and, with no information to go on, was favouring the longer route at this obstacle. However, as I approached the fence on Face the Music, I told myself not to be so feeble and kicked on for the straight route. At the very last second, I spotted some skid marks where a previous horse had run-out, but it was too late to change my mind by then. Face the Music put in a slight swerve, slipped and flipped over, catching a front leg in the fence as he did so.

I realised instantly, in a horrible moment, that the poor horse had broken his leg above the knee; he was standing there, so quietly, with the bone sticking out and the leg swinging, a ghastly sight that will stay with me for ever. The vet took 20 minutes to come and put him down, and it was the longest 20 minutes of my life. I was torn between rage at how long it was taking for the vet to arrive – I gave the unfortunate fence judge, who was completely blameless, a pretty hard time – and anguish at what I had done to my horse. I was in bits, trying to comfort him and saying over and over to him how sorry I was. In the end, a friend came and drove me back to the stables before the horse was shot.

It was a terrible day. Two other horses died: Karen Lende's Mr Maxwell broke a vertebra and William Fox-Pitt's ride, Briarlands Pippin, broke his neck in front of everyone at the Lake. William, a young British rider who was only starting out on his senior career then, probably had the worst time of everyone because it was so public. He had to hold the horse's head out of the water, and the pictures that reached the newspapers were dreadful.

I was absolutely numb when I got back to the stables, and sat in silence with Carolyn for a long time, drinking a cup of tea and hoping no one would come near me. No one put any pressure on me to ride Alfred, my second horse, but instinctively I felt it would be better to go out and face up to it. He gave me a brave and genuine ride, resulting in fifth place, which went a little way to mitigating the awfulness of the weekend.

One piece of good that came out of Badminton that year

was that there were significant improvements in take-offs and landings – several of the mishaps that occurred at Badminton that year were due to the edges of ditches crumbling – and also in designing fences that had less likelihood of a horse trapping a leg.

There was far worse to come in the run-up to Barcelona. Bill Hall, who had been like a father-figure to me, died of a brain tumour. He and Judy were perhaps my and Carolyn's closest friends; we did a lot together as a foursome and they were godparents to Lauren. Bill was only in his fifties, and had tried everything to find a cure but, with a terrible inevitability, it got him in the end.

* * *

For the first time, New Zealand were favourites to win a championship, and we set off for the Barcelona Olympics with high hopes. The team was myself on Greylag, Blyth on Messiah, Andrew on Spinning Rhombus and Vicky Latta on Chief. We felt like a properly established quartet now, accompanied by our vet, Wally Neiderer, and faithful *chef d'équipe* Dennis Pain. He was a high court judge in real life and had the nickname Auntie because he set such store on attention to detail.

The logistics were pretty shambolic. We were staying in the mountains, in a magnificent villa found for us by Santi near the cross-country course, but Double Take was stabled at the Real Polo Club in the city, where the jumping and dressage were staged, and Carolyn and Judy were staying in an apartment in Barcelona. The traffic was terrible and I spent a lot of time being driven around by useless bus drivers who didn't know where anything was and weren't prepared to be corrected.

The cross-country course was beautifully and imaginatively designed by Germany's Wolfgang Feld, who achieved the distinction of ensuring every single team completed, but the weather was boiling hot. At our first official briefing, there was a lot of pompous stuff about how riders must put their horses first, at which point, prompted by other riders I stood up, wearing my new hat as chairman of the International Event Riders Association (IERA). I pointed out that no rider who is in a position to win a medal, or even to complete for their team, is going to canter round an Olympic Games: it was up to the organisers to take some responsibility and adjust the distances and timings according to the climatic conditions. Until now, there had been very little rider interference with events – and very little adjustment by officials either – and it worked on this occasion, as they shortened the roads and tracks. Inevitably, though, there were some horses that struggled, and there was a particularly hideous sight of an exhausted Russian horse being winched into a truck.

As it happened, the adjustments to the endurance phase were academic for me. Greylag got as far as halfway around Phase C when I pulled him up because he felt unsound. He didn't feel right after the steeplechase and so I was expecting the worst anyway. One of the great anomalies of eventing is that you view the cross-country at major events with such dread, but then when you're suddenly not going to be doing it, the sense of emptiness is enormous. There was a palpable air of disappointment over the whole Kiwi camp, and I had this awful feeling of letting everyone down, the Welmans, the rest of the team, and all the supporters who had come over with such expectation. The only thing to be said is that by the time the competition ended, all four of us had a mishap which contributed to the loss of the team gold.

Blyth's problems started when Messiah went mysteriously lame before his dressage and then, as only old horses will, he played the fool in the arena, refusing to play ball and clocking up a cricket score. Blyth took some persuading that life was worth living, but in one of the most dramatic turnarounds, he eventually climbed up into individual bronze medal position.

Vicky went well across country but fell foul of a penalty zone which hadn't been properly marked. She incurred 20 penalties, which prevented her winning an individual medal; something I know still rankles with her. Andrew was in individual silver medal position, after an inspired display of cross-country riding, but by the time he got in the show jumping arena, Spinning Rhombus didn't want to know. Still, we had eight fences in hand over the Australians, so what could possibly go wrong? Quite a lot, unfortunately. Andrew experienced probably the worst day of his life when hitting *nine* fences; the owner Rosemary Barlow was mortified, hiding in a Portaloo, and that was the end of the gold medal.

I hadn't realised that I was feeling so stressed, but by the time a reporter had come up to me before the show jumping competition and asked me if I was feeling sad about Bill Hall not being there to see his horse, Double Take, compete I had snapped and walked off in tears. Still, at least I had something to look forward to after the disaster of the eventing.

Double Take had certainly earned his keep in the two years I'd had him and he'd developed into a charming character. We finished second to John Whitaker and Milton in the grand prix at Hickstead – and things don't get much better than that – and for a few heady days I was leading rider at the Spruce Meadows show in Calgary with a couple of third places. Another highlight was competing in the Paris Masters, and we reached the peak of our career on a Scandinavian tour with a win in the World Cup qualifier in Helsinki, beating the famous Austrian rider, Hugo Simon. First prize was a Volvo car, which was quite something for an eventer to win. John Whitaker has won so many cars that he's quite blasé about it – he even gave away a Maserati – but on the rare occasions an eventer manages to win a car, it's a big deal.

Bruce Goodin, who was only five and used to keep nagging me for bedtime stories back in the 1970s when his parents had employed me as a farmer's apprenticeship, based himself at Sydmonton and we travelled together on the jumping circuit. It was a great fun time, and inspiring to be competing against the big European names, but the schedule of jumping at night was an exhausting one, even for me, and I was in a state of collapse by the time I got back from Helsinki.

Double Take was small, just under 16hh, and cheeky just like Podge but, unlike Podge, he was easily rattled and I had to be careful not to upset him with a lack of accuracy. Chopping and changing between eventing and show jumping is a bit like playing tennis and squash – they look similar, but they're different techniques. If I was to do any good in Barcelona, Double Take would have to be at the top of his form, and it has to be said that he wasn't. However, we did finish the team competition as the best of the New Zealanders and, again, I was the only one to qualify for the individual contest, although we didn't make the final round of that either.

After Barcelona, it became clear that I hadn't got time to maintain a dual career properly, and Bill's estate needed settling so, after a spell with Nick Skelton, Double Take found a happy home with an Italian rider, Arnaldo Arrioldi, who rode him at the Atlanta Olympics in 1996. I was very sad to see Double Take leave Sydmonton because he was one of the nicest horses, but it was time for new beginnings all round.

CHAPTER
SIX

THE YEAR nineteen ninety-three was, in some ways, a
year of regeneration. Our son James was born and we
moved house. James arrived four weeks before Badminton, a very welcome baby because Carolyn had suffered
a miscarriage the year before. He was born by caesarean section, a strange experience in that you know precisely when and
where your baby will arrive – on 9th April at Basingstoke Hospital soon after 9am. James was named after Pop – James was
his real name, although he was known as Ted for some reason
– and it's also my middle name. Our ex-landlady Maria St Just
suggested we call him Wilbury after her house, but, luckily for
James, we resisted that one.

Lauren was thrilled with her baby brother, who was a lot
calmer than she had been at the same age although, in fairness,
it might have had something to do with the fact that Carolyn
and I were rather more expert by then. Having two children was
clearly going to be harder work than one, and it was a trigger in
my deciding to curtail my riding to just the discipline of eventing so as not to be leaving Carolyn alone too much, and to try
to restrict the number of horses I rode to around six or seven.

We were still bursting at the seams at Sydmonton, though,

with the addition of our working pupils – the Australian Brook Staples (who married my head girl, Debby Slinn), Fred Bergendorff from Sweden, the young British rider Nick Campbell and, also from Sweden and probably the most talented of the lot, Peder Frederickson, who is now show jumping full time. The Lloyd Webbers were developing their racing ambitions and it was clear there wasn't going to be room for all of us.

Chris Leigh – now Lord Leigh, whose family owned Stoneleigh Park – offered us his yard at Adlestrop near Stow-on-the-Wold in Gloucestershire, and found us a cottage to rent from Sir Anthony Bamford. The yard was previously occupied by Cynthia Haydon, the doyenne of Hackney driving, but she was retiring so the timing was ideal: it had 30 boxes, two staff flats and 25 acres, including an arena. The Cotswolds are arguably the epicentre of the equestrian world in the UK, and a beautiful area to boot. We loved the countryside, the ambience and browsing in the nearest market towns, Moreton-in-Marsh and Stow-on-the-Wold, and it was the area we were to call home for the rest of our time in England.

James's birth was easily the best moment of the spring; Badminton was a disaster. Kinvarra, whom I was riding for Santi, ducked out at the Mitsubishi Ms, a double of corner fences on the cross-country, and Just An Ace, on whom I could perhaps have won, clipped the top of a rail in the Quarry and somersaulted over it, rolling right over me in the process. Under present-day international rules, I would, of course, be eliminated. On this occasion, though, the doctor turned up and, to prove my fitness to carry on, I jogged up and down on the spot before vaulting back into the saddle, to the entertainment of the crowd. I was feeling far from amused, however, and as I gloomily watched Ginny notch up Badminton winner number three, on Welton Houdini, I wondered if I'd ever get my hands on the trophy again.

But I did, and it came, as these things often do, from a quirk of fate. On the Tuesday before Badminton 1994, a fellow rider, Lynne Bevan, telephoned to say that she had broken her collarbone but she was reluctant to withdraw her horse, Horton Point, from the event because he was 16 and it was probably his last run there. He was a real family pet and the Bevans had made many financial sacrifices to keep him on the road. I was touched when Lynne said she made the choice that Horton Point would get me instead because, 'He's a funny old horse. If he doesn't like you, he won't go at all, so I wouldn't put anyone else but Toddy.' Horton Point was beautifully produced and genuine, so I was delighted to get this bonus ride, but he was quite heavy in type and I doubted he'd go fast enough, so it never occurred to me that he had a better chance than Just An Ace.

Lynne chose Andrew Nicholson to ride her other horse, Buckley Province, but Badminton that year was operating a rule which said that all British riders had to take preference over foreigners, so we both had to wait to see if we'd get in. I did, but Andrew eventually lost out to Graham Law. I only got the green light on the Tuesday afternoon, the day before the first horse inspection, and finally got to sit on Horton Point on Wednesday morning.

As I expected, he was beautifully trained. Lynne was a talented all-round horsewoman who was good at flatwork – she is mainly a show jumper now and has won the Queen Elizabeth II Cup. On Thursday morning, I had a 40-minute warm-up and then, bang, it was into the arena as, somewhat cruelly, we were drawn number one to go. Horton Point was easy to ride and produced a lovely test for a mark of 40.6, which was only bettered by the German rider Marina Loheit (now Köhncke), on Sundance Kid. Just An Ace was placed fourth by the American judge Jack Le Goff and 37th by the German judge

Bernd Springorum – a pretty poor piece of judging – and was in 18th place on 57.2.

I popped Horton Point over a couple of jumps on the Friday, but that was the extent of our acquaintance and, come Saturday morning, I did wonder what on earth I was doing setting off around Badminton on a horse I'd sat on for less than two hours, in relative terms far less acquaintance than I'd had with The Irishman five years earlier. I was even more unnerved when Horton Point ploughed through the first steeplechase fence but that woke us both up and, after that, he was fine, finishing just couple of seconds over time. Rather disconcertingly, the old horse also had a tendency to bleed from the nose and I was slightly alarmed when Lynne's sister Ros discreetly handed me a wet rag with the instruction that when I was out of sight on Phase C, I was to clean his nose.

He jumped very neatly across country, but he wasn't the fastest thing, as he liked to set himself up for fences, and if I'd let him school round at his own speed we'd have accrued masses of time-penalties. He was such an obedient horse, though, that when I asked him to move forward to the fences and get away from them more quickly afterwards, he immediately responded, so well that we did the Centre Walk combination of hedges on three strides. I haven't done that on many horses, and Ian Stark's Murphy Himself is the only one to have managed it in two. We finished just inside the optimum time, the first time Horton Point had done that at a three-day event. Ros, who had previously competed Horton Point as well, and Lynne were both in floods of tears of relief and emotion, having been agonised watching the precious horse they'd known since a foal going round Badminton.

I was feeling in confident mood by the time I got on Just An Ace in the afternoon, and he made it feel like a Pony Club track, pulling up to seventh place. Poor Marina ended up on the deck at the second Luckington Lane crossing, which left me in the lead on Horton Point. This was a fairytale result, but there was a fairly tense wait for the happy ending. Horton Point was pretty jarred up after the cross-country and so it took a night of applying ice-packs and hosing him with cold water to get him right to trot up next day, and even then he was a little bit unlevel. By now, I felt drained; Lynne and Ros's anxiety and emotion was contagious and I desperately wanted it to be right for them.

Bless him, the old horse seemed to understand how much was riding on him, and he was foot-perfect at the trot-up. I was becoming more and more nervous, because I knew how much the prize-money, which was beyond the Bevans' wildest dreams, would mean. The girls were saying: 'Just relax, but don't screw up! Our life depends on this.' And they weren't really joking.

Luckily for me, Mary King was lying second on King William, who was at the height of his problems in the show jumping arena. All the attention from his win the year before had unnerved him, so that he would flatten in shape when he got into the ring and annihilate fences. This was one of his worst efforts – 26 faults – and Karen Dixon, who had been lying third on Get Smart, also dropped down with 15 faults, all of which gave me two fences in hand.

Horton Point must have been feeling tired, but he raised his game like a pro and jumped clear. I was obviously thrilled and relieved for myself, but the best feeling of all was being part of such a wonderful story. Another great result was that New Zealand riders took four out of the top five places – Blyth was second on Delta, Vaughn Jefferis third on Bounce and I was fifth on Just An Ace. It all augured pretty well for the second World Equestrian Games in The Hague, which were just a couple of months away.

* * *

So far, I hadn't managed to cover myself in glory at a world championship – and this one in 1994, my fourth attempt, was no better. It was a nightmare weekend. The Dutch had taken over running the show at an untried venue in The Hague after the French pulled out just 18 months earlier but, even so, it was extraordinarily badly organised by a country which has a heritage of running major shows and three-day events like clockwork. Everything was a hassle, nothing was properly built when we arrived, and the rules changed every day. The Dutch are normally good fun but on this occasion, perhaps unhinged by the chaos, they were terribly officious.

The cross-country was a couple of hours away on a heath, rather akin to Tweseldown in Hampshire, and claustrophobic with lots of confusing winding tracks through the scrub, with many of the cross-country jumps doubling as hazards for the carriage driving. The temporary stabling was hot and stuffy and the loos – or, rather, loo in the singular – and the grooms' accommodation were horrible. The roads and tracks were 10 kilometres in distance, far too long in the circumstances because the going was deep sand which had horses floundering and jelly-legged, and the steeplechase going was hard and extremely jarring. A heat wave had taken everyone, most notably the Dutch, by surprise, and the atmosphere was one of high humidity and high irritation.

The New Zealand team comprised myself on Ace, Blyth on Delta, Vaughn on Bounce and Andrew on Jagermeister, and, one by one, with the notable exception of Vaughn, we fell by the wayside. Even Vicky Latta, riding as an individual on Chief, had a run-out, to add insult to injury. Delta is normally a feisty little mare, but she was knocked out by the heat and the deep sand going and was flagging by the time Blyth reluctantly started her across country, eventually crumpling into a heap at fence six. Jagermeister was a very good jumper but Andrew, our trailblazer, had an uncharacteristic fall in the water and, before I knew it, Ace and I were head-butting the ground, too.

Ace hadn't enjoyed the roads and tracks either and I felt terrible having to push him on, but he started the cross-country fresh enough. He was a game and genuine horse and was going beautifully when he suddenly disappeared underneath me in the water, slamming against the bank head first. To this day, I don't know what happened, whether there was a hole, or he trod on his overreach boot, but that was the world title out of the window.

After the inevitable flash of rage and disappointment, demotivation is the next emotion to set in. Under present-day rules you have no choice but to walk home after a fall, but I somehow scraped myself off the floor and continued. I had to keep going, because we were now down to three men with the loss of Blyth, and we needed to qualify as a team for the Atlanta Olympics in 1996, which we achieved – just. This was mainly thanks to Vaughn Jefferis, a very talented rider over fences; he shone while the rest of us were eating dust and won the individual title, so at least that stayed in New Zealand hands while everything else went belly up.

New Zealand had been favourites for The Hague after our Badminton monopoly and, in an unusual twist, Britain the underdogs. But eventing is, thankfully, an endlessly unpredictable sport and their all girl-team, the only one to have four clear cross-country rounds, ended up quite deservedly the gold medallists.

But, as far I was concerned, it was the rotten end to a rotten summer. A few weeks before The Hague, there had been a dreadfully disturbing incident when Richard Adams, a former working pupil at Cholderton and a very nice lad, was killed at Windsor. I was watching his round with David Green and, in the distance, we saw Richard and his horse somersault over a table fence. There was an ominous stillness until an ambulance roared over the horizon. David, who is always good in a crisis, looked at me and we decided we'd better go over. We waited, helplessly, with Richard's family outside the ambulance.

It was a horrible, sobering incident which shook me greatly; I remembered Ace had rolled on me at Badminton and I realised, with a shudder, how lucky I'd been. I've never been back to Windsor since – it was never an entirely happy event because of the footing there, either rock hard or bottomless – and after that terrible day I couldn't face it.

Richard was one of four riders, including Scotty's former groom Mark Holliday, to be killed in accidents at horse trials that summer. It was an unprecedented run of tragedy in the sport, and there was some soul-searching about aspects of fence design for, apart from the family, the person who is in the worst position is the course-designer. However, I don't think the accidents had a particularly deep impact on the psyche of most riders; that was to come a few years later. Some of these accidents happened at table type fences and for a while there was a big discussion about their design; the front had to be lower than the back. Nowadays they have worked themselves back in to most courses, though they are always slightly ramped.

***

The summer of 1994 was also notable for the start of my ill-fated involvement with the late Trevor Banks, a colourful, entrepreneurial character who had owned such top show jumpers as Anglezarke, the 1982 world silver medallist ridden by Malcolm Pyrah. Trevor had involved Reg Bond, head of a large family-owned tyre distribution company in Hull, in equestrian sponsorship. I was the recipient of this generosity.

Trevor asked me to look for a good eventer, and the obvious choice was Bertie Blunt, a class horse who had faded from the spotlight. He was eighth at Badminton in 1993 with Nick Burton and the pair was subsequently chosen for the European Championships in Achselschwang. This competition was a mortifying disaster, the first time the British team had failed to complete, and Nick was partly to blame because he didn't continue after an early fall, reasoning that it was pointless. This went down very badly with the British hierarchy and, after an unsuccessful Badminton in 1994 when the horse stopped in the Quarry, their star was on the wane.

Trevor persuaded Nick to sell for £50,000, less than half the asking price of a year previously. It was now incumbent on me to turn the horse around and I was mildly apprehensive, as I sensed Trevor was not a man to cross. However, the horse's official owners were Robert and Melita Hall, with whom I got on well, and the whole enterprise seemed great fun, with a great coterie of Trevor's friends coming to support the horse, and lots of lavish hospitality.

Bertie Blunt was racing-bred by Suny Boy and had been in training with Nicky Henderson at one stage, though was too slow. He was a bit uncouth in the stable, but he was a lovely jumper, a smart mover and had been well schooled by Nick – he is now a top-level judge and invited onto the eventing ground jury at London 2012. I discovered, too late, that Bertie Blunt was a head shaker, which tends to be a great handicap in the dressage arena, especially when flies are bad. However, although warming-up could be a nightmare, he never did anything in the arena – apart from the disconcerting time he reared up in the rein-back on my first ride on him at Gatcombe. Still, we recovered to finish third, which seemed to augur well.

I nursed a vague hope of doing the Badminton–Burghley double in the same year, and this was looking a distinct possibility when I finished the cross-country at Burghley in second place behind William Fox-Pitt on Chaka. The usual celebrations were under way with Trevor and friends, when I heard an ominous announcement: 'Would Mark Todd please go to the secretary's tent.'

Trevor accompanied me, whereupon we were instructed to find Mark Phillips, the course-designer. I listened with a sinking heart as Mark broke it to me that it seemed I had missed a checkpoint flag on Phase C, which would mean elimination. Painfully aware of Trevor standing beside me, although fortunately he was crosser with the organisation than with me, I racked my brain for inspiration as to what might have happened. None came. There was a little loop on Phase C, the same every year that took about two minutes. I thought I knew the roads and tracks like the back of my hand after riding at Burghley for about a decade and a half, but who knows? It's still a moot point as to whether the checkpoint man forgot to tick me off or whether I never came past. Maybe he wasn't concentrating, or perhaps I was in a dream. The organisers argued I had arrived into the 10-minute box two minutes ahead of schedule, but that was not necessarily evidence, as I often arrived early in order to have more time to prepare for the cross-country.

Eventually, I had to accept the elimination, but it was extremely hard, being so well placed and feeling some pressure to impress my new sponsor. What I couldn't accept, though, was the incompetence of officials in allowing me to go more than four miles over one of the world's strongest courses and then eliminating me in hindsight. Trevor and company were sympathetic, but I still cringe to think of the episode, which cost me the lead in the Land Rover World Rankings – then the sport's most valuable series prize – and dented my reputation with my sponsor.

I took Bertie and Ace to Boekelo in the autumn, where they finished third and fifth, but it felt like feeble recompense. The final straw was when at the World Rankings awards dinner at Reims in France, Mark Phillips made a pompous speech criticising riders for chasing points 'at the expense of their horses'. He was clearly alluding to me and Andrew Nicholson for taking Ace and Jagermeister to Boekelo; we were furious because neither of us could be accused of failing to get our horses fit, and it still rankled that Mark was part of the team that had let me go round Burghley for nothing.

* * *

Things could only get better, and I was eager to ingratiate myself with Trevor by going well at Badminton in 1995, but this was not to be in yet another bizarre twist of fate.

Despite the hideous number of flies buzzing around before dressage, Bertie did a good test, and I was right up there with both him and Just An Ace. So far, so good. Our cross-country round was pleasantly incident-free until, landing in the dew-pond near the Luckington Lane, I felt my left leg slip down sharply. The stirrup leather had broken. My first thought was 'Oh my god, what is Trevor going to say now?' Instantly, I reasoned that I couldn't give up and would have to keep going somehow, despite the fact I was only a third of the way round with some of the hardest fences to come.

The immediate problem was the Vicarage Vee, before I remembered with dread the horrendous coffin with its short, awkward distances, but we got through that, too. It took a few minutes to work out a method – I didn't want to be banging around on the horse's back – and eventually I found a reasonable level of comfort by hitching my left leg right up to the pommel of the saddle for the galloping stretches and dropping it to put my leg on over the fences. The jumping was almost the least of my worries; the galloping was excruciating.

As we lurched towards the Lake, the situation was so surreal that I was laughing at the sheer ridiculousness of galloping down to one of the world's most difficult fences with only one stirrup. That year there was a bounce in and a drop to the water, three strides to a step up and another bounce to a rail. Once that was over, there was the mere task of the Beaufort Staircase, mercifully uphill, and the quarry, where, under the circumstances, I thought it was acceptable to take the easier route.

Bertie was heroic, lolloping along on a loose rein and never once thinking of deviating from his line, which was just as well because I was so exhausted I could hardly cling on. I have obviously had more stylish rounds, but that is the one that sticks in many people's memories. The press kindly treated it as a great feat – and it certainly felt like one as I staggered off afterwards – but the gutting thing was that it was all for nought. Bertie was, unsurprisingly, stiff after lumping me round with my weight unevenly distributed, and, despite all our efforts with massage and magnetic rugs, he wasn't great next morning either. I rode him out in the park, after which he felt fine, but when we brought him out for the horse inspection, he was hopping lame. It transpired he had pus in the foot. Although things remained civil in the owners' camp, there was, nonetheless, some palpable tension at the way things were turning out with Bertie.

The ever-reliable Ace, meanwhile, jumped a clear show jumping round and finished fourth. Sadly, it was my last ride on him. He tweaked a tendon at Badminton, so was out for the rest of the year, after which Robin Patrick wanted him nearer home and gave him back to Robert Lemieux, who was without a top horse. I was sad, because Ace was a sweet horse who, after a timid start, had learned to trust me to great effect, but it was a fair decision, seeing as Robert had ridden him as a young horse.

By coincidence, Ace was replaced by another former Robert Lemieux ride, Kayem, owned by Jayne and George Apter. Robert had upgraded the horse to advanced and ridden him, having changed to Canadian nationality, at the World Games and ending up on the deck at the same water complex as me. The horse was passed to the British rider Owen Moore, but he broke his collarbone at Badminton and asked me to take the horse to Punchestown. This wasn't a great success, because Kayem tied up on the steeplechase, but afterwards George and Jayne invited me to keep the ride.

Kayem was an attractive grey horse with a cheerful outlook, and Jayne adored and doted on her 'Coco'. He was also a terrific, honest, point-and-go jumper, and a great ride for me at the Open European Championships in Pratoni del Vivaro in Italy that September. It was the first time the Europeans had been open to the world, with two sets of medals – one set for everyone, and one for European riders only.

Pratoni is one of my favourite events. It's a beautiful site, in a mountainous national park south of Rome, and it has a great eventing tradition which stretches back to the 1960 Rome Olympics. The course-designer, Albino Garbari, was definitely one of the old school, producing big bold tracks which made full use of the undulating terrain. The precipitous slide fence, from 1960, soon wakes riders up.

Kayem wasn't the ideal shape for dressage and he found this phase difficult, but his jumping at Pratoni was superb and we rose to fourth place individually behind Ireland's Lucy Thompson, France's Marie-Christine Duroy and Mary King on King William, all of whom had produced much better tests. The New Zealand team finished second behind Britain and, as we had some inexperienced horses and the competition was a world championship in all but name, it was a pretty satisfactory result.

***

The most successful aspect of 1995 was buying our own home in England. Trevor Banks tipped us off about Poplars Farm, a lovely Cotswold stone farmhouse and 100 acres, most of which we leased out. It was owned by his friend Richard Sumner, a great all-round horseman who was master of the Heythrop Hunt. He was only selling because he was getting divorced and, thanks to Trevor's intervention, the property never went on the open market.

One of the best things about having our own home in England was that Charisma could live with me. He had been turned out at Whitehall, a farm Carolyn and I owned in New Zealand – and sold to buy Poplars Farm – and although he was in good hands, without anyone to ride him he would have got fatter and fatter.

I always loved riding him when I went home at Christmas. Lauren was lent a pony, Cheeky Charlie, by Jeff and Vicky McVean, and I thought it would be fun to take her out on the lead-rein. However, the idyllic afternoon turned into one of the most nerve-racking incidents I've ever experienced. Charisma, on turning for home, suddenly started to pull in anticipation. I only had him in a snaffle bridle and, riding one-handed, had no hope of holding him, so he got faster and faster, and so did Cheeky Charlie.

Soon, we were galloping, Lauren was wobbling around alarmingly and I could see that she was about to come off. I grabbed her and, in a move of which a Cossack rider would be proud, managed to lean down and drop her on the grass verge where she had a soft landing. On watching her father disappear into the distance on a bolting Charisma, she started to scream. I'm just glad there weren't any witnesses to this chaotic episode of parenting.

I had missed Charisma terribly and was thrilled when my former sponsors, Bell Tea, paid for him to be flown to England. He looked fantastic at 23, and was determined to ensure he was still the centre of attention. He clearly thought he should still be eventing and, as it didn't look as if Bertie Blunt would get me to the 1996 Olympics in Atlanta, it was sorely tempting.

I had been warned that niceties might not last with Trevor, and there was indeed a parting of the ways. He decided to sell Bertie, but the horse wasn't really in great shape post-Badminton and the price was astronomical for a head-shaker that had finished his last three-day event lame. I wasn't minded to prompt anyone to buy him. Unsurprisingly, a sort of Mexican stand-off ensued and the next thing I knew, Rob Howells was sending a dispatch rider over in the middle of the night to pick up the horse's passport. I knew what that meant. Even if I got to keep the ride, if my name wasn't on the passport by 1st January, 1996, I wouldn't be able to ride him at the Olympics.

Mainly thanks to Carolyn and Melita Howells maintaining friendly contact, I did get Bertie back in time for Badminton 1996, but only after an extraordinary reunion. I was taking a pre-season cross-country clinic near Lincoln for some friends, Tessa and Charlie Hood, who asked if I could liven it up by doing a demonstration on Bertie Blunt. The Howells agreed to bring him over on the day, and when he saw me, Bertie went mad with excitement, snorting, rearing and generally cavorting around. He had been doing some dressage and show jumping but cross-country was his thing, and when he saw me he seemed to be saying: 'Hurrah, now the fun bit's here.'

It seemed too good to be true when I was invited to ride the horse a few weeks later at the Lincolnshire one-day event in a class sponsored by Rob Howells's company, but we won it, and after that Bertie returned to Poplars Farm. This time, I was determined nothing should go wrong at Badminton and, anxious not to let down Rob and Melita, I left no stone unturned in my quest to produce the perfect performance.

After the last two mishaps, I paid extra attention to the flags on the roads and tracks and walked the cross-country over and over, because it was going in the same direction to 1994 and I was worried that Bertie, who obviously had a good memory, might have residual anxiety over his stop in the Quarry with Nick Burton.

Bertie did one of his best dressage tests and went superbly across country, although my good resolutions about concentrating didn't prevent me taking up a bet with David Green that I wouldn't wave and say 'Hi Mum' to the moving camera filming each horse gallop past Badminton House. There were jokes that the wave had cost me a couple of seconds – I finished with 0.8 of a time-penalty – but we finished the day a close second to Scotty on Stanwick Ghost.

Good friend though Scotty is, I couldn't help being aware that his horse, like Mary's King William two years before, wasn't the most reliable show jumper and I knew that if I could go clear, I would probably win. Bertie rose to the occasion in spades and jumped a lovely clear. Sure enough, the groan from the British crowd wasn't long coming, and a thunderous-looking Scotty emerged from the arena. I felt for him, because I understood only too well the frustration of losing a three-day after so much effort, but my overwhelming feeling was of being so pleased for my horse, finally having his moment in the spotlight. Rob Howells played the video nearly every night for a year. Sadly, he had to make the most of it, for Bertie Blunt went lame at Burghley, the last time I competed him. He was a horse who had tried so hard for me, and it still rankles that our partnership never reached the heights it deserved.

* * *

The Atlanta Olympic Games was a talking point in the horse world ever since they were awarded, especially for those who could remember the horror of the Kentucky World Championships in the next-door state 18 years earlier. There must have been many owners with mixed feelings about letting their horses compete in horrendously humid conditions in July in Georgia, and debate raged about the wisdom of going ahead. However, following an enormous amount of research on cooling horses by the Animal Health Trust in Newmarket, and political pressure applied in the States by the Humane Society, the predicted carnage thankfully never happened. There were cool misting fans everywhere you went and cross-country day started at dawn, so that it was over by the time the really steaming afternoon heat kicked in.

Another burning topic was that it had been decided to change the format of the Olympic three-day event to two separate competitions, team and individual, the reasoning being that no athlete should be able to win two medals for one performance. Everyone could see the anomalies. A rider who had gone brilliantly in the team competition might get no recognition and, if the team's chance went down the drain, they would clearly feel little motivation to struggle on if they had no chance of individual glory. And, as eventing nations have always put more emphasis on the team contest, the best riders and horses would clearly be in that, thus reducing the quality of the individual. It also meant the whole thing would go on for twice as long and cost twice as much to run, something unlikely to be in eventing's favour as a continuing Olympic sport.

My choice of horse came down to Kayem, but I was very happy as he had jumped out of his skin to win the competitive three-day event at Saumur in April and, as a result, he was earmarked as an individual prospect. I felt a bit weird about not being on the team that would have an obvious chance of gold, but was quite excited about Kayem. It was, therefore, a crushing disappointment when he went lame. He pulled up sore after galloping, and it turned out that he'd aggravated an old shoulder muscle injury from his racing days.

No rider ever wants to be trapped at an Olympics when they're not going to ride. I was lucky to be able to hang on to a form of accreditation, so at least I could still be with the team and walk the course. What usually happens is that you lose it instantly, as happened to poor Leslie Law of Britain when New Flavour went lame, and turn into a non-person, stuck away from home and twiddling your thumbs as a spectator. I'd rather have known this was going to happen and stayed away – at least that would have meant I could have accompanied Carolyn to her father Keith's funeral in New Zealand, which took place just before we had been due to depart for Atlanta, instead of leaving her to the sad experience of going on her own.

New Zealand had mixed fortunes. The team was Blyth, a brilliant pathfinder on the reliable Chesterfield in the slippery, dewy, early-morning ground; Andrew, who had a stop with the hard-pulling Jagermeister; Vaughn, who did well to nurse round a tiring Bounce in the hottest part of the day, and Vicky Latta. Vicky, who had done so brilliantly to produce yet another top-class horse, Broadcast News, for her last Olympics, had a frightening fall when going fast into a bounce. The horse broke his nose and she flipped over on her neck. Perhaps if she hadn't been so supple from her ballet-dancing days, things might have been worse. The team had no hope of catching the Australians, who galloped away with the gold medal, or the Americans, who were buoyed up by the exhausting atmosphere of patriotic fervour, while other nations were dithering. However, New Zealand did go home with bronze, quite an achievement in a tough competition.

My departure opened the door for Blyth to take his chance in the individual on Ready Teddy, a green eight-year-old who had really only come to make up the numbers. There was no way they were favourites, but Blyth is one of the world's great competitors who can assess a situation, work out what he needs to do, and then pull it off. His victory, a third individual gold for New Zealand in four Olympics, was extremely popular and, just to emphasise Kiwi supremacy, Sally Clark, a PE teacher and farmer's wife, shot up into silver with Squirrel Hill. I had to content myself with the knowledge that even if I wasn't part of this success, it was all part of the deeply satisfying rise to prominence of our tiny country.

CHAPTER
SEVEN

CHARISMA TAUGHT ME that small horses can be brilliant, so I don't know why I was hesitant about taking on Broadcast News from Vicky Latta, who returned to her real life as a lawyer. I went to Gatcombe, where she was based, to try the horse and realised immediately that he was a quality machine, prepared with all the individual care that Vicky applied to all her horses.

Like Charisma, Broadcast News – Andy – was also black and he also had unusual breeding, which can often give a horse its individuality and be the key to success. He was nearly full Thoroughbred but had a touch of Appaloosa, which only manifested itself in spots on his rump.

Andy didn't have any of Charisma's cheek – he was a rather timid, thin-skinned and slightly irritable horse who tended to stick his ears back rather than forward – but he was a high-quality galloper. I rode him under the banner of Team Husky, as Vicky had done, for the company's Italian owner, Guiseppe Veronesi.

Broadcast News missed a Badminton run, thanks to an unfortunate ruling. The event was inundated with entries and, in what some of us considered an extremely unfair and divisive move, foreign riders could only compete one horse. This seemed a pretty short-sighted rule for the world's most prestigious and best attended three-day event – an international competition, not a national, British-only affair – as surely the public should see the best horses in the world competing. The present-day rules are much fairer; the order of acceptance is simply based on horses' international points, and Broadcast News, with his seventh placing the year before with Vicky, would have been more than qualified.

After much agonising, I chose to ride Kayem, feeling that George and Jayne Apter deserved some good luck after Atlanta. It was a fateful decision; he landed on three legs at the penultimate steeplechase fence, a horrible feeling, and it transpired that he had cracked his pelvis, a sad end to his career.

I hoped to make it up to the Apters at Chantilly in France, a stylish event held in the beautiful grounds of the chateau and a great favourite with riders for its civilised atmosphere and £5,000 first prize. I was riding their other horse, Stunning, a big chestnut 11-year-old New Zealand Thoroughbred I had bought for them six months previously from Andrew Scott. Despite his age, Stunning was strangely green, and he had a tendency to either win or do something dramatic. It was the latter on this occasion, when he lost concentration and galloped straight through a fence, firing me head first into the ground. I got woozily to my feet, and first realised all might not be well when the fence judge started gabbling hysterically at me. Then Andrew turned up and started being unusually solicitous, taking me by the arm to a waiting ambulance. It turned out that Stunning had caught me on the forehead with a stud and blood was pouring all over the place.

However, I was well placed on my second horse, a chance ride given me by the Italian rider Roberto Rotatori, and after having my head stitched I was determined to carry on. The solution was to wind a bandage round my head and then stuff the crash-hat on top. It felt a bit tight, but it was better than nothing. Needless to say, Roberto's horse stopped at the water and I never got the £5,000 cheque, but it wasn't for want of trying. In a charming gesture typical of French events, the organisers awarded me a trophy for the most sporting competitor – it's still probably the nicest one I've ever had.

In this rather accident-prone summer, my next trip abroad, to Lummen in Belgium, was equally eventful, for different reasons. My wallet and passport were stolen on the ferry on the way out but, rather than doing something sensible about it, I spent the weekend feeling uneasy about what was going to happen on the way back. I hit upon a brilliant solution – Carlos Campon, my Spanish working pupil, could drive the lorry on and off the ferry while I hid in the back. The only snag was that he'd never driven the lorry before. The first part of the plan went off without incident, and as we approached the ferry terminal we slowed down for Carlos to leap into the driver's seat and for me to clamber up into the Luton. When he arrived at the ticket booth 200 yards later, Carlos pulled out the 'stop' button to shut off the engine, in order to hand over the paperwork which included how many people were on board.

But when it came to starting up again, he forgot what I'd told him. From my hiding place I hissed, 'Push the bloody button, for God's sake.' But Carlos, having quite an excitable Latin nature, started panicking and thought the ticket office could hear me so he hurriedly wound up the window and, putting the lorry in gear with the button still out, turned the key and wound the engine over, juddering forward in a series of kangaroo hops. Once out of earshot I was then able to climb down and get it going. The anxiety wasn't over yet; as we disembarked we realised they were flagging down every other lorry; but luckily for us they pulled over Matt Ryan, who was behind.

The 1997 European Championships, held at Burghley, were also open to the world, but, for the first time in my career, my team place was not a foregone conclusion. My choice of horse had come down to Broadcast News, but he had suffered a few minor setbacks, missing Badminton. Although we were second at Bramham, we were not the most in-form pair compared with the Olympic gold and silver medallists, Blyth and Sally, plus Andrew Nicholson, who had had some good results on Dawdle, a classy New Zealand Thoroughbred, and Vaughn on the ever consistent Bounce.

* * *

Andrew and I were both relaxed about which one of us should be an individual but, in a rare incident of New Zealand team dissention, Vaughn, who could be mercurial, objected to take the pathfinder role and was dropped from the team. He was about to put his horse on the lorry and head home but for Andrew charming him into staying and volunteering to take the first slot in the team. Blyth was entitled to go last, as Olympic champion, but felt Ready Teddy would explode if he went on the more atmospheric second day of dressage and so he was number two, followed by Sally. After all that, I got the advantageous anchorman slot.

The cross-country, designed by Mike Tucker, incorporated a new loop, taking in the water crossing nearest Burghley House and going under the Lion Bridge, which created some striking pictures. It was only meant to be of three-star dimensions and difficulty, as it was a European rather than a world championship, but the track was imaginative and big and caused a fair amount of drama.

I was sixth after dressage and all but one of those ahead of me – David O'Connor, the dressage leader, the good Finnish rider Pia Pantsu, Lucy Thompson, the reigning European Champion, and Christopher Bartle – fell off. Only Bettina Overesch and her lovely grey horse Watermill Stream were still there, but she had had time-faults on the steeplechase. Blyth had gone well but Andrew and Sally both had stops, which didn't improve Vaughn's mood – he and Bounce were, of course, clear and rising up the individual order – and it was down to me to keep us in the medals.

The one advantage was that although it had been a nerve-racking and long day's wait, at least I'd had a good chance to assess how the course was riding. As a result I decided I could afford the long route at two fences, the Leaf Pit, where the narrow fence after the drop had caused lots of problems, and the Lion Bridge.

If I had to name the great rides of my career, this one would be right up there. I was the very last rider on course and as the competition had been so dramatic, the crowds remained gripped to the end, which gave added atmosphere. The course was unrelenting in its demands for accuracy, bravery and scope – there were endless drops and steps up, requiring impulsion – and very little let-up. Broadcast News did everything I asked, and much more besides.

My caution in the early part meant I was 15 seconds behind on the time at halfway and I had to continually up the tempo as much as I dared. The little black horse's enthusiasm never wavered for a second and by the time we turned for home after the Lion Bridge, he was flying, faster than any other round in my life. One of my favourite photographs, which I still have on the wall, was taken by the *Horse & Hound* photographer Trevor Meeks, and it shows Broadcast News streaking home in front of Burghley House, looking like a sleek, shiny racehorse.

We were five seconds inside the time, which put us just 0.2 of a penalty ahead of Bettina and one ahead of William Fox-Pitt and Cosmopolitan. One rail down and I'd be nowhere, but nothing could dim my elation, and Carolyn and I headed off to The George in Stamford for a celebratory drink with Guiseppe and the Purbricks.

Broadcast News was prone to back problems, and he didn't react well to the cold of the iced water in the 'whirly boots' that we used to cool his legs and feet, but Wally Neiderer and physio Mary Bromiley did their usual amazing job and the trot-up passed without incident, although there were plenty of others who had an anxious time.

Phillip Dutton's horse was spun, which put out the Australian team, a decision some considered unfair when both Bettina and William's horses, after agonising periods in the holding box, were both passed. They both jumped clear, too, securing their individual medals, and, for William, the team gold as well.

I was determined after such an amazing cross-country ride that I wasn't going to lose the competition now. I had every stride planned and reminded myself firmly that I'd once show jumped to Olympic standard, so of course I could manage this, especially as Broadcast News was jumping superbly in the practice ring. He seemed to understand how much was at stake, as his exuberance and desire to please never faltered, and he rewarded me with a fluent clear.

I was crowned Open European Champion and Bettina European Champion – all a bit complicated, but if Bettina resented me for stealing the biggest moment of her career she didn't let it show and seemed ecstatic. I got a team silver medal as well – ironically, if Vaughn had been on the team, we'd have won – and one of the happiest days ended with my giving a BBC interview with a four-year-old James perched on my shoulders, grinning his head off. I couldn't quite call myself a world champion, although I'd beaten a truly competitive world-class field, but it was the next best thing – and the nearest I was going to get to the real thing.

* * *

The only way to go after such a triumph was down and, boy, was that painful. A week after Burghley, I had a crunching fall with a six-year-old, Hunter's Moon, at Gatcombe. He fell on top of me at a hanging log, squashing me into the gravel landing. I lay there winded and cursing, but it did dawn on me that I had been incredibly lucky not to have broken my pelvis, ribs or worse. I was 41, an age by which many riders had given up, and I think subconsciously the first thoughts of a future outside eventing were taking shape.

If that fall made me think, a real tragedy the following year certainly had an effect. On Easter Monday 1998, David Foster, a good friend, was killed at an Irish one-day event when his horse caught a leg at rails going into water, flipped over and landed on top of him in the water. My generation – the likes of Scotty and Andrew Nicholson – were devastated by his death and really shaken up by it, too. It sounds a terrible thing to say, but David was the first really top-flight rider to be killed, and that shook us all to the core. He was not only a talented, natural horseman but he was charismatic and added colour to the scene. He was a similar age to me, and had three young children and, for the first time, I think a lot of us – and our poor wives – identified with the tragedy and realised that perhaps we weren't infallible.

The Irish have their funerals very quickly after the death, but large numbers of the eventing community in Britain wanted to go and support his widow Sneezy, and so there was a mad dash for the airport or ferry. Andrew and Jayne Nicholson missed their ferry and chartered a private plane. Sneezy was incredibly composed, far more so than most of us. I can't remember a funeral where I have felt so distraught.

* * *

Broadcast News was an unnerving horse to look after, because his state of soundness was always on a knife-edge, and sometimes we wouldn't know until the moment of departure whether he was going to be able to go to an event. He was a gutsy little horse, though, and we had a brilliant Badminton in 1998. We led after cross-country but didn't have a rail in hand on the final day. Coming up to an oxer fence, I couldn't make him listen, so we had that down and finished second to Chris Bartle, who still held the accolade of being Britain's best ever Olympic dressage rider. It was frustrating, as I would have loved this horse to succeed where Charisma failed, but it wasn't to be, and Chris's win at the age of 47 made a great story.

I therefore had high hopes of back-to-back gold medals at the World Equestrian Games that October. They were held in Italy, with the dressage and show jumping taking place in Stadio Flaminio in Rome and the rest of it at Pratoni del Vivaro. Like the Dutch in 1994, the Italians had taken over the Games after another country – Ireland – pulled out but, unlike the Dutch, they pulled off a friendly and well-organised Games.

Despite its upgrade, Pratoni looked as rustic as usual, with the exception that the 'ladies of the night' who used to line the roads and tracks phases seemed to have been removed. There were still feral dogs everywhere, which kept you awake, sheep and goats which had to be shooed off the cross-country, and it was all pleasantly relaxed.

Albino Garbari had once more created a big, bold cross-country track although, perhaps under instruction, it wasn't quite as fearsome as the 1995 version. The ground was very wet and, after mutterings by other nations, a big drop corner was removed. Neither we nor the Brits wanted the fence removed, as we thought it would make the course too easy and, arguably, it did. Certainly the optimum time was lenient.

I was made to go first for the team, which really annoyed me, but there was no option. Sally Clark was given the number two slot, Blyth went third and Vaughn got his own way and went in the anchorman position, something he may have regretted when he got the worst of the weather.

Andrew was an individual this time, the first and only time he has filled that slot, on the relatively inexperienced New York, and Nick Larkin, a young lad who had won the inaugural four-star at Kentucky, made up the six. Spirits were high, and we all enjoyed the atmosphere of Vicky Glynn's Down Under Club tent throughout the weekend.

Vicky Latta acted as our *chef d'équipe* and, as the intellectual among us, tended to take life more seriously. She got particularly stressed by the fact that our team uniforms arrived late, so we decided to wind her up by swapping clothes. I put on Wally's trousers, which were way too short; Blyth wore mine, which were obviously ridiculously long, and so on. When Vicky got back to the lorry, we said: 'Look! Nothing fits!' She flew off in a panic to ring the New Zealand federation and it took quite a long time to get her to see the funny side.

I was so irritated at being first to go that it made me extra determined. I thought, 'I'll show you.' Broadcast News seemed to pick up the vibes and produced the most amazing test to score 34. Often at a championship, the judging can be cautious on the first day and then the marks go stratospheric on the second afternoon, but I wasn't overtaken until the end of the second day's dressage when Bettina and Watermill Stream, last to go for the German team, swept ahead. This put Germany into the lead, with us in second.

Broadcast News was a 15-year-old by now and he had had a few soundness issues, but once he'd warmed up over the first few cross-country fences, he still made it feel pretty easy and we managed the time without my having to push him – the first time I'd gone clear at a World Championship. It was a great day for New Zealand – Blyth, Vaughn and Andrew all flew round with outstanding rounds and only Sally had a bad day, Squirrel Hill throwing in the towel and baulking all the way, eventually getting eliminated for five refusals.

Bettina dropped to second with a few time-penalties, so I was in the individual lead for the world title, Stuart Tinney was third for Australia, Blyth was fourth, and the team looked unstoppable. Only Sally was understandably deflated, but we all tried to comfort her and she managed to join in with team celebrations that night.

It seems that drama is never very far away from poor Bettina, and next day Watermill Stream was eliminated at the horse inspection. This gave me a greater cushion and I really did think the title must be mine. I reasoned that it was exactly 20 years since I had been to my first world championship and it would be a neat result. Unfortunately, things didn't quite go to script. Broadcast News was normally a good jumper but the ground was soft and, like Charisma, he preferred it firm. Still, he warmed up well; I was reasonably confident and, although Blyth and Ready Teddy did a superb clear, Stuart Tinney – second at that point – took the pressure off with fences down.

The first fence was an oxer, which Broadcast News ballooned over and gave feet to spare. 'This is going well,' I thought. But the second fence involved a turn to a vertical upright and he failed to get high enough and hit it. 'Don't panic,' I thought, 'that'll wake him up.' But he hit the next fence and the gold was gone.

It was still a Kiwi walkover of embarrassing proportions: Blyth took his second gold after a true champion's perform-ance, I had the silver, Vaughn was fourth and Andrew fifth and we had a second team gold eight years after Stockholm, won by a ridiculous 45-penalty margin. In the immediate aftermath I did struggle to be philosophical, and was pretty monosyllabic at the press conference. I couldn't help dwelling on the mis-takes of the previous four world championships. The world title was the only thing I hadn't won and, yet again, I'd blown a golden opportunity. I was unlikely to have another chance.

CHAPTER
EIGHT

T HE INTERNATIONAL FLAVOUR of the British eventing scene was probably at its height in the mid-1990s,
not only with the New Zealand riders there, but also
Australians such as Matt Ryan, the 1992 Olympic gold medallist, Swedes, including Dag Albert and Anna Hermann (now
Hilton), the French rider Franck Bourny, plus Brazilians, Japa-
nese, Italians and Spanish. Event organisers would be delighted
to boast in their press releases that they had eight or nine
nations represented, including world and Olympic champions,
but not everyone viewed this in such a positive light.

Sue Benson went so far as to suggest in her column in
Eventing magazine that British owners were having their
heads turned by the presence of foreign medallists and should
be more loyal to British riders, and there were moves afoot
by some members of the British Horse Society's Horse Trials
Group (then the national governing body) to place a levy on
foreign riders. It was considered unfair that it was easier for
us to get into European events, due to the fact that there were
far fewer of us than British riders, a situation we could hardly
help.

Matters were made worse by some commentators making unflattering comparisons – even on television – between antipodean and British riders in the wake of the latter failing to win any Olympic medals in 1992 and 1996, and it was suggested that antipodean riders were more driven. That's not necessarily true, although if you have made the bold decision to sell up and cross the world, you are bound to be hungry for success.

A decade later, the topic still rankles. Both Kristina Cook, in her *Horse & Hound* column, and William Fox-Pitt in a newspaper article have said that foreign riders should pay a levy for the privilege of preparing for championships at British events. I try not to let it wind me up but it seems a little short-sighted. We pay British taxes and contribute to the British economy, and surely it makes the sport more interesting to have other nations here? It's what makes the eventing so much more vibrant in Britain than anywhere else.

At the height of the carping, in the 1990s, I had a lot of loyal British owners, such as the Welmans, the Apters, John and Pat Smith, Jane Starkey, Susan Lamb, Robin Patrick and Mike and Mary-Rose Cooney, and none were more indignant on my behalf than the Cooneys. They sponsored Carolyn and me through their eyewear company, Safilo, and were great fun to have around, so I was keen to find them a good horse. Their first with me, The Visionary, was a disaster. We nicknamed him Bad Vision, and he gave me more crashing falls than all my horses put together, so I wanted them (and myself) to have a better experience.

I found them a couple of New Zealand Thoroughbreds, Word for Word, a handsome seven-year-old ex-racehorse who had been showing and jumping with a friend, Andrea Rian, and Eye Spy, a six-year-old, who had been jumping with Joanne Bridgeman. Word for Word's show jumping was a major weakness – he really couldn't be bothered, which was a pity as he was a wonderful cross-country horse – but I had some good results on him in 1997 and 1998, including winning Saumur and my third British Open Championships at Gatcombe, and finishing second at Boekelo. As a result, the Cooneys were leading owners of the year, a really pleasing result.

* * *

Another new development in 1998 was the formation of PERA (Professional Event Riders Association), with the aim of promoting the sport, attracting sponsors and therefore raising prize-money levels. This was a smarter version of IERA (International Event Riders Association), which had been going for some while. Robert Lemieux, a rider who was always full of ideas and commercially aware, and Eddy Stibbe, who did a huge amount of work, were the driving forces and they, along with myself, Andrew Nicholson, Blyth Tait, Mary King and William Fox-Pitt, put in £3,000 each to kick-start it. We even had a PERA credit card, but eventually there were problems with a company we worked with and it all rather fell by the wayside.

We were full of optimism at first, but the problem is that riders are the worst people for being organised, committed and actually doing stuff, and most of us found it impossible to keep up momentum while riding full-time. Co-ordinating a united rider voice is a perennial problem. There used to be a culture of fear that speaking out would result in being penalised in some way and, for some people, that has stuck; others are only too keen to mumble and mutter but not stand up and be counted when it matters, and there are always those whose opinion is entirely swayed by the sort of horse they are riding at that particular competition.

However, PERA did get a rider representative on the FEI

Eventing Committee for the first time, and managed to make the point that we sometimes had more relevant experience than officials and should be consulted on certain issues at competitions. PERA is still going – now called ERA (Event Riders Association) – and has a role to play in decision-making but now, in my opinion, rider power has perhaps swung too far in the opposite direction.

* * *

One of the first occasions PERA exercised some real muscle was after Badminton in 1999. It was meant to be a major highlight, the 50th anniversary of the event which is still the oldest and most prestigious in the world, and the Queen was presenting the prizes. There was a big launch party in London, to which all top three finishers over the last 49 years were invited, and the plan was for us all to parade around the main arena in carriages. All sorts of greats turned up – from the 1960s and even 1950s, and I finally got to meet Anneli Drummond-Hay (now Mrs Wucherpfennig), the 1961 winner, whose picture had so inspired me as a child.

That year, the FEI was piloting a new scoring system, with the aim of simplifying the maths so it was easier for the public to follow. The co-efficient for working out dressage scores changed so that the marks were given in whole numbers, rather than with decimal points, and every second over the optimum cross-country time counted as a whole penalty – previously it was 0.4. Although you couldn't prove it scientifically, this had the psychological effect of riders going faster and faster across country to avoid incurring the greater amount of time-penalties.

The intention behind the system was understandable, but no one likes anything new, and scores became further and further spread and the relative influence of the three phases changed so much that, come the final jumping day, all tension would evaporate because the leading riders would be so far in front. We all moaned like mad.

No one could help the dispiriting, torrential rain which fell during Badminton, but that year the director Hugh Thomas had roped his course very tightly. There was a general feeling that the track had been getting easier over the last couple of years, and that, combined with good, fast going, too many people had been getting inside the optimum time, another factor that didn't make for a particularly gripping competition. Clearly, it had been decided that tight roping would sharpen-up the competition a bit and make it harder to get the time, but no one had considered the heavy rain. The turns were incredibly slippery, and riders were flying out of the side door – there were 27 falls. In the end, only 31 completed the event, a statistic at which no one would have batted an eyelid in the old days but which was considered a poor result in modern times.

Ian Stark and I were both there on our young New Zealand Thoroughbreds, Jaybee and Word for Word, and were drawn first and second. Both horses went well, but with massive time-faults yet, unbelievably, we were still first and second at the end of the day. Scotty, however, had four fences in hand in the show jumping – an example of how batty the system was – so I had no illusions that I would be anything but second – again.

Broadcast News, my second ride, led the dressage, but by the time we got to the steeplechase phase it was a bog and we incurred time-penalties ploughing around in the thick mud. The sensible thing would have been to call it a day, but there was so much carnage that if you could get round, you stood a good chance of being placed, as was proved when Pippa Funnell ended up sixth on Supreme Rock despite a refusal.

Poor Broadcast News hated it, and when we got to the

Vicarage Vee, he pulled himself up. Julian Seaman, who was interviewing me afterwards in the press tent, said: 'I think you missed there, Mark', but actually the horse just wouldn't take off at the spot I wanted and ran out to the side.

After Badminton, PERA called a meeting with Hugh Thomas, who was then chairman of the FEI Eventing Committee as well as director of Badminton, to complain about the scoring system and his course. For once, quite a few riders turned up. The atmosphere became quite heated, with some riders unnecessarily aggressive and I actually felt sorry for Hugh, who looked completely isolated. It had the desired effect in that the hated scoring system was dropped at the end of the year, and it made the point that riders weren't prepared to have ridiculous rules foisted upon them, but it was a highly unpleasant evening. Hugh later stepped down from his FEI position, citing a minor health problem, but it had no doubt been exacerbated by all the pressure and it was a pity, because he had a lot to offer in that role.

* * *

Stormy rider meetings were a theme of an *annus horribilis* for eventing in Britain. After the previous year's World Equestrian Games, rumours began to circulate that a horse in a medal-winning team had failed a dope test. Testing is a routine procedure that takes place at the end of any international competition when a selection, generally of the higher placed horses – and riders – are taken off for urine tests. We all know it's going to happen, but the problem is that the results cannot be instant, which means that if medals are involved, and other nations might stand to benefit, things can get nasty over a long period.

One rumour alleged it was a New Zealand horse, but we

knew that wasn't right and, eventually, it emerged that the horse was Coral Cove, ridden by Polly Phillipps for Britain, who won the bronze. The horse had tested positive for salicylic acid, a component of aspirin, and much later it was revealed that he had been injected with this substance to counteract soreness after cross-country.

The British federation fought this all the way, suggesting the substance had got into the horse's system through natural causes, and the case dragged on uncomfortably. It was months before information about the injection leaked out, leading to the resignations of some senior personnel, by which time everyone – competitors, members of the Horse Trials Group – felt deceived. There was also disbelief that Polly – herself a veterinary surgeon – hadn't been banned from competing. The rules are that no matter who administers a drug, the rider is the Person Responsible and takes the rap.

The whole thing boiled over at Bramham in June, where Polly finished third on Coral Cove. A group of frustrated riders made their way to the press conference, demanding that an uncomfortable Polly explain herself, which she couldn't. In hindsight, it was terrible to hound a fellow competitor and it is not an episode from which anyone – riders or officials – emerges with credit, but it reflected the hysteria gripping the sport at the time.

Five riders were killed in falls at British events in 1999. Peta Beckett, a lovely girl with two small children, died after a fall at Savernake, and Robert Slade, a young Australian rider who had spent some time with us, died at Wilton. Polly was number three, a dreadful end to an unnecessary saga when Coral Cove, going at speed, flipped over a fence at Thirlestane Castle in Scotland. Then Simon Long died at Burghley and Peter McLean, a young lad, at Somerleyton.

Suddenly, the sport went from everyone enjoying the thrills

and spills to holding your breath until a rider got up from a fall. Almost overnight, we went from laughing at someone hitting the deck to feeling terrible panic. Lorry parks, usually the centre of joking and sociability, became unhappy, tension-filled places. Everyone was hyped up and there was constant over-analysis of the sport. The message seemed to be: this used to be fun, but now people are being killed.

Talk was constantly of rider safety and eventing was cited in the newspapers as an irresponsible sport doing nothing about its reputation as the most dangerous of activities. In fact, nothing could have been further from the truth, as there was huge concern and Britain has done more than any other country to work on rider safety. There has been much investment in understanding the trajectory and velocity of a horse's jumping effort which led to the development of different types of frangible pin – devices that enable the fence to collapse under serious impact, and it has gone a long way to reducing the dangerous rotational falls. At times, I wondered why on earth I was carrying on, but you have to believe in your own ability. I had good horses, I felt I knew what I was doing, and I don't think I ever rode in a dangerous way. My crashing fall from Little Man when I was a teenager was probably a very good lesson, as it taught me early on that asking a horse to take off in the wrong place can have serious implications.

The aura of unhappiness reinforced my feeling that retirement, sooner rather than later, would be a good idea. Carolyn and I had already set 2000 as being a logical cut-off point. The Sydney Olympics that year were on our way home, it was the millennium, which seemed a pivotal moment to start a new life, and, most sensibly, Lauren would be 12 and ready to start big school, and we didn't want to uproot her at the wrong time.

Although my results were still good, Carolyn and I were

both losing motivation, and I wanted to stop while I was still doing well. The spate of accidents didn't in any way make me lose my nerve, and I certainly wasn't thinking about it when I was out on the cross-country course but, deep down, David Foster's death had affected me deeply. He was considering retiring when he was killed, and when it got close to my own retirement I started saying to myself: 'I've only got to survive a few more events and then I don't have to do this any more,' which is not a good way to be thinking.

Once I had made the decision, it was only fair to warn my owners and start thinking about what was best for their horses. Word for Word and Eye Spy eventually went to a British rider, Polly Stockton, who was second on the former at Burghley and rode at the 2002 WEG on the latter, and we sold Regal Scot, whom Carolyn had evented, to Karen O'Connor. He was one of my most prolific winners, having been successful at three-star level at Bonn-Rodderburg in Germany and Boekelo in 1998 and Punchestown in 1999. Karen was selected for the Sydney Olympics with him, but he didn't go through injury. Diamond Hall Red went next, to Leslie Law, before giving Kelly Macpherson a thrilling first Burghley.

Stunning also had done me proud, winning Achselschwang in 1998, and I decided it would be fairer for him to go to a new rider sooner rather than later. I advised the Apters that William Fox-Pitt would be the ideal rider; everyone respects William as a rider, and I felt he had the necessary calmness to deal with such a complicated character. At first, William didn't fare much better than me with Stunning at four-star level, but they went on to win Blenheim in 2000 and a European team gold medal in 2001, as well as Gatcombe.

In fact, William owes me one, because Mary Guinness asked me if I would ride her home-bred pride and joy, Tamarillo. I explained I was retiring, and suggested she contacted William.

Tamarillo turned out to be William's horse of a lifetime, winning Badminton and Burghley and four team medals.

***

Burghley in 1999 was another weird weekend. I was riding Word for Word and Pat and John Smith's Diamond Hall Red, a horse I'd had since novice. He was a really hot, difficult horse who was hard to control – he once took off out hunting with the Smiths' daughter, Rachel, and had crossed four fields before she could pull him up. He was bred as a jumper, by the Selle Française stallion Dallas, and he was very good and neat in that department, but his dire behaviour in the dressage meant that he had never really shone – we were actually last at Blenheim in 1998. However, for some strange reason, he produced the test of his life this weekend and beat Word for Word, a horse that consistently excelled on the flat.

I don't spend much time analysing why I've been successful, but when a cross-country course is really difficult, I can fall back on my show jumping training and my ability to be accurate. On this occasion, I knew I was riding two good horses, but if you can do your bit by being accurate and giving clear instructions, your horses will have confidence in you and that makes a huge difference when conditions are tough.

Burghley was particularly tough that year. It was very hot weather and Mark Phillips, the designer, had cranked up the difficulty of the cross-country. Everyone was worrying about the sunken water fence, and it was certainly a frightening, though not unfair, fence to ride. It comprised a downhill approach to a vertical rail, a bounce into the water, one stride and then a bounce up to a rail and drop. I told Mark that the fence sticks in my mind as one of the most difficult I've ever ridden but I had two very good rides through it. Word for Word went early and made it look easy, perhaps lulling people into a false sense of security, and Diamond Hall Red shuffled a clever little cat jump in the middle.

There were quite a few problems here, including for Blyth who broke his leg in a fall from Chesterfield, and it proved to be the most influential fence, but far worse was to come. Simon Long, a rider who enjoyed his hunting and team-chasing and evented for fun, had been thrilled to get to Burghley. He was going well when his horse Springleaze Macaroo stopped on the bank out of the complex, so Simon switched him right-handed to the alternative, a small rail. The horse took off from a standstill, caught the fence above the knee, and somersaulted agonisingly slowly, landing with his full weight on Simon. It was yet another fatal fall, and everyone saw it happen on the closed-circuit television in the riders' tent.

The final scoreboard made for fairly dramatic reading. My early round on Word for Word was the only one inside the time and so in the lead. Diamond Hall Red got 19 time-faults, but due to the amount of trouble, he was still in second place. The atmosphere had been jittery even before Simon's fall, due to the fact that in an awful twist, Polly Phillipps's funeral was taking place just down the road on the very afternoon when she should have been in the dressage arena. Things looked really black now, and it was not a night for celebrations.

Next day, in a sombre atmosphere, Word for Word was at his careless worst and hit four fences but, due to the ludicrous scoring system, he still finished third. Karen Dixon finished second on Too Smart and, to everyone's astonishment, Diamond Hall Red won, giving me Burghley number five, which equalled Ginny's record, and my 25th three-day event victory. John Smith was so taken by surprise at the result that he had to collect his owner's prize wearing shorts.

* * *

After such a fantastic run of success in the 1990s, the year 2000 was very low-key on the eventing front. I only won three competitions, all national: an advanced intermediate with Diamond Hall Red at Hoplands Court, an advanced at Weston Park with Eye Spy, and an open intermediate at Lincolnshire with High Street. I took Robin Patrick's big grey Just A Mission to Kentucky, where we finished eighth, and then headed to my last Badminton, on Eye Spy, who was fifth.

There was no fanfare about my last Badminton, 20 years after my first, and Mary-Rose Cooney was furious on my behalf but, actually, I was quite relieved. By the time I got there I was definitely in the grip of some sort of mid-life crisis. On the one hand, I couldn't wait to give up eventing and get on with my life; on the other, I was panicking that I was about to give up the one thing I was good at. And, although I was bored of all the grind that goes with the sport, Carolyn and I had so many good friends that I had the strong feeling that I didn't want to leave a country that had been generous and taken me to its heart. It was an uncomfortable period of limbo.

To use a modern cliché, I was in 'a strange place', and that is the only explanation I can give for a mistake which brought me to the lowest point of my life. That summer, as a result of naivety and impulsiveness, I was caught out by a tabloid newspaper sting, the deviousness of which still takes my breath away. Actors, politicians and footballers have to put up with this horrible kind of thing all the time but riders, I now realise, don't know they're born. There might be the odd sentence of criticism in the papers or magazines that is irritating or hurtful; generally, though, the equestrian press are friendly and genuine and enjoy the sport as much as anyone else, and riders are loyal to each other and close ranks.

It was a surreal, nightmarish time. Carolyn was put through hell, although she was heroic about it all and nothing but supportive. Some friends were clearly shocked, but everyone was kind. The absolute worst moment of all was having to ring my parents and warn them that I was about to be headline news in New Zealand, and not in a good way this time. There was also the issue of the forthcoming Olympics, and because the implication was drugs, it even went to parliament level as to whether I should be allowed to compete in Sydney, even though I hadn't failed a drugs test. In the end it was decided that a tabloid newspaper story wasn't proof of anything, and I was allowed to go to the Olympics.

The embarrassment I felt was huge, but fortunately I wasn't scheduled to go to too many events. When I did, it wasn't nearly as bad as I'd feared. People weren't at all judgemental; in fact they seemed quite indignant on my behalf. Everyone seemed very regretful that Carolyn and I were leaving England. We cracked on with a party that Tom and Mimi May had planned for me at their Wiltshire home, and it was a great night, with lots of laughs with people I liked and trusted.

And some lovely things happened. At Bicton, an event in Devon, they presented me with a collage of pictures of all the horses I'd ridden there over the years. It was an amazing effort, which was really touching. And at Burghley, the British Equestrian Writers Association, chaired by Alan Smith of the *Daily Telegraph*, gave me a picture and Amanda Clive, an owner of David Green's, a scrapbook. I was so choked I hardly knew what to do. I started a speech, broke down, at which point Carolyn shouted: 'Pull yourself together, Todd,' and I managed to mumble sincerely heartfelt thanks.

Fortunately for me, a lot of the attention at Burghley was centred on Vere Phillipps, Polly's widower, who had challenged himself to ride there on Coral Cove. Vere was a very able show jumper and hunting man, but he had to qualify from scratch for Burghley, which is virtually impossible in one year, something I was to be reminded of eight years later when I attempted to get to an Olympics from scratch in a similar timeframe.

In a fairytale ending, Vere finished fourth, and I was eighth on Just A Mission at my last event on English soil. Mark Phillips had toned down the cross-country, at the request of the FEI, but it was still meaty and, as I had competed so sparingly, it was a real confidence-booster for Sydney. The report in *Eventing* magazine read: 'Mark Todd was as quietly brilliant, professional, elegant, charming and unassuming as ever, but his final appearance on British soil was somehow tinged with sadness, both for him and his friends.' The good bit was that Andrew won on a tricky Mr Smiffy despite managing to do a handstand on the horse's back and still stay on.

The other cause of my fragile state at Burghley was that I had been asked to do a farewell parade on Charisma. Of course he loved the attention – I did some flying changes and galloped him, and he revelled in it – but I was an emotional wreck by then. Next day, we travelled to the airport to fly to Auckland, New Zealand, accompanied by 21 suitcases. It was a strange feeling, like the end of a story.

* * *

Sydney was not a glorious occasion for New Zealand eventing, and signalled the beginning of the team's decline at championships during the next decade. The first thing that went wrong was that neither of Andrew's horses, Dawdle and New York, were able to compete, and he is not a person that enjoys hanging around. Heelan Tompkins, the reserve, was steaming that she hadn't got a ride there, Blyth's second horse, Welton Envoy, threw a splint, and there were horrible snakes everywhere. The saving grace was that we're all pretty good mates and we were staying in a really lovely house on the outskirts of Sydney, near the Olympic site at Horsley Park.

We were assigned a press officer, a former shot-putter, the idea being to ward off any nosey tabloid journalists, but, fortunately, interest in me had died down and, anyway, Joan Gilchrist, the stoic editor of NZ *Horse & Pony*, would have seen them off.

As in Atlanta, there were two competitions, team and individual, and that brought its tensions as well. Blyth wasn't able to defend his individual title on Ready Teddy, as they were needed for the team, as was Vaughn with Bounce, and in the absence of Andrew we called in Blyth's partner, Paul O'Brien. Paul had had a brilliant first Badminton that spring on Enzed but the Olympics, and team pressure, was a big ask.

It wasn't long before things unravelled. Diamond Hall Red, my team horse, just about managed to keep the lid on in the dressage, and Carolyn lightened the atmosphere by holding up a home-made sign saying: 'Please don't clap, I'm nervous.' I was pleased to see banners saying: 'Toddy, we love you,' but the horse was spooky and tense and our score of 58 was, humiliatingly, the worst of the team. Only Vaughn pulled off a good mark, 40, so we were fifth as a team at that stage. The Australians had won their previous two Olympic team golds from sixth place after dressage, but this time they were in the driving seat from the word go, with an inspired Andrew Hoy on Darien Powers scoring 30, and there was to be no stopping them.

Mike Etherington-Smith had built a great cross-country course, big, bold and spectacular to watch, with a difficult coffin fence and strong water complexes, and it played into the hands of the Australians and Brits. It suited us pretty well too – we were the only nation to have three clears inside the time which brought us up into bronze, behind Australia and Britain. Vaughn, who likes to entertain the press, even suggested on television that we could still win because the Aussies' horses would be 'donkeys' in the show jumping, a remark which came back to bite him.

Next morning, both Enzed, who had had two stops, and Ready Teddy were lame. The sight of Blyth vainly trotting Ted up was particularly poignant and after he was spun, the team was down to just two, me and Vaughn, so we were eliminated. Vaughn was livid at having his worst fears confirmed and refused to show jump. I had some sympathy – if it had been a normal competition, he would have been in a medal position – but it probably wasn't quite the most graceful call at an Olympics. Even though it was a pointless exercise, I instinctively decided it was right to have my last ever ride on Diamond Hall Red and complete my last Olympics.

* * *

The individual bronze medal on Eye Spy came out of nowhere. The emphasis had been completely on the team, and if Andrew's horses had been sound, I probably wouldn't have had an individual ride. Eye Spy was an excitable, hot chestnut, who had the capacity to do odd things – he once flipped over backwards with me for no apparent reason at an event – and he certainly wasn't tipped for a medal.

I owe a great deal to Tracie Robinson, now the British team's dressage trainer, for all the work she did on him. Tracie had been riding the horses at home for a couple of years and we took it in turns to get frustrated with both Diamond Hall Red and Eye Spy.

The other problem was that I'd had Eye Spy on a low-energy feed, because that was the only hope of keeping him on an even keel but, for some reason, the Australian authorities wouldn't allow us access to our own feed. After a week on normal energy feed, Eye Spy was beside himself, like a child who had eaten too many E-numbers. I couldn't get him to do anything and I said to Carl Hester, who was helping me, 'Look, this is hopeless.' As a last resort, we decided to cut out all Eye Spy's grain, and so he lived on hay and carrots for the five days before his dressage. The difference in his demeanour was just amazing and he performed probably the best test of his life for a mark of 39, 10 behind the leader, David O'Connor on Custom Made. Eye Spy was certainly very pleased to have a feed that night, but I wasn't worried as I knew he was fit and could run on adrenalin.

I was really quite nervous about my last ever four-star cross-country run and longed for it to be over as soon as possible, but, with unbelievable irony, someone up above was obviously having a laugh. There were a lot of falls and I was held twice in my round, the second time for 20 minutes. I thought it would never end.

To my amazement, at the end of the day I found myself in bronze medal position, behind David and the Greek rider Heidi Antikatzides on Michaelmas, who subsequently dropped to sixth place with two show jumping fences down. I was so anxious to go clear that I rode with great deliberation and managed to incur three time-penalties – something I've never done at such a moment before, so perhaps someone really was trying to tell me to slow down. The penalties prevented me moving up to the silver position – that went to the unstoppable Andrew Hoy who overtook me with a clear on Swizzle In – but I really didn't mind too much. It was such a great note to finish on.

After all the dramas, it seemed inconceivable that I had ultimately enjoyed the best Olympics out of the whole squad and, to boot, had won New Zealand's first medal of the whole Games. Fortunately, no one could predict that it would be the country's last eventing medal for 10 years.

CHAPTER
NINE

OUR DEPARTURE FROM the Sydney was very discreet. It had felt like a very long summer and I was keen to be out of the public eye. I didn't want to go through lots of goodbyes, however kindly meant, so Caroline and I just slipped quietly away to the airport, to catch an early-morning flight to Auckland. We were both excited about the future, although it was tinged with trepidation at the thought of being so far from an affectionate and fun social circle and our home together for 12 years. Still, our friends in New Zealand were pleased to see us, and we had an engrossing project to look forward to.

The first thing was to collect the animals: Barney the cat, who gave us heart failure when going missing the week before our departure, even crossing the railway line in Moreton-in-Marsh, Rosie the Rottweiler and Winnie the Jack Russell terrier. They were in different sized cages and when they heard our voices, they were so excited that the place started shaking and rocking.

When we started house-hunting in New Zealand, Carolyn and I made a wish-list. We wanted to stay in the Waikato area, my home territory, we wanted to build our own house, to be surrounded by undulating farmland, trees and water, it had to have privacy, and be near good schools. Carolyn found the plot during a recce in 1999, and after I saw it that Christmas, we bought it. It had everything but the trees, and in our first year we planted 3,000 of them. A lot of the land was down to asparagus, and we had cattle as well.

We were completely united about Rivermonte Farm. It was 150 acres in a gorgeous setting, with a drive down to a kilometre of river frontage on the Waikato, a beautiful, wide, winding river and, in the distance, there were Kenny Browne's hills, where I used to charge about on Shamrock, Nugget and Little Man. The only sadness about returning was that Kenny, such a big influence on my early career, was now in a wheelchair. He had a terrible accident schooling a young horse, broke his neck and was paralysed from the neck down, unable even to breathe on his own. It was the one thing he had dreaded happening, having always said 'put me down', which made it even more poignant.

There was never any argument about the sort of house Carolyn and I would build. We wanted it to have a little bit of an English feel, but suitable to the outdoor New Zealand lifestyle. A lot of houses in New Zealand are single storey, but we wanted to take advantage of the views, so this was on two storeys on a slope down towards the river, with a patio area and infinity pool looking over the river. While our house was being built, we lived in a little bungalow which Carolyn had arranged to have done up, so it was clean and tidy and welcoming. It wasn't exactly a Cotswold farmhouse, but we didn't mind because we had this massive project to look forward to.

We had great fun designing the house – and attempting to keep within a budget. Carolyn and I share similar taste but I left a lot of it up to her. She took an interior design course in Bath when we were living at Cholderton, and is really talented and has a great eye. In the meantime, I concentrated on the farm. It needed post and rail fencing, a new driveway to the house, the planting out of gulleys, a lot in the way of earthworks, plus a gallop and stables.

The house was built partly on a Maori *pa* site – an old settlement – and there were several *kumara* (sweet potato) pits nearby. Just beyond the site was an old Maori lookout – they used the river for transport, and from that point you could see clearly up and downstream. And we had to get a blessing from the local *Iwi* (tribal chief). One of the old Maoris nearby was a diviner, and said bodies were buried at the lookout. He said: 'If you're sitting on your terrace and you see spirits walking across the field coming towards the house, tell them that you own the land now, and that they're to go away. You'll have to be really firm, though!'

Settling back into New Zealand life was, as we hoped, a very happy family time. We knew our neighbours, Brett Macdonald, a racehorse trainer, and his wife Diane, and their two boys James and Luke became great friends with our James. Across the river was Tim Bodle, who is from a big racing family who owned Empire Rose, a Melbourne Cup winner. Chele and the late Paul Clarkin of polo fame were also friends and near neighbours.

Lauren went to St Peter's, a good school which we could literally see across the river, and where she could travel by bus. Despite the bolting incident with Charisma, she had got going through the Heythrop Pony Club and, back in New Zealand, we got her a wonderful pony, Mr Pete, who was a saint. Ever a sociable child, she soon got into the local hunting, which she loved. We often went out as a family, joining up with the Macdonalds.

James, who was seven, went to the little local country school, which was lovely. They had a calf club, a regular day when the children could take in a pet, like a lamb or a bird, so we got him a calf from a local dairy farmer. Every year we reared a couple of calves and James would make pocket money on them.

Steadily, we began to acquire animals. One afternoon, not long after we arrived, we heard what sounded like a child crying from the river. It was a baby goat, which had fallen down the far side of the bank and was stranded at water level. The children said: 'Oh Dad, we can't leave it there.' So I rang up Brett, who had a boat. He's great like that, would drop what he was doing to help and was always game for a laugh. He came downstream, picked us up, we picked up the goat and then went for a cruise up and down the river with it on board.

I rang Tim Bodle, who owned the goat, and told him the children had fallen in love with it and could we keep it, to which he said: 'You can have the whole damn lot.' The kids named her Lucky, and James took her to calf club. Lucky was hilarious. She would tear round and round the house, round the veranda, and up onto the table. One day she flew around the house, jumped on Lauren's bed and peed, at which point Carolyn said, 'She's got to go.'

There was a local church group which ran summer camps with ponies which they then farmed out for the rest of the year. We had a couple of those for the children, and they were ploddy but safe, before we found Buccaneer, an amazing old pony, for James. Buccaneer was a really ancient dun – he'd even been at the Pony Club Championships with Charisma. He was a former Grade A show jumper and eventing pony who had done the rounds with several families. Even though he was 30, he still had plenty of go and we'd take him to little local gymkhanas where, often as not, he'd jump James off.

James and the Macdonald boys used to ride down the road to meet and they just had the most fun, galloping all around the place. Once, I was looking for them and found their ponies grazing by the gully near the house where we had a sandpit. They'd hopped off, dropped the reins on the ground, and were making a 12 foot slide down the bank. The ponies just stood and watched them.

It was very much the idyllic scenario we'd hoped for, and I was pleased to see the children learning to ride naturally and enjoying the sort of independence and fun I'd had as a child.

* * *

On the horse front, we obviously had Charisma, a youthful 28, and Sounds Like Fun, our former racehorse, who was coming towards the end of her breeding career. We also had a couple of mares brought over from England. I went to the December 1999 bloodstock sales with John Warren, who is now the Queen's racing manager, and chose two three-year-old fillies. One was an Irish River mare bred by Lady Tavistock, whom I was later to train for, and the other was a Night Shift mare called Little Gem. They had been sent to New Zealand ahead of us, and we had them in training with Jim Gibbs, although neither actually made it to the racetrack and they went to stud in the (New Zealand) spring of 2000.

Before I left England, I did a swap with Coolmore's owner John Magnier; he got Yeomans Point, a lovely big Thoroughbred intermediate event horse, later ridden at four-star level by Andrew Hoy, and we got a brood mare, Mer du Sud, by Bluebird. She was in foal to Danehill and we sold the yearling, later named The Duke. This might have been the better part of the deal, for The Duke went on to win the Group 1 Hong Kong mile, the richest race in Hong Kong, and was champion racehorse there.

We also had three horses to produce for eventing, to keep

me amused while the racing venture was developing. Jet, a chestnut by Jetball, and Steelbrook, a grey, were both sold to the American rider Michael Pollard, Carl Bouckaert's son-in-law, who is based in Georgia. They both ended up with Carl's partner, the leading Belgian rider Karin Donckers, and both got to four-star level, Jet becoming SS Jett.

The third horse was a pretty bay, Blue Moss, which Carolyn bought from Ray Knight. I didn't have any arena or jumps but I did one event on her. Blue Moss was sold to Louisa Clarke and then to the Italian team rider Susanna Bordone, who rode her at the 2011 European Championships. Both Blue Moss and SS Jett were at the four-star event at Pau in 2011.

The success of the New Zealand Thoroughbred on the eventing world stage – Bounce, Ready Teddy, Word for Word, Bahlua, New York and Ian Stark's pair, Arakai and Jaybee – meant this type of horse was at the height of its popularity with other nations. Reared on acres of rolling grassland all year round, the New Zealand Thoroughbred can have the advantage over European counterparts in toughness and naturally developed athletic ability, proven over and over again at major events in the 1990s. They might not be perfect on the flat, but they are lovely horses to ride across country. A sort of 'if you can't beat them, join them' mentality developed, and several European riders would make a buying pilgrimage to New Zealand every winter, which did the economy no harm at all. New Zealand was similar to Ireland in that way, in that most horses were sold on. In recent years, the warmblood has become more fashionable, but producers in New Zealand still did a good trade. Now, of course, it's in the doldrums, like everywhere else.

I also did a bit of teaching – Tim Price and Jonelle Richards, who are now based in England, came up from South Island for lessons, and I taught Bundy Philpott, who later travelled to Europe for a spell, and also Tim Rushbridge, who is now in England, too. The truth was, though, that I was sick of eventing. I tended to tell people enquiring about teaching that I needed some time to myself and that when I'd got the racing going, I'd see how much I wanted to be involved in eventing.

The circuit in Britain soon passed me by and I barely followed results on the internet. I kept up with Andrew, Blyth and another up-and-coming rider, Dan Jocelyn, when they came back to New Zealand in the winter, and was always pleased to hear news and gossip. I got used to the inevitable drunken phone calls from parties which, strangely enough, weren't nearly as funny in the cold light of lunchtime in New Zealand as they were to those making them at 1am in the northern hemisphere: – 'You must talk to so-and-so' – but we've all done it.

We had several visitors on horse-buying trips – William and Wiggy Fox-Pitt, Michael Pollard, plus Peter Thomsen and Kai and Petra Ruder from Germany and Laurent Bousquet, a French rider who is a great mate – he now trains the French team. Heather Holgate came every year and would sun herself by the pool. Eddy Stibbe and his partner Debbie Brooks had a share in a racehorse with us, and Kate Green, then editor of *Eventing*, and photographer Trevor Meeks came in the spring of 2001 to do a series for *Horse & Hound*. Kate loved being able to tell people that the last horse she'd ridden was Charisma, who was still in ebullient form and hogging the limelight.

I thought Charisma was immortal, so when the end came in 2002, it was devastating. Just a few days before, I took him down the road to the Clarkins' polo club, Mystery Creek, for a fund-raiser for Kenny Browne, who had always taken a great interest in Charisma. The horse was still in great shape – I still rode him once a week and I'd put him on the truck to accompany racehorses. He'd gone a bit saggy in the back, but he still looked amazing. I did some two-time flying changes and jumped the polo boards for our display, making him buck by touching him behind the saddle.

A week or so afterwards, we saw him lying in the field, not looking right. He couldn't get up and we think he must have rolled and broken his shoulder. It was just awful, and both Carolyn and I were in floods of tears. It was a terribly distressing day, but the only good thing to be said was that at least having him put down had to be an instant decision. He was buried on the farm with a headstone and, later, Winnie the terrier joined him – she was hit by a car while hunting.

* * *

I was raring to get going as a racehorse trainer. Racing was very much part of my life as a teenager but since then I'd only ever dabbled and I'd never trained a winner. I treated it as a challenge to see if I could make a go of it and despite the intention for it only to be a small enterprise, it grew and grew.

I had three horses and did it all myself. Carolyn would ride out with me a bit at first and was supportive, but she didn't really enjoy it as she didn't like the smaller exercise saddle or riding two-year-olds. We already owned Disco, by Dance Floor out of Sounds Abound, who was in training with Roger James, so I brought him home, along with a couple of progeny out of Sounds Like Fun: Askaban (by Maroof) – Lauren was reading *Harry Potter* at the time – and Crucio. Askaban was my first winner.

Gradually, the enterprise grew because, of course, I was madly enthusiastic. I love studying pedigrees and am fascinated by the whole bloodstock industry. At the start of 2001, I went to the yearling sales in Auckland at Karaka, run by New Zealand Bloodstock, with a view to getting some syndicates together for some nice young horses. I bought five yearlings and was keen to see if my judgement stacked up. There was a Sounds Like Fun colt, King Tango, and a dark brown filly by College Chapel, but the one that really caught my eye was a filly by Shinko King out of Images.

Every so often you see a horse that gives you a good feeling. We went back and looked at this one about four times, and every time she was really alert; a lot of horses at sales get fed up with being hauled out of their box, but her ears were pricked every time. Another factor in my enthusiasm was that Shinko King had stood at our friend Ray Knight's stud – he was a fairly new stallion who was starting to do reasonably well – and on the female side, it was a good family without being completely top of the range and out of my price bracket. I really bought her for ourselves but when we got home, the College Chapel filly had injured herself and so we put the Shinko King filly in the syndicate instead; we wanted the enterprise to get off to a good start. As it turned out, the College Chapel filly was useless, but the Shinko King one turned out to be Bramble Rose, who gave me success way beyond expectation.

Initially, I found watching someone else ride my horse quite a shock, and it made me realise the potential for frustration there must be for an eventing owner. It was a completely new experience for me and I felt quite powerless and found it hard to watch at first. I obviously tried to get the best jockey possible every time, but I still had the feeling that you do all the work and then you leg up the rider, whom you might not know very well, and they have all the fun. You're at their mercy, and sometimes that was frustrating and a weird feeling. However, I soon realised there's nothing like the adrenalin rush of winning – and I'm an adrenalin junkie. I even used to get excited about winning trials, and I found the whole planning and fitness process and build-up to a big race both thrilling and satisfying.

At first, Bramble Rose was a bit of a disappointment. When I broke her in, she felt awful. Cantering her was like driving a car with four square wheels, as rough as anything, and I didn't think she'd be any good after all. But as soon as I started doing some faster work with her, her stride got longer and the smoother she felt.

New Zealand has a useful system of trials, which are like race meetings but they're for educational purposes only and there's no money. A lot of horses get sold as a result and they're particularly helpful if you're a trainer operating on your own, or starting out, as I was. Although I was really too heavy, I did a three-quarter pace trial with her, and she felt amazing. She did a few more, and then became a bit shin-sore, so we turned her away and she did not race as a two-year-old.

When Bramble Rose came out as a three-year-old in the spring of 2002 – New Zealand Thoroughbreds have their birthdays on 1st August – I took her down to the Taupo trials; it had been quite wet and the racecourse is on volcanic soil so you always get a decent track. She was ridden by Rogan Novall, a Cambridge-based jockey and, thanks to her two-year-old trials, she knew what she was doing and bolted this one comfortably, which was very exciting, and meant she was ready for her first proper race, at Rotorua.

I booked the champion jockey Lance O'Sullivan and, probably on that basis and the strength of her last trial, she started favourite, which was flattering but slightly alarming. She ran third, a nice run – the form comment was 'out well, trailed fourth, fought on' – and I said to Lance: 'I'm thinking of running her in a stakes race for fillies about six weeks away. What do you think?' He replied: 'Nice filly, but on today's run I think it'll be a bit much.' I was a bit miffed, completely forgetting this was the sort of thing I would say to owners when I didn't think their event horse would make advanced.

For her next start, at Pukekohe, over 1,300 metres, I put Rogan back on her. From the angle I was watching from, I thought she finished third or fourth and was a bit disappointed but it was given out that she'd won. Suddenly, the dream was taking shape. It might only have been a maiden race, but it was a step in the right direction and confirmed my gut feeling that she could be an Oaks filly.

Bramble Rose could be a stroppy cow and, like a lot of good fillies, she was a little bit temperamental and on the hot side, but when she got to the races she knew her job and had a very good temperament for racing – she was very competitive. She confirmed my hopes by winning again, over six-and-a-half furlongs, on 12th October, this time in a big meeting with good money – $15,000 – and the distance was half a head. The comment was 'fifth or sixth on outer, wide on turn, strong finish'.

Two weeks later she was placed in the Gold Star Soliloquy Stakes, at seven furlongs, in Auckland. It was a Listed race, the first big one of the season for three-year-old fillies, and the form comment was 'second last, late clear, flashed through late'. I remember thinking Rogan had left it too late, as she looked really impressive and was unlucky not to have won or finished closer.

Then, as is typical with horses of any shape, there was a setback. Bramble Rose was turned out in the field and all of a sudden we heard this awful cracking sound. We looked out, and she was limping. Luckily, the vet was there but there was nothing to be seen and we think she must have whacked a splint bone while playing around. It took a bit of time to get her sorted; she had to have shock-wave treatment and was sore in the shins again, so I didn't get her back on the racetrack until 7th December.

This time, I took her down to Wellington, where the Oaks would be run, for a three-year-old race over seven furlongs, the idea being for her to get to know the racecourse and have a run on a left-handed track. Most of the northern tracks, where I was running her, are right-handed. The move to Wellington also seemed a reasonable excuse to put on a different jockey, one of the best in the area, Bruce Herd.

She was quite a gross sort of filly – she liked her grub – and I felt she was going into the race a bit under-done and I wasn't expecting her to win. She jumped out of the start and trailed in third, and then the other jockeys, obviously thinking she was the class filly of the field, tried to pin her against the rails and not let her out. Bruce had her in a stranglehold and I thought that was the end of the race, but then he just let her bump one of the fillies on her outside – casually but on purpose – after which she went whoosh and shot past and won by three lengths. I particularly liked the comment this time: 'ran third, pushed her way out, too classy'.

In the race before, I had another syndicate-owned three-year-old running, a colt, Vibhuti, whom I had given quite a good chance. Unfortunately, he got galloped on, cut his tendon and finished with it flopping horribly. The officials asked what I wanted to do with the horse, and as I could see that the poor horse would never work again, I reluctantly asked for him to be put down. It was gut-wrenching, but there was no time to dwell on it as I had to rush off and saddle Bramble Rose. This rather brought it home to me that I was a racehorse trainer proper; it was one of those emotional rollercoaster days, such as the big-time trainers experience all the time.

Some good friends, Kit and Genevieve Davison, had flown down from Cambridge because they owned a good horse that had won the Derby and was on the comeback trail. However, it rained and rained and they didn't want to risk him, so they scratched. By this stage I'd had a lorry built which, by New Zealand standards, was quite smart, so they came home in the lorry with us, and we both drowned our sorrows and celebrated Bramble Rose's win with a couple of bottles of champagne.

* * *

As the Oaks is one-and-a-half miles, and Bramble Rose hadn't gone beyond seven furlongs yet, I needed to step her up in distance, although I wasn't worried because her pedigree indicated that she'd stay and everything she'd done suggested that she would get the trip. On Boxing Day there was the Auckland Racing Carnival, and so I ran her in the Eight Carat Mile, a $100,000 Group 2 race. She ran third, and it was a good run, but the field ran spread out all the way so she ended up running wide and covering a lot of ground. Still, she finished two lengths off the winner and a nose behind the second; I was slightly disappointed, but third place in a Group 2 race was still a pretty good result.

On 2nd January, the distance was stepped up again, this time to one-and-a-quarter miles in the $120,000 New Zealand Bloodstock Royal Stakes, a Group 2 for the country's top fillies. I was struggling slightly with her fitness and again she ran third and again I was a bit disappointed. Rogan had got her at the back early on so she'd had to go wide and come at it with a strong late run. It was a good trial but I felt that we could have done better because she was only a head and neck behind the winner, Lafleur, owned by New Zealand Bloodstock's director Peter Vela, and had had to cover a lot of extra ground.

The Oaks itself, on 16th January, was a wonderful occasion. Many owners – and trainers – never get a run in a Classic and here I was doing it after only two years with a licence. But I expected nothing less – just like the eventing, I wanted to challenge myself to see how far I could go.

The build-up was hugely exciting. Lauren came down with a friend, Carolyn was there and her mother, Betty, later donned the Filly of the Year sash at the celebratory party. Our family accountant, Graham Wrigley, a part-owner came and two of Bramble Rose's owners were there, Teresa Gatting, the head of NZ Telecom, and Terry Serepisos, a major property developer in Wellington who went on to own the country's only football team.

Not everything went according to plan. Our jockey, Bruce Herd, was riding in the two-year-old race before the Oaks, and the colt he was riding jumped out of the barriers and crushed his foot, so he wasn't able to ride. Luckily, I had lots of knowledgeable back-up; Roger James, who had trained Disco for us, was with me and Sounds Like Fun's trainer Jim Gibbs was helping as well. I knew there were two or three good jockeys who didn't have rides but didn't know whom to ask. They suggested Opie Bosson. He was a leading jockey who had been out for a while and was on the comeback, and Roger and Jim said he was top class, which I said was good enough for me.

Another worrying aspect was that Bramble Rose was drawn two from the outside in a capacity field. The start wasn't far from the finishing post, and it could be a bit of a mad dash to the first bend in which horses that are caught out wide can get pushed out. I said to Opie: 'Look, she's really fit, so you make the decision as to what to do.'

Bramble Rose jumped out of the gates really well, went round the first bend a little wide, but Opie let her stride forward. He got up into a lovely position, in third place one horse off the rails, and, luckily, a good strong pace helped spread the field out a bit. She had a lovely stride and a very high cruising speed, so he let her come up on the outside of the horse in front and, as they turned for home, took over the lead, kicked clear and won by a length and a half from the favourite, The

Jewel, the 1000 Guineas winner. Nothing could get near her. We were screaming our heads off; it was just the most exciting thing – as good as winning Badminton. I felt incredibly sorry for poor Bruce, who had never won the Oaks, but Opie had given the horse a brilliant ride and, after his troubles, it was a fantastic day for him.

The rest of the syndicate missed the Oaks; as none of them had been involved in racing before, they hadn't really been following what was going on and, in hindsight I had probably been reluctant to build up our chances too much. One, television presenter Paul Holmes, watched it on television and then rang me up to say: 'I didn't realise what a big deal this was, but everyone's congratulating me!'

Bramble Rose came through the race incredibly well and although I hadn't planned to run her again so soon, there was a race at Te Rapa, near home, on 8th February which was the last in the New Zealand Bloodstock Filly of the Year series; if she got a good placing she'd win the title. Neither Opie nor Bruce was available, so I put up Lance O'Sullivan again. She was second, beaten by Lafleur again, a filly we'd beaten in the Oaks, but she fought on really well and it was good enough to win the series, which I was thrilled about.

* * *

Our next target was to conquer Australia. The prize-money is much better – the AJC Oaks is worth $715,000 – and, although you can't always compare New Zealand and Australian form, it was clearly worth a crack. After a break, I ran Bramble Rose at Tauranga in an open-class mile race. It was raining and the track was a bit soft, which she didn't like, but she showed her class and Opie didn't have to do a lot on her to win, and so we headed off across to Australia with high hopes.

The Australian racing scene, I knew, would be a whole different ball game, but we were made to feel very welcome. The idea was to run her in the Arrowfield, a Group I race which takes place during the Sydney Carnival, a huge affair, and I decided to get an Australian jockey. It's good to have local knowledge and Paddy Payne, whom I engaged, was one of the leading riders in the region.

Suddenly we were up against all the top Australian fillies, and it can be hard to gauge where you stand. Still, Bramble Rose did not let me down and we were second to a very good filly of Gay Waterhouse's, Shower of Roses from the Eight Carat family, and a famous broodmare of Patrick Hogan's. We were unlucky in that Shower of Roses took off and built up a big lead and Paddy had Bramble Rose three horses back and boxed in. The others just let Shower of Roses go on so she built up too big a lead and Paddy couldn't get out of the melee to get going after her. Bramble Rose did her best to wear her opponent down, but the finishing post came too soon and she was beaten three-quarters of a length. It was a huge run, though, and very exciting. I thought she would improve for it and couldn't have been happier with her.

The Australian Oaks was both a thrill and a disappointment. It was thrilling to be there, but the ending was deflating. I had gone home in between the two races, leaving Bramble Rose in the charge of Kirstin Richardson. She needed re-shoeing before the Oaks, so in a bid to be efficient, Kirstin arranged it while I was away. When I returned to Australia I wasn't happy that the new farrier had got the balance of her feet quite right and became slightly paranoid about it as the day approached. As I watched her walk towards me in the parade ring I wished I'd done something about it before the race.

She went off second favourite and, although she looked as if she'd got the winning run halfway down the straight, she didn't make any further progress and finished third behind Sunday Joy and Shower of Roses, both trained by Gay Waterhouse. When Paddy came back, he said: 'I don't think she's quite right.' Carolyn and I went back to the stables with her and, and sure enough, the leg was filling. I had to break the news to the owners and found, to my horror, that this time Paul Holmes had been on the case and had lost a small fortune punting on her. So although I'd trained a horse to run third in the biggest race for fillies in the Southern Hemisphere, it was also devastating. I was particularly gutted because I knew Bramble Rose was slightly offset and had always been careful of the way she was shod.

There was one possible solution, however. We had become friends with Wayne McIlwraith, a New Zealander who lives in the USA, where he is head of veterinary research at Colorado State University. By chance, he was in New Zealand so I got him to have a look at her. It was just when stem cell treatment was taking off and she was the first horse in New Zealand to have it. The process has now been more refined – at that stage it involved taking fat from the sternum and injecting it into the core lesion.

Bramble Rose had 12 months off, but the treatment worked. She ended up with a thicker leg, but the tendon was good and hard and strong. She came back into work in September 2004 and had a trial, after which we raced her six more times. Although her work was good, and she still had the speed, she seemed to have lost her competitive edge. As I didn't want her racing career to peter out, and wanted her to be remembered for her brilliance, I sold her to Australia as a brood mare prospect.

* * *

Although Bramble Rose was easily the high spot of my race-horse training career – four wins, two seconds, four thirds, one fourth and one fifth from 17 starts and prize-money totalling $414,298 – there was another major highlight. This was Willie Smith, a lovely big horse by Volksraad out of a Sound Reason mare. He had been trained by a friend, Richard Dee, who had given up, and I took him over midway through 2005. He was owned by Merran Hain, my Gawler team-mate and the owner of my Olympic jumper Double Take, in partnership with her brother Murray McPhail. By the time I got him as a four-year-old, he had won one race. He always looked as if he had a bit of ability, but was a great big horse and needed time to mature.

I had a couple working for me, Vic Booth, a former trainer, and his partner Debbie Hughes, a jockey. She didn't want to race-ride any more but agreed to ride Willie Smith in his first trial where he showed an amazing amount of dash. This came as a considerable surprise because on the training track he'd shown us nothing – he was the laziest of the lot.

I entered him for a race at Avondale and I got a call from the agent of Leith Innes, the leading jockey of the season, asking for the ride. I said: 'Well, yes, you can have the ride, but I must warn you that he's shown me nothing on the track, and if you get a better offer, go for it.' Leith decided to get on something else, so I engaged another good jockey, Michael Walker, who was known as a bit of a rebel but was talented. Willie Smith idled out of the gates, ran around the outside of the field, then flew home and won by two lengths. I was flabbergasted.

A few weeks later, the same thing happened. Willie Smith wandered along at the back, swept round the outside and won again by two-and-half lengths. Merran was over the moon. He was an exciting horse to watch because, as he had no early speed, it was no good trying to make him hold a good place early on – you had to let him amble along at the back, make his way round the outside and then he would fly home. He won two more races that season, including a one-and-half mile race, the Virginia Turner Summer Cup which was part of the Wellington Cup meeting, this time with Scott Seamer, an Australian jockey, in the saddle.

Then we stepped him up to a Group 1 race in Auckland, but he didn't do any good, as he liked going left-handed. He didn't get the best of runs, got bumped, and his run was too late. I also took him to Australia, but he was past his best by then, so I turned him out for a spell. He was a funny horse – he either liked his jockey or he didn't. If you were relaxed, he was fine, but if you took hold of him, he'd pull like anything.

He got on well with a young jockey called Matthew Cameron, who had been a good apprentice but had gone off the rails a bit and was getting his career back on track. I put Matthew up on Willie Smith at Te Rapa, where he finished second. He then ran in a Group 2 race in Auckland where we were unlucky – he got interfered with a furlong out and finished third, but got promoted to second after a stewards' enquiry. I don't think he could have actually won, but it was a good race.

The following year, 2007, I took Willie Smith down to Wellington for the Trentham Stakes (one-and-a-half miles) on the first day of the summer carnival, and then the plan was to stay down and run him in the Wellington Cup a week later, which is a staying race at two miles. It sounds a lot to run a horse in two races a week apart, but the record of horses doing both is good and we'd primed him specially to do this.

We stayed with a friend, David Howarth, and worked the horse on the beach between races. Matthew was riding him in both races and I said to him before the Trentham Stakes: 'I believe the horse is very fit and will run well, but the main one we want to win is next week.' In hindsight, if Matthew had gone a little bit sooner on him in the first race, he could have won both, but it was the perfect warm-up. The horse loved the big roomy track at Wellington which has a long straight that suits horses that like to come from behind. The encouraging form comment was: 'just warming up, top run'.

He did very little in between races. We took him to the beach and he did one piece of fast work, on the Thursday. He was in peak form and I went to the Wellington Cup feeling confident. I got a bit of stick for putting Matthew up rather than a top jockey, but I had faith that he would do as he was told and, most importantly, the horse liked him.

It was hugely exciting to watch. It's quite nerve-racking with a horse that dawdles along at the back, but Willie Smith had an amazing finishing burst as long as you wound him up carefully. You had to start setting him alight about four furlongs from home and let him gather speed, and Matthew used to do it beautifully, going round the field so as to get an uninterrupted run. Matthew rode the race to perfection, and came charging home. I was watching with Merran in the stands and we were cheering like mad, but we were at a bad angle and couldn't see that he'd won. When he was called the winner, we went mad. I was thrilled to win a big race for Merran because we went back a long way and it was also Matthew's first Group 1 winner. And, although I didn't know it at the time, it was to be my last winner in North Island.

Willie Smith had one more run in the Auckland Cup, another two-mile race, but struck a wet track and only plodded home. When he came back into work in 2008 there was a bit of heat in his leg. After that, the horse went to David Howarth, and though he got some good placings he never won another race.

After Bramble Rose's Oaks win, I got offered a lot more horses to train, including from some of the major studs. This meant a great deal more paperwork and commitment; Carolyn did a lot of the entries and Sheryl Lang acted as my secretary. She was married to a trainer, Roger, so she knew what she was doing, which is just as well as I used to be really nervous about missing nominations for races; otherwise it costs a fortune to get in.

I trained some horses for Peter Vela, the head of New Zealand Bloodstock, which he owns with his brother Philip. The best one was Stanica, a filly. She was by Zabeel, the champion sire, out of a Japanese-bred mare by the leading sire in Japan, Sunday Silence. I hoped she might be an Oaks filly, and she was talented, if rather tricky – Peter always sent me the difficult ones to train. She won four races for us and I entered her in a Group 1, the Avondale Gold Cup, at just over one-and-a-quarter miles. It was a step up in class, but I felt she was up for it, as she was a real stayer. The Velas flew over Scott Seamer, who had won the Caulfield–Melbourne Cup double on Ethereal for them, and I felt a bit bad for Rogan getting jocked off. I felt even worse when she just got beaten by a head and half a head, probably because Scott didn't know her very well.

Another horse that gave us a lot of fun was Izzat, by Almutawakel out of Wauwinet, a half-sister to Sounds Abound, Disco's dam. I bought him as a yearling, as I knew the family. He was a big raw-boned plain sort of yearling but he reminded me of Disco and looked as if he would furnish into a nice three-year-old. He was a big staying sort but showed a lot of ability as a two-year-old, winning a trial. His first race was five-and-a-half furlongs, an open two-year-old race with some useful horses in it, as there wasn't a decent maiden available. Izzat was dead green, last out of the gates and last round the final bend, but he had an experienced jockey, Jamie Bullard, who pulled him wide and, suddenly, he flew down the outside and got up and won by a nose. We were astounded.

He was third in a Listed race over six furlongs, and then we put him away for the winter. He looked like an exciting prospect as a three-year-old, but when he came out in the spring he ran a very ordinary race first up. I scratched my head and then ran him again a fortnight later on the same track, and he came through and won nicely. There was a lot of talk about him then and we got offers from Hong Kong, but we'd decided he was a Derby horse and kept him in the hope of getting more money. His next race was a Group 1 over a mile. We knew it would be a difficult race to win as a lot of the best three-year-olds were in it. He was slow away again and had to weave his way through the field, but he got up and was only beaten by a nose and half a length. As a result, the offer from Hong Kong doubled, so we sold him. He went on to win the Hong Kong Derby and earn prize-money of $1.75 million dollars. I felt very chuffed and enjoyed following him.

We were also concurrently running a breeding operation, with the two mares from England, plus Sounds Like Fun and a Zabeel mare from the family of Empire Rose, the Melbourne Cup winner, and a daughter of Sounds Like Fun, Cantango. Her colt, Tamhamkke, by Dance Floor, went on to win some 22 races in Korea. His owners came to Rivermonte Farm to ask if we had any relatives; we asked how he was doing and they said: 'He is champion.' He won the equivalent of $1 million in prize-money, and they had just bought him out of the paddock.

* * *

By this stage, I had rather dropped out of the eventing world and hadn't had any involvement in the 2006 World Equestrian Games in Aachen, another disappointing occasion for the New Zealand team. I'd had two cracks at being a team trainer by that stage and neither had been at all successful.

In 2002, I was appointed advisor to the New Zealand squad,

quite an eye-opener and which I can't boast was an unqualified success. I was training a rider in New Zealand, Kate Lambie, whom I had known for ages. She was from a farming family and worked hard at her eventing, and the good mare she had at the time, Alibi, was her big chance to shine on the international stage.

She brought the mare over to Badminton and I went over to help, and to catch up with the rest of the team. Kate did really well; she finished fifth, and earned her place as an individual at the World Equestrian Games in Jerez, Spain. I was slightly dreading the trip to Badminton, as I was worried I'd think, 'Oh God, I wish I was riding,' but although it was great fun to see everyone, especially Tom and Mimi May with whom I was staying, the trip reiterated that I had made the right decision. I was relieved to find that my main emotion was merely contentment with what I was doing.

I found Jerez quite a strange experience. I was in a 'non-role' really, the idea being that rather than acting as a team coach, I would just offer advice if necessary. I had so recently been on the team myself that this felt a bit awkward, and the riders presented a disparate group, the camaraderie of our early days apparently lost. Blyth, as ever, was totally relaxed about it – he has always been a great team player – and Andrew always gets on with it, so I wasn't about to tell him what to do either.

The result was something of a car crash really. It was very hot, the ground on the cross-country was like a road, and there was a water complex which was rather a lottery. Andrew, who had a broken stirrup crisis, finished ninth on Fenicio, the first of a family of Spanish-bred horses he rode for Ramon Beca, a Spanish rider who had been my contemporary. Dan, making his team debut, was 12th on Silence, a horse bred at the Mamaku Stud where Charisma came from, and the team was fifth. There was a lot of drama and it wasn't the happiest of weekends. Heelan Tompkins, also making her debut, had a stop on Classic Hits Crusada. Blyth, trying to defend his title on Ready Teddy, had a horrible fall at the water, and Kate finished 17th after an upsetting argument about a refusal.

Two years later, my role was more defined for the Athens Olympics in 2004, where I was officially team trainer. I came over a couple of times to England to work with the riders, two of whom had been based in New Zealand; Heelan, who had been doing a degree and working in local radio, and Matthew Grayling, a dairy farmer who evented – just like I had 20 years before.

We had high hopes: Andrew had obvious credentials on Fenicio, who was capable of a really smart result; Blyth had Ready Teddy back to his best and had won Punchestown that spring – this was to be their joint retirement event; Matthew had had some good results on Riva; Heelan had a lovely little horse, Glengarrick, who was good in all three phases, and we knew Dan, as pathfinder, would set them up with a good clear on Silence.

The Olympic format had reverted to one competition, much to everyone's relief, the only difference to the original being that there were two show jumping rounds, the first to determine the team result and the second for the top 25 individuals. It was also the first Olympics in short format, with no roads and tracks or steeplechase phases, and this was to be to our disadvantage.

The team's chances were dashed as soon as the dressage phase. Heelan and Matthew both scored in the forties, which was great, but the other three were in the sixties, a disaster. Ready Teddy became unnerved by the occasion, reared up in fright and scored 63, a devastating result for Blyth. Then to our dismay, Andrew, our anchorman, scored the same on Fenicio, who was strangely lacklustre. The mood in the camp slumped into an atmosphere of sullen disunity, with Andrew beating himself up for not rescuing the situation with a better dressage mark.

The cross-country was short – up and down a stretch of grass resembling an airstrip – and lacked technicality, to say the least. We knew it would be too easy and uninfluential and that we would have no hope of making any headway on the leader board. As Blyth put it ruefully: 'This is no Barcelona.' We had three cross-country clears inside the time, from Dan, Heelan and Matthew, and Blyth just clocked 1.2 time-penalties, but it didn't do us any good. Our Olympic spirit further deserted us when Fenicio left a leg at a Greek urn fence near the end and unshipped Andrew.

About the best thing that could be said about it was that we were staying in a very nice house near the beach, with our *chef d'équipe* Chris Hodgson and his wife Lowell. In 'real life', they are both high up in the legal world in New Zealand and I should think the whole experience was a nightmare for them, but they were great fun company. There was a nightclub nearby, the Kahlua club, where most nations congregated. My credit card bill was enormous by the time I got home. Before the competition started, we collected the grooms to take them out for a meal and go to the club. In the early hours of the morning, Dan and I, plus David Green's wife Jackie, who was looking after Glengarrick, and Fiona Fraser, Blyth's groom, were emerging from the club when Dan and I decided to go for a swim. We stripped off and then had the very mature idea of throwing the girls in. Chris probably knew that he should stop us, but he had done quite well in the club and wasn't really up to articulating the right instructions. All this took place as our head of the New Zealand federation was leaving to go to the airport to meet Dan's mother, and was rather startled to see us running naked down the high street. We bundled the girls into a car, all of us dripping wet, and dropped them off at the stables, shouting: 'Thanks for a great night out!' The security guards obviously thought they were a couple of hookers.

The whole episode brought home to me the fact that being a rider is much easier than managing a rider. As a competitor at a championship, you just have to focus on your horse and everyone will run around after you. Managing people who just want to do their own thing came as quite a shock to me; I realised it probably wasn't my forte and, for the first time in four years, I felt a twinge of envy for the riders.

CHAPTER
TEN

I N THE APRIL OF 2007, Carolyn and I made the decision
to change our lives again, and moved to South Island. We
were in search of a more tranquil way of life: the racing
had taken off in a way that neither of us had expected and,
ironically, I was probably busier during those few years than
when I was eventing.

When we returned to New Zealand in 2000, the original
idea was just to breed and race a handful of horses of our
own but, in hindsight, it was unrealistic that at the age of 44 I
would just retire and potter about. Carolyn hoped I'd be less
busy, but I don't like not being busy. There will be plenty of
time for that when I'm old! I am not the sort of person who is
happy playing golf; I naturally want to be competitive, and I
found seeing how far I could go with the training to be addic-
tive. I know I probably wasn't the best husband all the time,
and it got to the stage where Carolyn wasn't enjoying either
the racing lifestyle or living in Waikato, which was always my
home territory rather more than hers.

The idea for the move came about when we went on a trip
around South Island with the aim of rekindling our relationship, which had been suffering. Carolyn found a beach house

to rent on top of the hill overlooking Kaiteriteri, in the Tasman Bay area; it was owned by Michael and Karen Moss, who have since become friends. We fell in love with the area, which has the most sunshine hours in New Zealand. It was a gorgeous setting, and the beach was once voted one of the five most beautiful in the world by a British travel magazine. The rest of the Bay can only be accessed by boat or on foot, so a lot of people miss it. It's a wine-growing area and has a bit of a hippie colony feel, like a step back in time.

We spent quite a bit of time in a pub called the Beached Whale and the guy who owns it, Anthony, has also become a good friend. He sings and plays the piano and guitar and is a really good entertainer. There was one great night when an American guy who had been with a big band was there, and the pair of them had an impromptu jamming session. It was a happy, feel-good place.

Carolyn and I decided to meet up with an estate agent who showed us one property that as soon as we saw it, we both knew we wanted. Carolyn and I have always been compatible about places we like – it was one of the great strengths of our marriage – and this place just had an atmosphere which worked for us. The problem was working out how we could afford it, as it was beyond the budget we had planned – like everything we did always was. After some discussion, we sold 50 acres off Rivermonte Farm, the asparagus fields that we didn't really need, to David and Maisie Benjamin who had owned a stud and wanted land for the few horses they had kept on. They also bought a house down the road that Carolyn had been doing up as a project, so it all worked perfectly.

So we bought this magical piece of land, which was less than an acre but had 270 degree views all round to the ocean to Nelson, about an hour away, and two little bays on either side. We got the plans drawn up, but never got round to building anything because, ultimately, it was too much money for something we'd only visit for a couple of weeks a year.

Throughout our married life, we've always moved around – up until now, five years was the longest we've stayed anywhere. By now, we'd turned Rivermonte Farm into a beautiful place; the trees had grown and it was looking stunning. Chatting together one day, we discovered that we both wanted a new challenge. We knew we didn't want to move to Auckland or Wellington, and we had really enjoyed the times we'd spent in South Island. But we knew that a move there needed a bit of thought, because South Island is more remote and logistically difficult, and that we should plan to be near a major airport. Christchurch was the obvious area, so we contacted people we'd met while travelling around there and went down to take a look.

We stayed with Humphrey and Deborah Rolleston, and Johnny and Mary Hutton, and they put on a dinner party for us; they aren't horsey, but they invited all their horsey friends and called it The Horse & Hound evening. Deborah made it her challenge to find us somewhere, the idea being that we'd move in a year or two. But things moved a lot faster than that. Deborah got on to a friend, Dennis Hazlett, who was a property finder and, within two months, we got a call saying: 'We think we've found the ideal place, but you'll have to move quickly.'

She had found us Hillcrest, 481 Mount Thomas Road, Fernside, one of the historic houses in Christchurch – Mark Twain stayed there. It was colonial in style and, as Carolyn said, just needed a lick of paint. It had 60 acres, no stabling, and was only 15 minutes from the sea with panoramic views of the surrounding countryside. The view of the mountains was amazing, so clear that we could see the skiing conditions and go straight up there if we wanted. It was half an hour from the centre of Christchurch and from the airport.

We both really liked it, decided to go for it, and our offer was accepted, which all took place quickly. So the move suddenly came forward and we had to think about selling Rivermonte Farm. It was hard to tell my parents that we were off again, albeit only to South Island, and I did have mixed feelings, but it was such a lovely place that I was optimistic it would all turn out all right.

The lick of paint turned into major alterations; we added onto the kitchen and redid that, then we discovered a ceiling was made of asbestos and redid that, and we put in a new patio. Carolyn is very talented at interior design and, yet again, we had a beautiful home.

I did find the move quite a big adjustment. South Island has a very different feel to North Island and, although New Zealand is not exactly a hectic country overall, the pace of life in South Island is a lot steadier. I'm used to rushing around so it took me a while to get used to it, although I did like the fact that people were so friendly and had time to stop and chat.

The idea was that I would give up my public training licence and cut right back on the racing, concentrate on breeding, have one or two of our own to race, and get back to the ideal we'd started with seven years before. We were lucky in that we had no debt; all we just had to do was keep ticking over. By this stage, Lauren had left school to do a law and psychology degree at Canterbury University and, as she has always been outward-going, chatty and confident, we felt the move would not be a problem for her. Conversely, James, who is out of a quite different mould, was only 14 and did not want to leave Waikato, where he had great friends and had spent the most significant part of his childhood. We felt awful because by the time we moved, his term had already started. He would have to be a boarder at a new school, St Andrew's, a factor which took some persuasion on our part and involved much bargaining.

We had to promise him that as soon as we moved down to Christchurch, he could come home and go daily to school, and if at the end of the first year he didn't like it, he could move back to St Peter's. However, when we arrived in South Island, he said he might as well stay until the end of term and, as there was a group of new boys all starting boarding at the same time, we agreed it was the best thing. We chose St Andrew's because it had a good reputation and a lovely family atmosphere. Boarding schools now are brilliant and, after that first term, we couldn't drag him home – there was so much going on that he enjoyed.

* * *

It was quite a bizarre experience, moving horses and our life down south, but we managed it. The brood mares went back up north in June to foal or get in foal, and, although my racing involvement was coming to a close, I took a gorgeous little filly, Kate Cross (by Cape Cross, the sire of the 2009 Triple Crown winner Sea The Stars), to race.

James Macdonald, my James's friend with whom he mucked around on ponies, had become an apprentice jockey. He was 15 and just the nicest kid. I'd given him a few lessons and I said to him: 'When I've got a horse I think will win, I'll get you down and you can have the ride.'

Kate Cross was racing at Motukarara and I thought she would win, so I got in touch with his mother and said I'd try and organise him some other rides. He came to stay, had a few other rides and won on them, and then he won on my filly as well. It was a great day.

James is now the leading jockey in New Zealand; he's broken

lots of records and has spent time in Australia, Hong Kong and Ireland, where Jessie Harrington, a former Irish international event rider who is now a successful dual purpose trainer, was impressed. I'm very proud of him, having known him since he was a little kid, because he is now the racing sensation in New Zealand. He's kept his head, he's very professional, and I think he'll be world class.

Training racehorses on a public licence is not something I expect to do again, though I still own two in partnership – both retained because they came back from the sales. I'm Your Venus, a four-year-old (by Show A Heart), whose dam we bought in foal, is in training with Matt and Mary Brown on South Island and, at the time of writing, has won twice and been second twice in eleven starts. Then there's a five-year-old Kullu (by Elvstroem), bought as a weanling in Australia, who is in North Island with Stephen McKee and has to date won $75,000.

* * *

In November 2007, Tinks Pottinger, my former team-mate, and Erik Duvander, my one-time working pupil, were down in South Island doing some clinics and came to stay. During dinner one evening, and after a few glasses of wine, the conversation turned to the Beijing Olympics the next year, and New Zealand's not very starry prospects. They said: 'Why don't you have a go for next year's Olympics?' And I replied: 'Well, find me a horse, then.'

New Zealand eventing was in the doldrums as far as championships were concerned. It hadn't won a medal of any kind since mine in Sydney, and the team was struggling. There didn't seem to be enough young riders coming through and wanting to travel to England as we had, and apart from

Andrew, on a number of horses, there was no stand-out combination. It sounds big-headed, but I knew that if I could get myself together, I could be in contention for the team. I knew I wouldn't be an individual medal chance, but if I could put up a solid double clear, I could contribute usefully to a team effort. I'd only ever won one team Olympic medal, bronze in 1988 with Tinks, which was niggling me. And, I reasoned, if I couldn't get qualified in time – and that would be a tall order – I wouldn't be on the team anyway. It was a fun idea, but it wasn't at the forefront of my mind.

The Christmas holidays arrived and we went up to Kaiteri-teri, taking the little boat we'd bought. On Boxing Day, I got a call from Mary Derby, my team-mate in 1978 and 1984 and now the chairman of selectors. She said: 'I hear you want a horse for the Olympics?' I said: 'What? Not really.' And Mary said: 'Well, there's this horse called Gandalf ...' Paul O'Brien, Blyth's partner, was also a selector, and he knew the horse, so I rang him to discuss it. I also talked with Carolyn about it. If she had said 'no way', I wouldn't have done it, but we both viewed it as a short-term challenge. I had obviously been riding all the time, but I hadn't competed in eventing apart from a one-off novice ride in 2001 and at all since Blenheim in 2004 when I rode Andy Griffiths's daughter's horse and partnered Ginny in a fun event.

Despite my past achievements, there would be no dispensation from the FEI; I would have to qualify in the proper way, and that meant completing two- and three-star events, both three-day events and CICs (international one-day events), to a certain standard, all within a few months. It meant getting an unknown horse to Olympic standard, and it all hinged on absolutely nothing going wrong. I reasoned, though, that I was a fairly good judge of a horse, and if I could go to England with him and clock up some form, then I might be able to make some money on him. We had a family discussion about the fact that the whole project meant I would be away for four months, but everyone was in agreement that I should give it a go.

We decided that when we finished our holiday in January, we'd fly to Auckland to see the horse and if we didn't like him that would be the end of it. I was aware that Gandalf wasn't a superstar, but he had a good record up to three-star level, and a good cross-country reputation.

He was a nice-looking grey, but when I tried him, he felt a bit lazy. He was all right on the flat and I felt I could improve his dressage. Most importantly, he felt safe jumping. I didn't jump anything too big – 1.10m felt pretty big and, when it was suggested the jumps were put up, I said hastily: 'No, that's fine, I've got a good feel of him', the truth being that I didn't want to jump any higher.

Carolyn and I went back to the South Island, chatted some more, and decided to get the horse vetted – he'll probably fail, we said. But, of course, he passed. I wondered what on earth I'd done. Fairly quickly, it dawned on me that the project was going to cost a fair amount, and that I urgently needed sponsorship. I immediately thought of Peter Vela and his brother, who ran New Zealand Bloodstock. They have a lot of interests in Hong Kong, which is where the Olympic equestrian events were going to be held due to quarantine restrictions in mainland China. It seemed a good fit, and Peter had always been an approachable man.

I rang Peter and told him of my plan and that he was the first person I'd thought of. Peter replied: 'Look, I'm at the races and I've just had my first bottle of champagne. I'll think about it.' Five minutes later, he rang back and said: 'Yes, we'll do it.'

New Zealand Bloodstock is only part of the Velas' empire – it's a large and very successful company and racing is only one of Peter's interests and passions. In fact, his main interest was fishing. He and his brother hadn't been involved in eventing before, but they are entrepreneurial, generous and they like winning, and Carolyn and I were friends with both Peter and his wife Pam. It seemed that we were all set up – all I had to do was qualify!

I had Gandalf to ride at home for a couple of weeks before going back up to North Island to compete him. New Zealand Eventing got into the spirit of the thing and was very accommodating; doing everything they could to help. Mary Derby, however, got some flak from other riders saying that I was getting favouritism.

The first thing I had to do was a national advanced competition on a horse I'd had for a mere two weeks. As I needed to have two qualifying results at this level, I had to ride a strange horse as well, and, in case one went wrong, Mary organised two loan horses for me. They were Judges' Decision, owned by Chris Hodgson's wife, Lowell, and Tom Collins, owned by Nathalie Page. The competition was Aran Station at Takapau.

It was a tall order in so many ways. I never was one for keeping up to date about what you could use and had to dig around to find equipment – we'd given so much of ours away when we left England. I still had my old dressage saddle but the seat was hard, and I would be using leg muscles that hadn't been tested for ages, because of the long length you ride at. I hadn't really jumped or schooled across country, either, yet I felt remarkably calm about it. I managed to get a qualifying score on both horses, but it was quite terrifying. Fortunately, it wasn't the most difficult cross-country course but it looked huge to me and it was a first advanced class for Judges' Decision. Tom Collins wasn't particularly good at dressage but he was a brilliant little jumper, and Gandalf also went clear across country. The relief was that, once I got going, it really was like riding a bike. I still seemed to be able to see a stride and, although I must have looked a bit rough, it didn't feel too bad.

Helen Christie, another selector and now a technical delegate, was also in on the project and kindly invited me to an annual fun event right at the bottom of South Island, a kind of Pony Club event at Wakatipu, which they allowed a few ancient riders to go round. I rode a horse belonging to Clarke Johnstone and that was a useful bit of practice.

I didn't want publicity, but of course the gossip got round when we bought Gandalf and got the sponsorship, and some people were fascinated. It all felt a bit weird, because I honestly never anticipated eventing again, but it was fun. Carolyn enjoyed it, too, and it was all rather romantic, just the two of us travelling around with our one horse in a funny little truck, camping out with friends along the way.

We went to stay with David Howarth near Wellington for a night, and got Gandalf off the truck for a graze. All of a sudden, he threw his head in the air, curled his lip and staggered backwards. We put it down to a bee sting, but it was, sadly, to come back and haunt us.

On our way north to the three-day event at Puhinui, I did an event in Rotorua, an open intermediate class, for more practice. I rode Judges' Decision again, whom I pulled up, but Gandalf once more produced the goods. His dressage was starting to improve – or, at least, I was getting to grips with it – and I was starting to feel more confident about across country. Slowly, the idea that I was really starting to enjoy eventing again was creeping up on me. I then went to the Horse of the Year Show at Hastings, as they had a big dressage and show jumping class. It was a huge arena with plenty of atmosphere, and we were placed in a 1.30m jumping class.

The crunch came at Puhinui, a CIC in March, where I had to get my first international three-star qualification. I hadn't ridden there since an invitation event about 10 years previously but my entry seemed to give the sport a shot in the arm in New Zealand. It sounds conceited, but I think there was a feeling of 'well, if he's going to be on the team, I want to be on it too', and people got bound up in the fact that it was undoubtedly a good story. There was a lot of goodwill towards me, and people clearly wanted me to do well, but there was also a bit of nervousness from other riders; some of their connections were saying, 'Why should he take the place of one of these young ones?' They were, of course, assuming an awful lot about me and Gandalf at that stage. Going to the Olympics isn't about 'it's my turn', it's about excellence, and it would be down to whoever was best.

Incredibly, I won the event. The main arena at Puhinui, which is like a natural amphitheatre near the sea outside Auckland, can cause a lot of horses to get upset, but nothing fazed Gandalf. Although our dressage test wasn't exactly good, it was steady. The cross-country was pretty decent, and you needed to kick on, but we were inside the time and then we followed it up with a clear show jumping round. I might, perhaps, have been marked a little leniently in the dressage, but no one else could have helped me ride a double clear, and we also survived a dispiriting amount of new rules to do with things like length of whip and boots, which the stewards were only too keen to impose.

Then it was all stations go to get myself and the horse to England. Eddy Stibbe, as excited about the whole thing as anyone else, kindly invited me to stay at his base, Waresley Park in Bedfordshire. I knew that things would be much more competitive when I got to England and that I only had a small window of opportunity. If anything went wrong and I missed a qualification, that would be the end of it, and I was very aware of this, but I felt no pressure because I thought the chances of it all coming off were so slim that I decided I was going to enjoy it all. However, my competitive instincts were as strong as ever, and I wasn't intending to throw away a single opportunity.

* * *

When I returned to eventing in England, it was as if I'd never been away. There were, of course, a lot of young riders I didn't know, but also an awful lot I did. Pippa Funnell (who won Kentucky and Burghley on Primmore's Pride, a son of my stallion Mayhill) and William Fox-Pitt had become the Ginny and Ian of their day. Mary King was still very much to the fore, and starting her own horse-breeding empire – I was pleased that she had been using Mayhill as well. Andrew Nicholson was as hard-working and successful as ever and, I think, was genuinely pleased to see me back. He was now with Wiggy Channer (formerly Fox-Pitt) and had started a second family, and William had married again, to Alice Plunkett, a former rider and now a presenter on Channel 4 Racing.

On the international front the children of my contemporaries – Buck Davidson, son of Bruce, Sam Watson, son of John, and Mark Phillips's daughter Zara, the reigning world champion – were making their presence felt. Lucinda and Clayton Fredericks of Australia were the golden couple; Phillip Dutton, who won an Olympic team gold medal for Australia in Sydney, had switched to American nationality and was dominating the US scene; Andrew Hoy, who stood on the individual podium with me, and his wife Bettina were now living in Germany, and David O'Connor, the Sydney gold medallist, had retired and was making a career out of coaching. The Germans, who were nowhere when I left England, were now the team to beat. Trained by Chris Bartle, who beat me at Badminton in 1998, and with riders like Ingrid Klimke, Frank Ostholt, Andreas

Dibowski and Hinny Romeike, a dentist who had a brilliant grey horse, Marius, they were conquering Europe, if not the rest of the world.

I don't really know why I thought the eventing scene in England should have changed – the lovely thing was that it was all so familiar. Bill Allen and Peter Lamont were still in the start box, Justin Llewelyn, Richard Clapham and Giles Rowsell in the control box, and all the same stewards, commentators and fence judges, being so friendly and greeting me as if I hadn't been away. Ann Allen and many other secretaries were still there.

My first event was Osberton in Nottinghamshire in May for a two-star CIC, and we travelled there in style. Eddy had won a helicopter ride and thought it would be fun to use the trip to get there, so I got some ribbing about making a grand entrance. Gandalf got a 58 in dressage, had one fence down show jumping and went clear with 5.2 time-penalties – a respectable result, I felt. Dusky Moon, the last of Eddy's advanced horses which he kindly lent me to help get my eye in, finished eighth. I duly turned up to prize-giving to collect my rosette, and it all felt very warm and welcoming.

I realised that people were surreptitiously fascinated to see if I could still ride, and that there was a whole generation who had never seen me ride and wanted to see what the fuss was about, so I felt a bit of pressure to live up to my reputation. I was conscious there would be an expectation that I would just take up where I had left off but, in truth, I was feeling pretty rusty. Although Gandalf was a good horse, he wasn't a brilliant one; the most important thing at the time was that I felt confident and safe on him.

The next excitement, a few weeks later, was Saumur, an event I'd won three times in my previous life. It is always competitive; the cross-country, designed by Pierre Michelet, is never a walkover and, worryingly, this was my one and only chance of clinching my Olympic qualification, as Bramham in June would have been cutting it too fine.

It had been a long time since the New Zealand team picked itself – in the days of Los Angeles a sound horse that had done a clear round would get you into the team. But, sadly, that did seem to be the mentality among some of the riders, who were only thinking about getting an automatic ticket to an Olympics, rather than whether they had a chance of actually doing any good. There was some mumbling about my presence by one or two of their connections, and one person actually wrote a rather unpleasant letter to the selectors.

Considering Saumur was a completely different ball game to Puhinui, we did quite well. I did a 53.9 dressage on Gandalf, incurred 16 time-faults across country and then show jumped clear, pulling up to sixth place. This was considered a credible result, and it was good enough to secure me a place at the Olympics. Dusky Moon, a horse that had been having a few problems with Eddy, was eliminated for three refusals, which was less helpful, but all mileage was useful at that stage.

I was thrilled with the event and with the horse. Another bonus was that Peter, Pam and Philip Vela were all there to watch, the first time they had ever been to a horse trial. Saumur is in the glorious Loire region and I thought it would be a good introduction as it is always very social and the restaurants, food and wine are outstanding. I put the Velas in a hotel on the hill just outside the town and they loved it, giving the wine cellar a fair thrashing. Philip even commented that he would like to buy a place in the area.

I did three more events with Gandalf in England before going to Hong Kong. We did the open intermediate class at Salperton, where we got a reasonable dressage mark of 38 and jumped a double clear with just a few time-penalties. Then there was Barbury Castle, a very good event in Wiltshire which had developed with David Green's involvement while I was away; it was a bit like Gatcombe in that it had an amphitheatre-like arena and a hilly cross-country run in reverse order of merit. Gandalf ran out at a skinny fence on the lip of a hill; he had always been very genuine about narrow fences, but I don't think he locked onto the idea that he had to jump this one. Although it was annoying, I wasn't particularly worried; it was the first little hiccup with him, and acted as a good wake-up call.

Our final run was at Aston-le-Walls. Our dressage continued to improve, mostly thanks to help from Carl Hester, Britain's leading dressage rider and an old mate of mine; he is a great teacher and very good at having an overview. We scored 36 in an advanced class at Aston, had one fence down in the show jumping and went clear across country to finish 10th.

It was a fun summer. Eddy and Debbie were extremely generous and helpful and the facilities were fantastic – you couldn't wish for better. As I only had the one horse, I rode a couple of their spare horses just to get riding fit. It was good fun on the social side, too. There were lots of parties and I found I was really enjoying being part of the circuit again.

I was also pleased to hear from Carlos Campon, who had worked for me at Poplars Farm and in New Zealand, having married a Kiwi, Vicki. She was already in racing and also came to work for us. Carlos is very Latin – he'd call me Basil and I'd call him Manuel – and we used to have huge barneys, but he is hilarious company. We got on very well and he is excellent at his job. He wanted to work for me again. I reckoned we could last three months, which we did – just.

* * *

The team went into quarantine at Ben and Lucy Sangster's racehorse training centre at Manton, near Andrew. It was supposedly a team-bonding session, although I'm not convinced of its success. This time Blyth was our *chef d'équipe*, with the unenviable task of trying to make us behave like a united team which, sadly, we weren't. The team comprised me on Gandalf; Andrew on Lord Killinghurst, one of the most consistent four-star horses ever who had finished in the top four at Badminton and Burghley numerous times over the last six years; Heelan Tompkins on the successor to Glengarrick, a relatively inexperienced young horse, Sugoi; Caroline Powell, who had been living in Scotland for years and had a great four-star record with a lovely little grey, Lenamore; and Joe Meyer, the grandson of Charisma's breeders, Peter and Daphne Williams, on another nice grey, Snip, who had been placed at Badminton. Annabel Wigley, based in England for a while, was reserve on Black Drum.

By this stage, Carolyn and I weren't getting on too well either, and she decided she didn't want to come to the Olympics. Lauren was dead keen and, as I thought it would be my last, we decided it would be fun for her to come. She stayed with an old school mate in Hong Kong and had a great time. Peter Vela and Humphrey and Deborah Rolleston, our friends from Christchurch, came out to support.

Running the Olympics in Hong Kong in August attracted as much heated discussion as Atlanta 12 years before. The humidity would be even worse, which is why there is no racing in Hong Kong in August and September, and there were horror tales of clothes going black with sweat within half an hour. It was certainly uncomfortable; even riders of the fitness levels of Andrew were streaming with sweat after just a few minutes working in, never mind a dressage test in top hat and tails. And I have never seen rain like it; it was like standing under a waterfall, a vertical sheet of warm water.

However, there is probably more technical and veterinary knowledge massed together there than anywhere else in the world. The facilities at Sha Tin racecourse, where the equestrian events were based, were amazing. You could not wish for better. There was even an adjustable air-conditioning system which got progressively colder as you went from outside into the stables and indoor arenas.For once, the grooms had great accommodation and we, as riders, probably had our best ever facilities. The hotel was a bus ride from the racecourse, and all the volunteers, who had apparently had training in waving, smiling and saying 'have a nice day', were very friendly. I'd never been to Hong Kong and I loved the buzz of the place. We were soon making the most of it, having foot massages, tailor-made suits, and a trip out to the coast which was fascinating, and surprisingly rural, beautiful and properly Asian once you got away from the skyscrapers.

To my horror, it was broken to me that I was going to be first to go for the team. I had assumed that as I had the least form, I would be going second or third, which is traditionally where the least secure partnership goes. I knew I wouldn't be last – Caroline and Andrew had the best form – but Heelan was on a young horse and Joe didn't want to go first, so I had no choice. There was more bad news to come. When the team order was drawn, New Zealand came out as first to go. So, after eight years out of the sport and a sum total of eight competitions, I was first rider out at the Olympics. Surreal.

The only good thing was that my dressage would be at 6.30am, which would be marginally less uncomfortable than for everyone else. But it was still disgustingly close and humid, and when I took off my hat and jacket, sweat poured down my face in rivulets and my shirt could have been wrung out.

Gandalf did his absolute best and we scored 49.4 which, for the first rider, was pretty good. Perhaps it would have been three marks better on day two, but for him it was very respectable, and I felt that we certainly hadn't let anyone down.

The Germans and Australians ran away with the dressage, and we lay fifth behind the USA and Britain, but we had good enough horses to have a chance of improving into a medal position.

Mike Etherington-Smith, the cross-country course-designer, and his team had done a great job on the course, about an hour out of town at the Beas River Country Club where elderly Chinese on golf buggies looked on disapprovingly at the horses thundering over the fairway. The track wasn't overly difficult, and it was only eight minutes – although no one managed to come within half a minute of the optimum time. We had a lot of instructions about heat and humidity and looking after our horses, and it certainly made us aware of our responsibility to present good pictures to the watching world. We were told that if the day went badly, eventing's place in the Olympic movement would be jeopardised.

With all this ringing in my ears, I probably set off too cautiously. The thing I was most nervous about was that I didn't really know Gandalf. I hadn't had to really push him before and he wasn't a natural galloper. With a short course, you need to set out quickly from the beginning, but I had no information to go on and I didn't want to run out of petrol too quickly.

As it turned out, the predicted heat didn't materialise; it was still clammy, but relatively cool considering what we'd had the day before, and horses finished well. By the halfway stage, I realised that Gandalf was full of running, but it was too late to catch up. I got 27 time-faults which, had I had a bit more knowledge, might have been 10 fewer. However, I was touched when Ginny – now Ginny Elliot – wrote in *Horse*

& *Hound*: 'The two outstanding cross-country rounds for me were Mark Todd's and Mary King's. Toddy, who was first to go, was amazing – it was the horse's first four-star ever and Mark's first for eight years, but he set the tone with a round that gave the riders – and organisers – confidence. Had he been a little later in the day, he might have gone for the direct route at the penultimate fence, the Pagodas, and been a bit quicker.'

As I came into the Pagodas complex, two narrow brushes on a diagonal line, I thought 'will I, won't I?' But I knew it would be such a stupid place to have a run-out, so I didn't risk it.

Unfortunately, our team result began to disintegrate. Caroline and Joe, who both had better dressage marks than me, incurred 21 time-penalties apiece – you needed to be around the 17 mark to be competitive – and Heelan had two run-outs at the ninth fence, a downhill brush to a pair of skinnies. By the time Andrew set out, there had only been two really fast rounds, Hinrich Romeike (12.8 penalties) and William Fox-Pitt, who had 10, and this spurred him to try and do better. There was no point in Andrew being cautious, either for the team, or for himself, as he had a good dressage mark and he and Lord Killinghurst were an established partnership. Andrew was completely on a mission, and they were well up on the clock despite living dangerously once or twice, but when they came to the Pagodas, the horse didn't get a great jump over the first fence, twisted awkwardly over the second and crumpled to the floor. With a new FEI rule that a fall of any kind was instant elimination, that was another Olympics over for Andrew.

The mood was pretty down by now and we were miles off the pace, but we crawled up a place to fifth in the show jumping, thanks to the Italians having a couple of spectacularly bad jumping rounds, and Caroline, myself and Joe qualified for the second, individual, round of show jumping. However, although our team result was a disappointment, the show jumping phase was a personal triumph. Gandalf jumped two clear rounds, with just one time-fault in the first, and we finished 18th, a rise of 11 places after cross-country. Caroline was 14th, so I was the second best New Zealander. Yet, instead of being elated, I felt underwhelmed and wished I could have done better.

Hong Kong was perhaps the most sociable Olympics I've been to. Because we were thousands of miles away from the real thing in Beijing, there was less segregation of teams, officials and supporters, and a good atmosphere with everyone mixing. And a lack of medals in the New Zealand camp didn't prevent us joining the party in the local hotel. Hinrich Romeike, who won the individual title and is a really popular guy, was brought in shoulder high. The Germans, who won the team gold, went mad, bopping away up on stage to 'We are the Champions', which was playing on a long loop, but we couldn't let them have it all their own way and soon it was a pretty international scene.

The upshot to Hong Kong was that although Peter and Philip Vela were rather more used to their horses winning than finishing 18th, they were incredibly enthusiastic. Racing people often don't understand why eventers are pleased with their horses even if they don't win, but they grasped the situation immediately, and were wonderfully encouraging.

When Gandalf was in quarantine, some people had been looking at him with a view to buying after Hong Kong, but we pulled the plug when the Velas said: 'If you want to carry on for the next four years, we'll back you to do it properly. But you're not going to win a grand prix in a Mini, so we need to get a good team of horses together.' As they said that, I realised how much I was enjoying being back in the sport and riding.

And that I felt exactly the same way I had after the Kentucky World Championships 30 years ago when I worked out that if only things had gone slightly differently, I could have won! I knew then that I could be competitive, and it was the same feeling this time.

CHAPTER
ELEVEN

AVING MADE THE momentous decision to return to England and a career I'd given up, a major setback nearly curtailed the whole thing. I was doing some fencing at home, when a piece of wood flew up and hit me in the eye. It was absolute agony and my eye immediately filled with blood, so that for a short but terrifying period I thought I'd lost the eye. Somehow I managed to run back up to the house and find Carolyn, who took me to hospital.

The doctors thought it was just a trauma, so they bandaged me up, gave me some painkillers and told me to keep still and not get on an aeroplane, which was inconvenient because I wanted to buy some horses. However, the blood cleared, I started getting my sight back and, after three weeks, I was cleared to fly.

David Green (Greeny) and Andrew Nicholson had both rung independently to tell me about a really smart horse. This was Land Vision, owned by Oliver Townend, one of a new wave of young British rising stars and considered something of a breath of fresh air. Oli was very popular with owners and the press, if not always with his team-mates, for his tendency to say what he thinks, and he was great mates with Andrew;

they're very quick-witted, professional and competitive and both, at times, like to kick back against the establishment.

Greeny picked me up from the airport and drove me to Leicestershire to see Land Vision. Normally, I travel pretty well, but on this occasion I felt knackered. I had a quick ride on the horse and liked him, and then Oli offered to take me out for a Chinese with friends in Market Harborough. This turned into quite a session and the next day I felt dreadful: a combination of a hangover, lack of sleep and a dodgy eye. However, I knew that I should ride the horse again so I forced myself to get going.

Land Vision – Ben at home – is a striking-looking grey who moves beautifully and really jumps. Although he doesn't have a lot of Thoroughbred blood, he still looks quality. I could quite understand why the horse had been recommended. He had clearly been a winner from day one, doing well in dressage competitions with Daniel Henson and upgrading very fast from novice to advanced with Oli, who had won the British Intermediate Championships at Gatcombe with him and an international competition at Hartpury.

After striking the deal, I flew home. A few days later, I noticed I couldn't see out of the main part of my eye. In fact, when I closed my good eye, I could only see a tiny amount out of the side of my left eye and that was pretty blurry. In a panic, I rushed back to the eye specialist. As luck would have it, Christchurch has one of the best eye surgeons in New Zealand, Dr Borthwick. It turned out that the trauma had caused three little tears in the retina, and fluid from the eye had seeped in behind, which had caused the retina to peel off. It all sounded pretty alarming.

I was given the choice of local or general anaesthetic for the operation, in which the surgeon would stick a needle in, drain the fluid out, put another needle in to reattach the retina and fill my eye with gas. Unsurprisingly, I didn't want to be conscious for this. When I woke up, I had a band around the eye to hold it all together and I had to stay face down for 48 hours so that the gas could help the retina reattach itself, which was pretty unpleasant in itself. Dr Borthwick explained that it would be at least a year before the sight really improved. And eventually it did, but the damaged eye became short-sighted and the other one was very long, so I struggled to judge distances; I'd try to pour a drink and miss the glass completely.

The situation was worrying, to say the least. When I eventually started riding, I couldn't see a stride at all, and I thought there was no way I'd be able to ride competitively, the last thing I wanted to admit to having just signed a four-year sponsorship deal with New Zealand Bloodstock and bought an expensive horse. So there was yet more panic as I worried what I was going to tell everyone. However, Dr Borthwick assured me that my eyes would adjust and so would the brain, and gradually it did. My right eye has now become the strongest; when going downstairs in a bad light, I still have to look carefully what I'm doing and I seem to bump into people and things on my left. I got so used to the status quo that I was worried about adjusting to a further change. I have now had the cataract removed and the lens replaced to balance my vision.

* * *

After a family Christmas, I headed back to England in February, the plan being that Carolyn would commute in between James's school holidays. It seems unbelievable that I was so excited about restarting a life I'd been so desperate to give up, but I couldn't wait to build up a string of horses and get stuck in.

My starting base was Bruno Goyens de Heutsch's place near

Wootton Bassett in Wiltshire, which he shares with his wife Dominique, a dressage rider. Bruno has been one of my most consistent and generous friends; he is a Belgian rider, a hugely successful businessman – he markets and sells the Mark Todd Collection, a range of clothing and saddlery which we started back in the 1990s when Bruno was bored and trained with us at Evenlode. He continues to keep dabbling in competing, threatening regular comebacks.

I lived in a tiny flat at the end of his drive at first which was fine for just me, but when Carolyn saw it, she wasn't having any of that and we rented a three-bedroomed house at the golf club next door. Gandalf had been turned out at Bruno's over the winter, and when I got Land Vision, Oli's head girl Charlie Gardener came too; she told me she was planning to look for a new job and asked me if she could come to me, so that worked very well.

My other horse, who had also wintered out at Bruno's, was Grass Valley, which I bought from a young American rider, Julian – Jules – Stiller, who had come over to base herself in England a few years earlier. Grass Valley – 'Riley' – had come from the veteran Irish team rider Eric Smiley, who is now a four-star judge, but Jules found the horse too big and other riders had also tried him without success. My introduction to Riley came through Susie Pragnell, who lives in Henley and acts as a sort-of matchmaker between horses and riders. She's very talented at it – the American riders are particularly devoted to her – and she has a lot of contacts in Ireland. I'd rung her after Hong Kong to ask if she knew any horses I could buy.

I have to admit that I mistakenly thought Riley moved rather better than he did, but he is a lovely big horse who jumps really well and is an absolute gentleman and everyone's favourite. The latter was an important factor in my search, as I was still a long way from getting back to the way I rode in

2000, and I needed horses that weren't too tricky and would give me both confidence and mileage.

My first outing as a full-time event rider was not exactly successful. I took Gandalf, who was then being aimed at Badminton, to Tweseldown, where I managed to miss a cross-country fence and get eliminated. Afterwards, when we were cooling the horse off and he was picking grass, he threw his head in the air, staggered backwards and went over, with his neck bent under him. Somehow he missed hitting all the nearby cars, but it was a horrendous incident. We thought he was having a heart attack. As I tried to keep everyone calm, he lay twitching for what seemed an endless period but was really only 30 or 40 seconds. Then he sat up, looking a bit shaken. He got to his feet and seemed to be quite normal. None of us had seen anything like it before – it was most bizarre.

I got him checked out by the vet, but they couldn't find anything untoward, and the following week I took him to another competition, at Lincoln. I got him off the lorry and, as he was grazing and I was taking his travel boots off, the same thing happened. He stuck his head in the air, curled his top lip, staggered and went over. Again, he picked himself up and seemed normal, so I competed him the next day and he finished third. Obviously things were not right, though. On talking to Bruno and Dominique, they said that during the winter they'd seen him, out of the window, staggering into a fence. It all seemed to coincide with that strange incident back in New Zealand when we just assumed he'd been stung.

My vet, Buffy Shirley-Beavan, decided to send him to Newmarket, where he underwent loads of tests, all of which proved inconclusive. I was asked if I could get a video of him doing it, but the timing proved impossible. I also involved Wayne McIlwraith, who had operated on Bramble Rose. He showed me a clip of a horse having an epileptic fit and it looked just like Gandalf. You can treat the condition with drugs, just as you can a human, but obviously this would have precluded him from competing, as he wouldn't have passed a dope test. We tried all sorts of things – cranial osteopathy, different kinds of massage, and we looked into homeopathy, which is right up Carolyn's alley – she did a lot of research into it – and he seemed fine for a bit. But then he came in from the field one day with grass stains between his ears and down his face and a very stiff neck, so we could only assume he'd had another seizure.

Lucinda Green rode him for her *Horse & Hound* series, Lucinda Rides, and complained he was hard work, but then he always was, and he wouldn't have been her sort of horse anyway, as Lucinda has always liked quick-moving, sharp horses. It was all very baffling. Badminton was obviously out of the question, so the great comeback would have to wait. Looking back, I now realise the poor horse must have perpetually been in discomfort. All the alternative medicine practitioners said he was like a person with a continual nagging headache.

Grass Valley, however, went well on his first two events, before I took him to Burnham Market, a new advanced event in Norfolk. There, I had serious control issues and had two run-outs. I realised that I would have to be put him in something stronger than the snaffle to have any real effect; he had a tendency to panic in front of a fence and take control, sometimes getting himself in trouble. Once I'd put him in a Pelham bit, it was like magic. I suddenly had him under control. We went to Belton, traditionally a major pre-Badminton advanced event, and we won.

* * *

It wasn't long before some of the less welcome aspects of the sport – the ones I intended to leave behind in 2000 – reared their heads again, and the first, and most tragic, was that weekend at Belton.

I was just getting ready to go across country, when a heavy silence descended. News filtered through that the course was being held, and we knew it wasn't for a good reason. Ian Olding, an Irish rider who was one of the great characters in the sport, not top level but highly experienced, had suffered a bad fall, and there was an ominous cluster of paramedic vehicles around the fence. We all knew what had happened. He'd been killed when the horse landed on him.

The fence made you scratch your head, with a tricky distance, but none of us had thought it needed to be changed. It involved three obstacles, with two strides from the first to an upright table and then two strides on an angle to the third element. The line was quite difficult, because there were some distracting life-size figures between the second and third elements. It was a long two strides, which was never going to be three, which is probably what Ian's horse had attempted to do, and I remember thinking that I should keep moving Riley forward to get the two strides.

Eventually, the competition was restarted – without that fence – and I won my section, my first advanced win in England since my return. That must sound extraordinarily hard-nosed to people outside the sport, but it doesn't mean that none of us care what happened. It's just that riders develop a way of disassociating themselves from such an incident, or else none of us would be able to carry on. I presume racing drivers and other people in risk sports must think the same. No one in their right mind would set off across country thinking they were going to die, and if you do, then it's time to stop.

Generally, though, riders are beginning to have more and more say about cross-country courses. In the old days, if you didn't like something, you retired and went home. Things were less politically correct and perhaps the officials were more frightening. But since then the sport has become much more professional and now there is more at stake in terms of the value of prize-money and of horseflesh.

There are occasions when riders are having a bit too much say – especially some riders, who tend to base their opinions entirely on the type of horse they are riding and what they would personally like to happen. The ground conditions also cause a lot of debate; obviously all events should make an effort to present as good going as they can, but there are occasions when riders forget it is a cross-country test and expect it to be like a bowling green in all circumstances. Perhaps I'm being old-fashioned, but riders used to ride a bit more thoughtfully at difficult fences and let the horse 'hunt' its way through, finding his own way; now everyone is hung up on counting strides, and they don't like it if it's not an exact science. Too much rider power can be a dangerous thing and in instances where the course-designer or technical delegate has been a bit weak you end up with riders virtually redesigning courses, which is ridiculous.

The problem is that if a fence causes trouble, even if it is due to riders tackling it incorrectly, officials are placed in an impossible position. They are damned either way, and if they stick to their guns and leave a controversial fence unchanged and then someone has an accident, the repercussions would be terrible.

This situation arose that summer of 2009, in the World Cup qualifier at Tattersalls in Ireland. The water complex has always been a bit controversial and hasn't always ridden well, particularly at speed, and on this occasion there were a couple of early falls. Then an Italian, Alberto Guigni, fell and his horse broke a leg and had to be put down which, although discreetly handled, was hugely distressing all round.

I arrived at the cross-country start on Gandalf to find a mutiny. A group, both Irish and British, had refused point blank to start unless the fence was removed. My view is that if you don't want to run, you needn't, but don't ruin the competition, as it ends up making it a nonsense. Some, such as Pippa Funnell, who had already negotiated the fence beautifully, were happy for it to stay in, and I was prepared to jump it myself as I didn't think it was dangerous.

The organisers were put under huge pressure and the fence was removed, but it was all academic for me as Gandalf ran out early on the course and I retired him because, again, he didn't feel happy in the very heavy ground conditions.

The biggest change in the sport was the loss of the old-style three-day event, with the roads and tracks and steeplechase format. It used to be like a military campaign and a real test of horsemanship, fun in an occasionally masochistic way, and it definitely added to the atmosphere. I felt sad about its demise, but I can see that for horses' longevity and for the modern sport, the present situation is better. Realistically, they were tests that went unnoticed and meant nothing to Joe Public. They were expensive to put on, in terms of land and officials, and their necessity precluded a lot of events around the world from progressing in status because they couldn't afford to do it.

Back in the days of long format, the cross-country arguably used to be a better test of horsemanship and judgement because the courses were longer with the jumping efforts more spread out. You couldn't set out too fast, the idea being that you should gradually pick up pace while still reserving some energy for the last part, and you had to be constantly aware of what was coming the next day in terms of the veterinary inspection and the horse needing to be supple enough to clear the show jumps. Horses certainly got more tired in the old days.

Now you have to set out faster, hoping that you have judged your horse's fitness and that he can maintain the pace until the end. It's certainly true that horses are coming out of the stable fresher next morning and lasting longer. There are far more old horses in the sport – a 16-year-old medallist, as Charisma was, isn't a talking point any more – which all adds to the horses' popularity and makes following the sport more enjoyable for the public.

In the old days, the Thoroughbred was the predominant type, because it was likely to be the toughest and fastest. New Zealand horses certainly proved this adage in the 1990s, and that was why people flocked to buy them because they saw us being so successful. Now, more people want a warmblood horse from Europe, which is likely to have more elegant movement in the dressage and a rounder, cleaner, if more deliberate, jumping action. What riders forget, though, is that you still need enough 'blood' to get the speed and to cope in extremes of weather; a lot of people now get hung up on European blood and forget about the sharpness required.

In my absence, fence profiles had changed almost out of recognition. As part of the safety revolution post-1999, they were all much friendlier; either rounded, if they were made of wood or willow, or constructed with brush. Anything upright, like a gate or a set of rails, will have the frangible pin.

At Belton, there used to be a proper coffin fence (rails with a sloping landing to a ditch and then another set of rails on rising ground) and you knew that before you got to the fence, you had to be careful and get your horse into what Lady Hugh Russell would have called a 'coffin canter' – a short-striding, powerful, energetic canter.

After I'd ridden this fence on my first horse, I was astonished by how many time-faults I'd accrued, so I went back out and watched some other riders. I realised that because the fence was made of brush, riders were galloping at it, and that I was going to have to change my riding style and be much more aggressive if I was going to keep up.

Another feature of the last 10 years, which I had pretty much missed, was the continual experimentation with 'quick-fix' novelty competitions designed to take eventing to a wider audience and into more flexible settings, often with eye-watering prize-money. The Hickstead Eventers Grand Prix, in which riders complete a knock-down cross-country course as well as some of the late Douglas Bunn's famous show jumping features, is probably the most successful – and I did compete in a couple before I retired – but there have been other variations which have received a mixed response.

These competitions are fun as a one-off, but I don't really think the public has a consistent appetite for them and I can't see these cheaper versions ever replacing spectators' or riders' desire for beautiful parkland settings such as Burghley, Badminton, Bramham, Chatsworth and Gatcombe, combined with shopping and perhaps a country fair atmosphere.

However, in 2008 we all had our heads turned by an ambitious new venture in the Millennium Stadium in Cardiff in November. A number of international riders were invited, including me; Phillip Dutton and Buck Davidson even came over from the States, Karin Donckers from Belgium and Rodolphe Scherer and Nicolas Touzaint from France.

We were all promised appearance money of £3,000, and were treated to a gala dinner and a night in a smart hotel. The competition comprised a freestyle dressage to music, which some riders spent a fortune on choreographing, with artistic interpretation judged by Andrew Lloyd Webber and Arlene Phillips from television's *Strictly Come Dancing*. Then there was a jumping phase, a 'pit-stop', which involved pulling a fiddly, stretchy shirt over your head and then a so-called cross-country course. The first prize was a life-changing £100,000, and riders went mad for it.

The dressage to music phase went off OK, a whole new experience for most of us; the level of difficulty somewhat amusing, with tempi changes and canter pirouettes among compulsory movements. But the cross-country was a complete disaster. We were all a bit uneasy about the slightly unstable feeling of the built-up arena surface and the first rider, Rodolphe, fell off heavily when his horse slid across a built-up bank. The course was unstringed and incredibly complicated with 40 jumping efforts, which we had only had a very short time to assess because the venue had hosted an international rugby match the day before, and several riders quickly got eliminated for taking the wrong course. Riders became panicked about losing time in the pit-stop and hitherto sensible horses became lit-up and lost their heads. Both Andrew Nicholson, riding Rosemary Barlow's lovely young Avebury, and Tina Cook on her Olympic bronze medallist Miners Frolic, were eliminated for three run-outs, something which neither horse had shown any sign of doing before.

I had a complete disaster when Gandalf banked a filled corner fence and made a huge hole in the top. We destroyed the fence, and the horse could easily have broken his leg. We continued but then had several run-outs at a corner and were eliminated. I felt terrible for subjecting him to this awful competition, but much worse was to come, when Mary King lost her best horse, Call Again Cavalier. He broke his leg, in front of everyone, when falling at a double of corners and, thanks to the 'one seat sees all' philosophy, the audience could look right down onto the poor horse being loaded into a trailer.

All the riders had been asked to sign media agreements

beforehand, so it was difficult to be outwardly critical. It was a brave experiment by Stuart Buntine, who organised it, and John Peace, who underwrote it, but in hindsight it was too new, too big and too difficult, and the horses were confused by it. Oli Townend, who won it on Flint Curtis, the horse with which he won Badminton in 2009, totally deserved to do so as his round was superb. Those who went well made it look easy but too many didn't. Suffice it to say, however, that the venture has not been repeated on anything like that scale since, and a watered-down version, with a final at the Horse of the Year Show, has received only moderate support to date.

***

During the 2009 season, I persevered with Gandalf and his odd quirks. We won an open intermediate class at Aston-le-Walls, then came Tattersalls, and after that Bramham, where we could have been really well placed. He went well across country with only four time-faults, but then, like an idiot, I managed to jump the wrong fence in the show jumping and got eliminated. This rather brought it home to me that I was some way off the top of my game and was going to have to practise harder if I was going regain my touch.

However, Gandalf had gone so well at Bramham, and had not had a seizure for some time because, we thought, all the natural treatment he was getting had been a success. So I decided that whatever had been wrong was under control and I took him to the three-star CIC at Aachen, the premier German show where a cross-country course had been built specially for the 2006 World Equestrian Games. Here he did a reasonable dressage, had one fence down show jumping, and then ran out across country at a skinny fence in the water. There was a big drop into the water, then two long strides across the water to the narrow fence. He had landed so awkwardly he couldn't make the distance to the fence and so ran out, an excusable mistake. Afterwards, we were cooling him off and leading him back to the stables when he had another seizure.

When he ran out, it was always to the left of fences. He did it again at Gatcombe, at a left-handed brush corner, and again, really oddly, at a similar fence at the World Cup final at Strzegom in Poland. There, he had done his best ever dressage test and was going really well and in contention to win, when one minute the fence was right in front of us and the next, to my shock, he'd ducked out and I was left sitting on the ground. The prize-money for the final was very good, so it seemed a particularly long and dismal 24-hour journey home. The whole thing was so puzzling because he wasn't a dishonest horse.

After that, he suffered a minor injury which ruled out taking him to the four-star at Pau in France, another new event that had sprung up in my absence. So we sent him to Jackie Green near Marlborough for a rest. She rang me and said: 'There's something strange about this horse. He keeps banging into things.' I went down to see Gandalf and tested his eyes by gently flicking at them. There was no reaction from the left. We got the vet, who confirmed that he was blind in it. Amazingly, the vet thought the blindness had been a gradual progression, perhaps because he had damaged his optic nerve at some stage, and this is why he had started to run-out. I felt terrible because I knew people thought the horse was dishonest and letting me down.

After that, Gandalf had a couple more seizures and we realised that it wasn't safe to turn him out in the field. He could fall on someone handling him, or cause a serious accident, so eventually we decided that it would be kinder to have him put down. We arranged various autopsies and through Wayne

McIlwraith some of the best equine neuro-surgeons were involved, but no one found anything conclusive. It remains a mystery why this brave horse had these terrible seizures. I hate losing any horse but I was particularly affected by the loss of Gandalf, because he was so genuine. He may not have been the most brilliant horse in the world but what he had done for me was amazing. It was a very sad end to what had started as such an exciting project.

* * *

Before Gandalf's demise, I had bought Mouse, by the good Irish sire Cavalier. Jules Stiller had asked me for some lessons and, during one, she mentioned that she had this horse that she wanted to sell. It was currently with Andy Austin, the show jumper, and I was keen to have a go because I knew the horse was highly thought of. Jules had another horse to sell, Walk the Line, which she had bought from William Fox-Pitt. Bruno wanted him, so we did a package deal on the two – Bruno got Walk the Line and I took Mouse.

Mouse was in a difficult state, napping and behaving badly. Although he was qualified to advanced level and an intelligent horse, he was really tricky. The first day I rode him in the school, he got in a muck lather after just five minutes of walking on a loose rein, so I realised it wasn't going to be that quick a turnaround.

However, I like a challenge, and by the time I took him to the two-star three-day event at Houghton Hall in Suffolk, we had formed a much better partnership and he gave me a great ride to finish fourth. I won on Walk the Line, lent to me by Bruno, and it was very exciting to claim a British three-day event again, even at two-star level. It was a hugely satisfying weekend, especially as we beat the horse's former rider,

William Fox-Pitt, which isn't the easiest thing to do nowadays.

Other than that boost to morale, 2009 wasn't entirely going to plan: my best horse, Gandalf, was in trouble, Land Vision was too young to do any major events, and I wanted to give him a consolidating year anyway, so Riley would have to step up a level if I was to have a horse for the World Equestrian Games in 2010. There was a bit of a race to get Riley qualified for three-star level, but he did the advanced section at Withington Manor and came fifth in the two-star CIC at Tattersalls and eighth in the three-star CIC at Blair Castle in Scotland. He seemed to be getting better and better, so I took him and Land Vision to Blenheim.

The ground was firm and Riley looked a bit scratchy at the first trot-up, but Leigh Miller, the physio, did some work and he performed an adequate dressage test. As I warmed him up for the cross-country, I realised he didn't feel quite right. He's quite a heavy-striding horse, so I dithered about starting him across country. In the end I did, but he had a run-out early on, which was most unlike him, so I pulled him up.

I found afterwards that Riley was rather jarred up and sore, so no wonder he hadn't felt himself. After he'd recovered, I took him to Boekelo where he finished 21st and got his four-star qualification, so I was really pleased with him.

Land Vision (Ben), the great white hope, finished 14th at Blenheim. He'd had an interesting season. On our first outing, at Lincoln, he felt pretty green, which I wasn't expecting with his record. He was inattentive in the dressage, spooking and gawping, and then he had five fences down in the show jumping. I had generally more trouble in the jumping with Ben than with any of the other horses all season, which was strange, seeing as he was the class jumper of them all. This was somewhat unnerving, considering the cheque New Zealand Bloodstock had written for him, but after a bit of schooling he won the two-star CIC at Somerley Park in April, which was a bit of a relief. Peter and Philip Vela are brilliant owners though – they never interfere and they understand horses.

Summing up my first year back competing, although I was firmly on a mission and absolutely determined to be competitive again, I eventually realised that I had to view 2009 as a building year. Most of the horses were actually placed quite regularly, some had problems to overcome and some were inexperienced, but it was a case of my having to get to know them and all of us gaining mileage together. One advantage was that in contrast to the 1990s, I had fewer owners and, therefore, less pressure. I was confident that I'd found the horses to take me back to the top, and I felt reinvigorated and re-enthused with the sport.

Unfortunately, the same could not be said of my marriage. After Boekelo, Carolyn and I separated officially. She went on holiday to Portugal with friends, and when I went to pick her up from the airport, she greeted me with the news that she wanted a divorce. On one level, I was terribly shocked. We had been looking at properties to buy in England and, in many respects, were getting on well. We had been married for 23 years and, although we'd been through a lot we were, at base, very close friends and it felt incredibly sad. I couldn't deny, though, that it was a difficult year; Carolyn had a tough time going backwards and forwards a lot, and she was very torn between supporting me and being with the children back at home.

There was no getting away from the fact that returning to a full-on eventing lifestyle was chiefly my project and my idea; Carolyn hadn't really expected it all to take off again and she was realising that she didn't want to go back to that kind of life. I knew she wasn't happy, and I knew that I probably hadn't done enough to rectify that.

Our break-up has made me a lot more observant about the lot of an eventing wife. Often, when you win, they are the last person to get hugged, and they can't get near you for friends, team-mates, grooms and press crowding round you. You return from a three-day event, often on a high and having had an intensely fun, sociable time, with a lot of like-minded people with whom you inevitably become close friends because you're thrown together – and this must be the same of all international sports – while they've been worrying about you breaking your neck. You're the centre of attention and they are in the background, even though without their hard work and support and negotiating with owners, the whole thing might not have been possible. In hindsight, I was so enthused about restarting my career, and was so much the centre of attention because of it, that Carolyn must have felt left out.

* * *

So Carolyn packed up and went home to New Zealand, and I packed up and moved to the smart new yard Jules Stiller had bought, Headley Stud, near Newbury. Jules said she'd got more stables than she needed and asked if I'd like to take over part of the yard. It seemed a good option; it was an area I knew well and I hoped it would be a mutually beneficial arrangement: a lovely yard for me and, hopefully, my presence would be of help to Jules in building her career.

Then there was the question of where I was going to live. There were flats at Headley but I was reluctant to revert to the lifestyle of my twenties. I got together with some old friends from my Sydmonton days, Hinny and Jo White, who now live in the house we once had on the estate, and whose sons James and Harry are great mates with our children. We looked on the internet for a potential property, finding one a stone's throw from the stud. It was a pretty little white cottage with an attractive front and, as the owner was, sadly, dying of cancer, they wanted a quick sale.

After living in a series of large houses, it did feel rather small, but I was keen to get something sorted and it needed a lot doing to it, so from that perspective, it was ideal. Carolyn and I had always enjoyed doing up houses together, so I thought it would keep me occupied and be a challenge to see if I could do it on my own.

In the interim, I went back to New Zealand for Christmas, and we managed to have a relatively normal family time. It was good that we could get on well enough for that, but it did hit home that for the first time in more than 50 years I wouldn't have a home of my own in New Zealand. Carolyn got the farm in the split and, as with every separation, there were times when sorting out who was to have what was both ghastly and sad.

I returned to my little cottage in February, and went straight to the local community shop to buy two chairs. The only other furniture I had was a bed and a dining-room table, which we had brought over from New Zealand. It has a glass top and it neither fitted back at home nor in my cottage.

A few days later, it was my 54th birthday. Hinny and Jo came round, plus Bruno and Dominique, Dan Jocelyn and his partner Tanya Cleverly, who live in the next village, Moysie Barton, Charlie, my head girl, and the Italian rider Giovanni Ugolotti (Joe) and his Canadian girlfriend Katherine Robinson, who also had their horses at Headley. We sat on the floor or on boxes, eating fish and chips. It felt a bit weird, this newly single state, but there was an element of anticipation in it as well.

Jules and I went on a shopping trip to Germany, mostly looking for horses for her, but I came home with Campino from Dirk Schrade, a successful rider who spent some time with Andrew and Bettina Hoy and is now a mainstay of the German squad. Campino was a seven-year-old, a warmblood but with quite a lot of Thoroughbred in him, and he had done a few pre-novice events. He had also been show jumping as well, and he was a horse that I thought would fast-track quite quickly, which he did, winning the two-star three-day event at Hartpury that summer.

Jules and I went on another buying trip, this time up north with Rachel Wakefield, a former amateur rider who had given up corporate life to be a horse-finder with her partner Michael Wynne. Jules tried Regent Lad, a nine-year-old owned by Carly Reid who had done one advanced event with him, but she didn't really get on with him. Rachel had warned me that I wouldn't like the horse, and he was smaller than I had been led to believe, but I liked him. He's a chunky little thing, he moves and jumps well and I was taken by his big personality. I bought him for my New Zealand Bloodstock team.

A week later, I took Regent Lad to 'Little' Gatcombe, the spring one-day event run by the Princess Royal in the top part of the park. He was already entered, so I thought I might as well run him, but I didn't want him to upgrade too fast, so I turned a circle between two corners and got 20 penalties. A few weeks later he won the advanced intermediate class at Brigstock and a couple of months later an advanced class at Aston-le-Walls.

I had thought of taking Land Vision to Badminton, but he spent the spring on the sidelines after tweaking a ligament behind his knee, so it all came down to Grass Valley. It was a big ask because Riley had only done the one three-star, but I had nothing else for the World Games. He had a run-out at Belton, for which I blame myself, but he was becoming more and more genuine. Ten years is quite a long time not to ride at Badminton, yet it felt as if I'd never been away, which was bizarre really. I was slightly worried about riding a horse that was so inexperienced, but I did trust him. I knew he had enough scope to jump the big jumps; the question was whether our partnership had cemented enough for him to trust me on the accuracy fences. I'd also had a bit of a wake-up call a couple of weeks before when I was eliminated on Mouse for jumping the wrong last fence at Burnham Market. Following on from my blunder at Bramham the year before, it dawned on me that perhaps I needed to be concentrating more.

We finished 18th, the event being won, for the first time, by Paul Tapner, an Australian rider. Andreas Dibowski, a prolific German who hadn't really got going by the time I retired in 2000, was second and British team rider Daisy Dick was third on Springalong, one of the best cross-country horses in the world.

Riley did the best he could in the dressage for a score of 55 and gave me a really nice ride across country. He had never done a course of 11 minutes 30 seconds before and, as he wasn't full Thoroughbred, I didn't know what would happen and took it easy in the beginning. As he grew in confidence, I felt I could push on, and I didn't think our resulting 8.8 time-faults were too bad. Next day, he only had one show jump down.

As it was my first four-star for 10 years – I couldn't really count Hong Kong as a proper four-star track – it didn't seem a bad start. The whole process felt normal – I didn't feel I was struggling or outclassed, and I quietly felt I'd done a good job on a young and inexperienced horse. And more importantly the result had put us in contention for the World Equestrian Games that year. The whole outing seemed so natural that I didn't even really find it odd that there were no roads and tracks. In fact, I was probably relieved, as they used to go on for ever. My abiding memory from the old days at Badminton, though, was when you finished the roads and tracks and you rode down Worcester Avenue towards Badminton House, the crowds getting nearer and nearer and louder and louder and the moment of starting the cross-country more inevitable.

It was both daunting and atmospheric, and the closer you got the more you became aware that you'd got to face up to the cross-country. It was nerve-racking, but an incredible feeling, and I feel sorry for riders who will never know such an extraordinary experience. The warm-up now is a bit like a one-day event, which rather detracts from being at the world's most famous three-day event. I'm also sad that the Badminton course has lost its individualistic character. I read Mary King's autobiography, in which she describes her first ride at Badminton, mentally ticking off all those evocative fences: Tom Smith's Walls, the Luckington Lane crossing, the Normandy Bank, the Vicarage Vee. I can relate exactly to how she felt. Now all those have gone, and the Quarry and Coffin are nothing like they used to be.

It's a shame, and yet Badminton is still an amazing event. Even if you don't feel as physically terrified, there are still plenty of opportunities to make a mistake, and the huge crowds and enormity of the occasion, on which so much still rests, make it a significant test. And Badminton 2010 certainly had huge significance for me, because I was desperate to ride at the World Equestrian Games in Kentucky that September. It would be 32 years since my first world championships there, and I would be the only rider to have done the double. It was all thanks to dear Riley that it would be possible, plus the fact that there weren't many proven four-star horses on the New Zealand squad, really rather like the early years when one clear round at top level was enough to get you selected. The big difference between now and 1978, though, was that this time I did appreciate just how lucky I was.

***

The slightly alarming thing was that despite all the horse-acquiring, I didn't have a useful back-up to Riley, especially because Land Vision had been off. I had a desperate time trying to get Mouse to a three-star three-day event. The CIC at Chatsworth, which I would have used as a qualifier, was rained off, so the organisers put on an extra section at Bramham so that people could qualify.

My old mate Ian Stark was the course-designer there for the first time, having taken over from Sue Benson. It's quite a strange feeling when your contemporaries start taking on grown-up positions like this, but Scotty is doing a good job designing bold courses which feel like cross-country the way it used to be. I could have done without one of his designs though: a meaty double of very narrow brushes on two long strides where Mouse ran out at the second; infuriating, as I'd been having a brilliant ride.

Eventually, I got a three-day result out of him, at Blenheim, where he completed with a slow cross-country as he felt a bit off colour. I sold him to Pietro Sandei, who subsequently got into the Italian Young Rider team at the 2011 Europeans at Blair Castle and finished 20th. He used to send me hilarious emails updating me on Mouse's progress. One read: 'Fantastic Mouse. He is a warrior. Fantastico. The horse is fantastic, but I am rubbish.' I think Pietro is doing a brilliant job with him.

In June, I went back to New Zealand for my father's 90th birthday at my brother Martyn's place. I've missed a lot of my parents' birthdays, but this was a fairly momentous occasion. There were lots of family there and I had to make a speech, which I found very hard and it choked me up. It was an emotional evening, not just because of my own altered family situation but because it came home to me what great parents they have been. My dear mother is now in a rest home, as she suffers from Parkinson's and Alzheimer's, but my father is still independent and quite amazing.

On returning to England, I was pleased to hear that I'd fit in one more four-star ride before Kentucky. I had a new ride, Major Milestone ('Milo'), who had a slightly chequered career. He started life in Ireland and was ridden by Oli Townend before being sold to Philip Adkins, an American businessman living in Leicestershire who used to be trained by Ginny Elliot. The horse then went to the Australian rider Bill Levett, then back to Oli, before being sold to his present owners, Diane Blunsden and Peter Cattel.

Di sent Milo to Owen Moore, a kind rider clever at producing and rehabilitating horses, and then he came to me in July 2010. Milo is a big, long-backed horse with a complicated personality. He's not so much hot as worried; once, I was schooling him and he got so wound up that he began staling (peeing) as he went along.

My first ride was an open novice section at Purston Manor, and six days later we went to Barbury Castle for the three-star CIC, in which he finished 18th amid strong competition, before being third in an advanced class at Gatcombe. Owen hadn't tried going particularly fast on him, mainly because he was trying to get him settled. The first time I really let him go was around Barbury, where he felt very strong and almost a little dangerous. He can be quite flippant about the fences towards the end, and that wasn't a good feeling.

Fortunately, Milo is a good jumper. We only had one sticky moment at Burghley, when he hit the table fence alarmingly hard, and we finished 11th. He is an honest horse who keeps his line and, although he is sometimes maligned for his erratic dressage, he has never had a single cross-country fault with me, and only two show jumps down. It's just the dressage that is the problem. He's the wrong shape for a start, he hasn't got a good canter and tends to go four-time instead of three, and he panics about the flying changes, but he's getting better. The shame of it is that his trot is amazing and if he'd just take a deep breath and relax, he could do a good test. I've still got high hopes for him.

Milo can be exasperating, but he is a useful horse to have around and he was providing me with an unexpected four-star ride. If you're going to be competitive at that level, you need to be consistently part of it. I wouldn't have been at Burghley without him, and Peter and Di are such nice and enthusiastic owners that they were over the moon with him.

I was thrilled to be back at Burghley, always my favourite three-day event. I love the setting; it's friendly and good fun, and it doesn't have the nervousness of Badminton where riders are scrabbling for team places. It's pure competition without the politics. It's also the nearest you get to an old-fashioned three-day event now. Mark Phillips is quite a fearless designer who still has the ability to make both spectators and riders gasp. The terrain is more difficult than Badminton, and it took me quite a while to win my first one, but the place has been good to me.

Friends from New Zealand, Janice and Grey Keyte, stayed one night and we had a barbecue at the lorry with Brendan and Sally Corscadden and Dot Love. Madeleine Lloyd Webber had brought her daughter Bella and friends for the weekend and was staying in a caravan, an experiment I suspect she won't repeat – they were at The George the next year!

Caroline Powell won on the 17-year-old Lenamore, which made her the first New Zealand female rider to win a four-star – and the 10th Kiwi win since my first in 1987. This was a great fillip for her before Kentucky, to which she had decided not to take Lenamore, saying that he hadn't really travelled well to his last two championships.

Caroline is from Christchurch, so both she and I were a bit preoccupied with news of the earthquake that had taken place there, although it was nothing like as bad as the awful one a year later.

After Burghley, it was a quick turnaround to Blenheim. This was to be an exciting weekend when Land Vision finally showed what he was made of. He didn't get his first run of 2010 until July, at Aston-le-Walls, and then after another couple, he won the advanced section at Highclere. This turned out to be quite a significant result, as he beat Cool Mountain, the horse on which William Fox-Pitt had won the Kentucky four-star in the spring and went on to be world silver medallist. It felt like confirmation that Land Vision really was going to be competitive with the best horses.

At Blenheim, he led from the start to win the three-star CIC for young horses, which was a very competitive class with some lovely horses in it. He did a beautiful dressage test, show jumped clear, and I was particularly encouraged by how good he was across country. Only two or three of us got the time, and he did it quite easily, which pleased me because it is a hilly course and it showed that he was learning to gallop in a much better way. He'd got over being spooky, he didn't pull and he was easy to ride and, being a good jumper, I felt I could trust him. It was a really exciting result.

By a stroke of good timing, Peter Vela was able to be there, and he was delighted with Land Vision. I'd kept some champagne in the lorry especially for him, and as it was Dan Jocelyn's 40th birthday, we had a great party in the lorry field.

* * *

For the first time in years, the New Zealand squad actually felt happy, motivated and united, and I think we all felt positive about gelling as a team. The five of us selected for the World Equestrian Games in Kentucky were me, Andrew and Caroline, plus two new boys, Jonathan (Jock) Paget, who had been competing in the USA, and Clarke Johnstone, who was only 22 and hadn't been further afield than Australia, but had some useful form. Jock was selected on the basis of getting round Kentucky clear in the spring, and he had come over to England the previous summer to stay with Andrew. He came to me for some help as well, and we worked on the dressage. He's very good to teach, desperate to get better and highly motivated. Andrew and I have been very cheered by the arrival of Jock and Clarke.

Before the competition started, we decided that we should go into town in Lexington and have a boys' bonding session – Caroline wisely gave this one a miss. We found a pub, had a few bottles of wine and got quite merry. When we came out, I decided it would be hilarious to make some calls to the team officials and pretend we were in trouble.

The story went like this: our team van was going to be towed away by parking wardens, but they'd ripped out the front of the van. The police had arrived and Andrew was going off on one. What should we do? I rang Sarah Harris, our performance manager, then Jock rang Erik Duvander, the *chef d'équipe,* and told him a similar story, and by the time Clarke rang Wally Neiderer, the story had got more elaborate. By this time, giggling helplessly, we told them that Andrew had decked a police officer and been arrested – all totally believable. The best reaction was from Olly Penn, our vet, who took it very seriously and calmly said: 'OK! Don't move! I'm on my way.' All very juvenile, but it was certainly successful in setting an upbeat tone for the week and had us laughing for days.

A few days later, there was another outing, which was slightly wilder. After the first day of dressage, Caroline and I had done our tests so we went for a night out, as we'd have the next day off. She went to dinner with her owners, the idea being that we'd meet up later. I was with our team farrier, Andrew Nicholls, who, to avoid confusion with Andrew Nicholson, we simply called 'Farrier'. (I had known him since he was a child, because I had ridden with his late father Grant, who had coincidentally worked for my father.) Also with us was Olly, who is English and works in a Newmarket practice and is known as 'Vetinary'. The two of them look alike and often get mistaken for each other. We decided that instead of pudding, we'd have a few shots, the favoured one being Baileys and butterscotch which had a spectacularly rude name. I hasten to add that, at this stage, we did have a driver.

Caroline turned up and we all headed off to find the next place, at which point we lucked upon a nightclub which was giving away free shots. By this stage, Farrier was a bit the worse for wear. We'd been told about another nightclub but Farrier, looking green, didn't think he could go on. He needed to lie down so the best place was on the floor in the back of the van. We put him in, locked the van and headed off to the next club. He managed not to throw up in the van, although as soon as we let him out into fresh air a few hours later he was violently sick.

In many ways, the Kentucky Horse Park looked very familiar 32 years after my first visit. Of course the arenas were much more modern and there were more barns, but the rolling landscape is timeless – acres and acres of grassland, with painted white rails dividing paddocks containing millions of dollars worth of horseflesh. It's an area of massive wealth, but also of great insularity and poverty, being so landlocked.

I was surprised by how chaotic things were in the horse park, considering this was supposed to be a World Championship on a tried and tested site with ready-made equestrian facilities. There were no gallops and, following a dry spell, you could even see from the air the green strip of watered grass for the cross-country course snaking its way through the park. But aside from the cross-country course, which we obviously weren't allowed on, there was nowhere to canter that wasn't rock hard, so some people rightly did get a bit upset.

Some of the arenas were in a bad state too, but it all eventually settled down and we got used to where we could go and what we could do. The set-up was a bit officious and there seemed to be more volunteers than horses, all of them mainly saying 'No'. One of the most annoying things was that we couldn't park our team van near the stables. The system wasn't well thought out and there was little flexibility, but it was a fun atmosphere between competitors and at least we were getting on well within our own team camp.

I was in training for the New York marathon, and was intending to use my spare time at Kentucky to run. I am a patron of the Catwalk Trust, along with the champion jockey Lance O'Sullivan, Ritchie McCaw, the captain of the All Blacks, and Zara Phillips. The trust was started by Cat McLeod, a New Zealand event rider who was part of our squad in 1995. She returned home, married a first-class bloke called Sam Williams, and then became paralysed in a terrible fall at Kihikihi horse trials. It was one of those awful senseless incidents in which a life is irrevocably changed in one second; she was riding for someone else, landed on her head and, because her hat had a stiff peak, broke her neck. Cat has turned into the most remarkable person, never complaining, and has raised a lot of money for spinal research. It had been organised that a group would run in aid of the trust, and Cat would do it in a hand-cycle.

I had sort of been training, but it had been a bit sporadic. I'm not really a keen runner – I used to do it at school, but hadn't done it for years. Olly, who has run in a couple of marathons, volunteered to go out with me every morning. One morning we decided to run home from the horse park to the hotel, five or six miles. I got about three-quarters of the way and felt a twinge in my leg. I tried to ignore it, but then realised I definitely wasn't right. Olly made me stay still and ran back to the hotel to get the van.

The next day, the leg really didn't feel that good and Olly suggested it ought to be scanned, so we went to the veterinary hospital, as you do. The leading man there, a French vet, did a scan and told me that I had a 30 per cent tear in my Achilles tendon. Farrier made me a wedge for my shoes and the acupuncturist, Holly, who was there to treat Riley, was switched to treat me with electro acupuncture.

Holly was absolutely gorgeous and on the first day she was treating the horses there was no room in the stable for men who had suddenly become fascinated by acupuncture. Even Andrew, who normally has no truck with any sort of natural medicine, was taking a close interest.

I did feel vaguely nervous when Holly, who by this time had me face down in a bed of shavings bags, pulled out the manual on treating humans to check where to put the needle, but I was game for anything. She stuck the needles in, turned on the power and asked me if I could feel anything, which I couldn't. So she kept turning it up more and more and I still felt nothing until suddenly there was a terrific jolt, which felt like I had been plugged into the mains. I yelled and it felt like my leg flew into the air. Holly leapt back in fright. There must have been a faulty connection to the battery which had suddenly reconnected at full power. It was absolutely excruciating, but all I could do was laugh at the farcical nature of the situation. Needless to say, that was the end of the acupuncture idea.

Then there was a pow-wow about team order, and I soon

had this horrible feeling that I was destined to be the cannon fodder again. It was fairly obvious that Andrew had the right to go last on Nereo, a hugely talented horse who had won Bramham and was a full-brother to his Athens horse, Fenicio. It wouldn't be fair to put Clarke first at his first major international; Jock was getting the individual slot, mainly on the basis that his horse, Clifton Promise, had had a few issues before leaving the UK, and Caroline didn't want to go first either, on Mac Macdonald.

I never had any expectation that Riley would be an individual chance, but I hoped he would post a useful dressage score, and he seemed to have this way of continually stepping up to the plate with whatever was required. He has such a brilliant temperament; he might get nervous and a little tight, but he doesn't blow up.

Charlotte Dujardin, who works with Carl and is now a European team gold medallist and the new British dressage sensation, is an excellent trainer as well. As she was out there, she gave me a hand. He scored 48.5 and I was really pleased with him; the best test he'd ever done. He could not have gone any better and he certainly chose the right moment to do it.

The standard of dressage was, as is to be expected at world championships, very high and our team was only sixth at that stage, despite three scores under 50 – Andrew on 43.5, Clarke on 46.3 with Orient Express and me. The Germans were in front again, and looked unstoppable, with the Brits just behind.

We liked the cross-country which, typically for a Mike Etherington-Smith course, was very fair, big and bold. It was a proper championship track and had a few rider-frighteners, including a throwback to the Normandy Bank. There was a big double of hedges with ditches in front as the third last fence; they were a bit skinny and on three strides, and there was a lot of talk about them. Quite a few people were planning to do the long way, but as Riley isn't a speed machine, it was obviously imperative that I take all the direct routes.

Riley, bless him, is a wonderful jumper and so honest, and he gave me a really good ride all the way round. I was amazed I was on time at every minute marker, but coming to that key third last fence, he felt a bit tired, so I thought I'd play safe and take the long option. I probably wasted a few seconds and it made the difference between getting the time and missing it, but I was only four seconds over and, as number one for the team, the clear round was the most important thing. The relief and the thrill were amazing, a wonderful feeling.

The course was causing all sorts of problems but Caroline rode a really classy clear inside the time on Mac Macdonald, a horse that was very much her second string; Clarke's horse got tired towards the end and he had a refusal at the fourth last, a double of angled fences, purely down to an understandable lack of experience. Then Andrew, who had a long wait for his round due to all the drama, stormed round easily on Nereo. Jock had a great day too; he had done the best dressage test of his life to score 44 and went round with just 2.4 time-faults to ultimately finish seventh individually on Clifton Promise, a brilliant result.

Although things went smoothly for the USA, and for the Brits, there was a lot of drama elsewhere. The Germans fell to pieces, with the exception of Michael Jung, who remained miles ahead on La Biosthetique Sam, the horse with which he has such a brilliant partnership. Dirk Schrade fell off at the penultimate fence, Andreas Dibowski had a run-out and Simone Deitermann, an individual who had been lying second after dressage, had the misfortune to tip up at the very last fence. The Australians fell apart when the Badminton winner, Paul Tapner's horse Inonothing went lame and Sam

Griffiths had a crashing fall at a big corner on Happy Times. The Swedes and Irish had a catalogue of mishaps as well, and an Italian team horse, ridden by Juan Carlos Garcia, staked itself, causing a long hold up. Officials stopped another Italian horse because it had blood in its mouth but, after they checked it out, the rider didn't understand that he could go on so he retired and that was the end of their team, too.

We saw that we had risen to fourth place behind Britain, who had a brilliant day, the USA and Canada. I was in a respectable 16th place and Andrew was fifth. There was a feeling of excitement and quiet optimism in the camp, as we knew we had a chance of moving up and that Andrew might get an individual medal, which we all really wanted to happen. We knew we were on pretty good jumpers and that some of the other teams maybe were not.

These things are all in the lap of the gods, but we were aware that the American team horse Courageous Comet, ridden by Becky Holder in third place, might not pass the vet and we also knew that Ingrid Klimke's horse Butts Abraxxas, fourth, wasn't a reliable show jumper.

We had a fairly quiet evening, at least in relation to some other nights out. The restaurant next door to our hotel didn't serve alcohol – Lexington is right on the border of a dry state – but we decided we'd smuggle in the red wine that an American friend, Joe Giannamore, had sent. We all ordered raspberry juice and, once we'd drunk that, surreptitiously filled our glasses with wine. I suspect the waiters cottoned on, but fortunately they seemed to think it was quite funny and turned a blind eye.

Next day, all our horses trotted up fine, and I met up with the New Zealand veteran show jumper Jeff McVean, who was out there as his daughter Katie was competing in the show jumping. He had helped me in the late 1980s so I asked him

Diamond Hall Red (left) pictured here with Word for Word, third, was an unlikely candidate to give me Burghley win number five

Ride of a lifetime: Broadcast News clears the last fence at Burghley (the Open Europeans, 1997) to give me a third individual title

A happy day: Lauren and James wearing Kiwi medals at the press conference at Burghley, 1997

James and Lucky at his calf club – his friend in the background, James Macdonald, is now a champion jockey!

Lauren and Mushroom at a local gymkhana

James out hunting on the perfect pony, Mr Pete

Podge was far more cheerful than me on his farewell at Burghley in 2000

Eye Spy does the best test of his life at the right moment (Sydney Olympics, 2000)

Signing off with a medal – with Andrew Hoy (silver) and David O'Connor (gold) at the Sydney Olympics, 2000

The last ever cross-country ride? With Eye Spy at the Sydney Olympics, 2000

The lucky mascot that worked – with groom Becky Bulley in Sydney

Willy Smith astounds me by winning the Wellington Cup, 2001

Holding the Wellington Cup, 2001

A dream result for a new trainer: Bramble Rose wins the NZ Oaks and post-race
debrief with Carolyn and jockey Opie Bosson

A proud day: James and Lauren at their grandfather Norman Todd's 90th birthday – June 2011

The new generation: Laura Collett and Nicola Wilson with Andrew Nicholson and me at the Badminton press conference, 2011

Thirty-one years' experience can come in handy: NZB Land Vision wins
Badminton, 2011

Blues brothers: Erik Duvander (*chef d'équipe*), Andrew Nicholson and Clarke
Johnstone at the Greenwich Test Event

My grown-up children: James and Lauren at Riccarton Races, 2012

Peter Vela (right) receiving the Badminton trophy from Princess Haya and Lance Bradley, Managing Director of Mitsubishi Motors UK.

if he'd help us warm up. Riley warmed up really well, even though he was a little tired, and he came out and jumped a nice, safe clear round to boost our team chances.

It was incredibly tense, as the prospect of a team medal, after 12 years in the wilderness, was so precious. As Clarke had had a refusal, we had to count Caroline's less good dressage score, and she had one fence down. Then, in a rollercoaster few minutes poor Karen O'Connor, riding for the US team, had a disaster when Mandiba stopped at a gate. That opened the door for us, and when Andrew jumped clear, and Ingrid had two down, he clinched not only our team bronze and his own bronze, but unbelievably, his first individual medal.

Michael Jung finished an outstanding nine penalties ahead of William Fox-Pitt in the individual rankings, the British team were unstoppable for the gold medals, and the Canadians were incredulous at moving up to team silver – only three penalties ahead of us. We were on a high of our own. It felt such an achievement.

As a team, we were a complete mixture of young and old; Andrew and I had more than 50 years experience between us, yet I was riding a young horse rushed through the grades. Caroline had left her best horse at home; Clarke had never been to anything like this before, not to mention Jock, who had done brilliantly.

For me, it was overwhelming for Riley to have finished 11th in the world, and to be part of New Zealand's comeback and the country's first medal for 12 years. I was also so pleased for Andrew after all our history together that he was having his moment on the podium. We knew we had better horses at home and things could only get better. It was a great experience for Jock and Clarke, both of whom have been spurred on to increase their experience – Clarke is determined he won't be the discard score next time. He and Jock both want to beat

Andrew and me and that has led to some healthy rivalry which is keeping us on our toes, as we both want to win individual medals, too.

Afterwards we went to the international supporters' tent along with the other successful teams, but the party after that was the best bit. We went back to the stables where all the New Zealand supporters had gathered for their first championship celebrations in a long time. Someone had got in champagne, so an impromptu party took off. The atmosphere was brilliant; it felt like a rebirth.

CHAPTER
TWELVE

———————————

THE FINAL EVENT OF 2010 was Boekelo, important in that it confirmed that Land Vision was the real deal. We were second after the dressage behind the newly crowned world champion Michael Jung on River of Joy, a horse that does a very good test and often beats his top horse, Sam, when he runs them together. To be second to this pair was no disgrace and I was thrilled.

I took over the lead after cross-country, because I had the faster time, and felt very excited that I might become the first rider to win Boekelo three times, something I would still love to achieve.

Frans van Meggelen, an irrepressible Dutchman who is part of the organising team, took Michael and me off to a press conference, then ushered us into the Grolsch hospitality tent for a few beers. Before we knew it, Michael and I were fairly merry, and although his English isn't that great, we had a very funny time. It also occurred to me that he might not be used to jumping with a hangover, so I made sure everyone bought him plenty of drinks.

Next day, both Michael and I had a fence down, which would have been fine except that unfortunately I'd forgotten that a talented young Frenchman was lurking, Donatien Schauly, and he went clear and beat the pair of us, a scenario I hadn't envisaged at all!

It was interesting to meet Michael properly. He is very driven yet still an extremely nice guy. He apparently took up eventing because he came to Burghley on a school trip and saw me win and he decided that was what he wanted to do. He is perhaps the most brilliant natural horseman to break onto the eventing scene for a long time, but, although he's nearly 30 years younger than me, I am determined to beat him!

Considering Holland is a country that doesn't really like eventing, Boekelo is probably the most welcoming event in the world. The cross-country course covers several farms, and they promote the event as a commercial opportunity for the farmers and local businesses and run conferences. They look after riders better than anywhere, but it's just as well it's held at the end of the season, as you need a holiday to get over it. There were a couple of serious parties in my lorry, and the next year I learned my lesson and locked my lorry, as there was no way I was allowing that volume of visitors in again. I felt terrible as there was a young baby in the next-door lorry – embarrassingly, in the morning the mother apologised to me for asking us to keep the noise down the night before.

The season finished with a bang at Jules's 'stable-warming' party. I had anticipated a bunch of people having a glass of wine in the gallery in the indoor school but had underestimated party-giving on Jules's epic American scale, and so had most of the rest of the eventing circuit. None of us could believe it when we saw the indoor school lined with a marquee, with a velvet ceiling with twinkling lights in it. There was a vast cocktail bar, with every drink under the sun and a few more besides, fantastic finger food, dancing, a vodka luge, pole-dancing, bucking bronco and even valet parking. Lots of riders turned up in their lorries and settled in for the night.

Lauren had arrived, along with a friend, Emma Newton, who is a very nice girl and something of a soothing foil for Lauren. Some old friends from Ireland came over – Brendan and Sally, Sneezy Foster and Dot Love – plus Mary and Finn Guinness, who happened to have Barry Humphries of Dame Edna Everage fame staying with them, racing's Ian and Emma Balding and their son Andrew, whose gallops I sometimes use, and the Lloyd Webbers. I walked in at 7.30pm and walked out the following morning at 7.30am. It was a really good night, and one which I think will become an institution.

***

I was still suffering from the Achilles heel injury I'd sustained in Kentucky, so when the doctor said I wasn't to run the New York Marathon in November 2010, I was half disappointed and half relieved. I had never had any ambition to do a marathon, but once I've said I'm going to do something, I like to do it and it had became a box to be ticked. However, Cat McLeod, on whose behalf I was meant to be running, said that she'd still like me to be there to show support and, as my ticket was paid for, I thought 'what the heck?' The day before the marathon there's a five-kilometre slow jog around Central Park, and the New York Marathon Club had invited me to be in it, carrying the Kiwi flag, so I took my running gear to do that, at least.

As I was still entered for the real thing, I thought I might as well pick up my runner's pack. The organisation of that was amazing. There were thousands of people, but the queue kept moving and it happened like clockwork. The pack had a number, information and drink bottles, and a magnetic device for your shoe so that people can follow you, and other bits and bobs.

The night before the fun run, the clothing company Ice-breaker, who make merino wool base layer wear and sponsor Cat's charity, Catwalk, put on a cocktail party for all the Kiwis. As I wasn't running, I had a few drinks and got chatting to a couple of fellow supporters who suggested I join them at another bar. 'No, I mustn't. I'm doing the fun run,' I said. 'No, *come on*, we'll make sure you're home early,' they said. You can guess what happened: I got to bed at 4am.

My room was so high up in the hotel that there was no mobile reception and the internal phone didn't work, so no one could wake me. I slept through the fun run, for which I was supposed to be up at 7am, and, as I was the only one with the card to get the New Zealand flag, no one else could replace me. Not only did I feel terribly ill, but awful that I had let everyone down. I spent the rest of the day wandering around New York in a state of misery until I realised there was only one way to redeem myself. On the previous afternoon, the Kiwi contingent had all met at the office of the former New Zealand Prime Minister, Helen Clarke. The runners included a former rugby player with only one leg and women considerably older than me who clearly weren't fit. I thought: 'God, if they're having a go, I can.'

So I fronted up at 6am on Sunday morning, joining the hordes walking silently in the freezing temperatures to get on the buses for the start at Staten Island. Not having a clue about the reality of marathon times when I'd entered 12 months before, I put down three-and-a-half hours as my estimated time which meant, ridiculously, I was placed on the front row, just behind the racing group of athletes.

I got chatting to an Irish guy while waiting for the start who said he was also injured so we set off at a slow jog and were very soon at the back. We chugged along and I actually managed to keep running for the first 10 miles before I had to keep switching into walking breaks. The streets were lined three or four deep with people and 120 bands; the music was so great that you felt like stopping and joining the party. Everyone was cheering: 'You can do it.' A river of people drew you along. I passed a guy with only one leg on crutches with the stump stuck in the handle, and another man doing it backwards in a wheelchair. Near the end, I overtook the Chilean miner, a survivor of the terrible accident a few months earlier; a little hole in my tendon didn't seem very much in comparison.

I was thrilled to get halfway – apart from the awful realisation that I had the next half to do. I carried on with a mix of jogging and walking at the mile markers where you could get energy drinks and gels, and got into quite a comfortable routine, slowly ticking off the miles. A woman with a load of fresh-baked cookies gave me a couple. I also had a couple of energy sachets and, by 20 miles, I felt quite good. Then I hit the last three miles, which are slightly uphill and rather dispiriting, but I battled on. I have never been so relieved to see a finish line, after four-and-a-half hours. All around me, people were bursting into tears and I very nearly did the same. It was so lonely – as no one knew I'd decided to run, there was nobody there to meet me.

I'd put $30 in my pocket for a taxi back to the hotel but first, wrapped in my standard issue tin-foil cloak, I just had to find a hot-dog stand. I was starving. There wasn't a regular yellow cab to be had and I flagged down a black cab, but he wanted $60 for the journey so wouldn't give me the ride. By this time I was seizing up and could barely walk. I had no idea where I was but someone directed me to a metro station two blocks away where I could use the free tickets we were all given. I struggled down the stairs into the metro and then up at the other end and after that there was another two blocks to the hotel. It was like a nightmare that would never end.

We all met up for dinner, and everyone was thrilled that I'd run in the end. I've never been in so much agony but I was so pleased to have done it, and to have redeemed myself for my feckless over-sleeping.

* * *

Two days later I flew back to England, still feeling like death, only to be held at immigration for five hours. They eventually let me go but told me I must get my visa sorted. When we lived in England, we got British passports for the children, but Carolyn and I had never bothered for ourselves because we were returning to New Zealand. This turned out to be a mistake. I couldn't get a sporting visa and had to get an entrepreneurial one instead, which involves a whole load more paperwork. Apparently, all my previous years in Britain didn't count.

It was infuriating, because Lauren had just arrived for Christmas and here I had to go back to New Zealand, but there was no other way. I arranged it to coincide with some teaching, the idea being that I would fly into Auckland and, that same afternoon, send my passport to Canberra in Australia, the nearest British consul. Of course the traffic was terrible and I arrived at the visa office three minutes late for what is literally a two-minute process, but they were completely inflexible.

I was supposed to be going straight to Whangerei to teach, but I realised I'd have to put my teaching start-time back a few hours the next day. I stayed in Auckland with Cindy and John Tootill, owners of Nightlife from way back, and then tried the visa office again at 9am before heading off to teach my understanding pupils.

I went to see my parents – Dad was in great shape and still drives to see my mother in the rest home every day – and then on to Christchurch to stay with Carolyn and catch up with

James. There, I started to get nervous because I hadn't heard from the visa people and I knew that if there was the smallest problem, I wouldn't have time to redo it before Christmas, and I'd be trapped in New Zealand and unable to be with Lauren. It turned out that they had indeed lost track of my application, but eventually they promised it would be couriered over to New Zealand where I could pick it up at the airport before catching my flight. It did work, but I was sweating.

Having left Lauren and Emma to their own devices in my house – which I think Becky Elvin, my PA, had hastily tidied up – I was impressed to find that they certainly hadn't been blobbing out; Lauren had been showing Emma around London and they'd been to lots of shows and exhibitions.

We had Christmas drinks with Madeleine and Andrew Lloyd Webber and then spent the day with our old friends Hinny and Jo White. Harry, their son, had spent a couple of Christmases with us in New Zealand, and Lauren is like a surrogate sister to him and his brother, so it was a very nice time. Then James arrived with his friend Luke Macdonald, the son of our neighbours at Rivermonte Farm, who has been like a third child to us. We did all sorts of things – a visit to Highclere Castle, go-karting in Swindon and a trip on the Eurostar to Paris, where we did the Eiffel Tower and the usual attractions, went ice-skating, cycling round the city and out to Versailles.

Then there was a skiing trip to Les Arcs with Mick and Mel Duff and one of their sons, my godson Ollie, plus James White and his girlfriend Rachel Quirke and Jo Preston, an old friend, and her two children, Ben and Jess, and Jess's fiancé, Joe. We rented a lovely chalet and stayed in every evening playing games. What was really nice was that the children seemed happy to be with us, rather than out clubbing. I was anxious to spend as much time as possible with them and it was rather comforting that we all got on so well and had a fabulous time.

The holiday was not without incident and I nearly managed to do myself another injury. The kids had found a snow park where they were doing flips and spins and, in embarrassing father mode, I thought I'd join them. I went down the novice track of jumps, but thought that was quite small and boring, so I lined up with Lauren to do the intermediate line. 'Dad, don't that – you'll kill yourself,' said Lauren, but it was too late. I went down quite gingerly the first time, but as I did all four of the jumps quite well and it was so much fun, I thought I'd do it again, but this time a bit faster. I sailed over the first bump, flew the second, gathered so much speed that I cleared the third all in one and landed smack on the hard snow. I landed on my skis, but the whiplash sent me over backwards and I hit my head. I felt a bit shaken when I got up and decided I might not try that again.

It was hard seeing off Lauren and James and their friends when they returned to New Zealand, a situation I was to feel even more keenly following the disastrous earthquake in Christchurch in February. When Carolyn rang to say: 'We've had another earthquake, but we're all right,' I didn't really register at first. Then I turned on the news and saw the pictures, and realised what they'd been through. Several hundred lost their lives in this latest quake and the city was left like a bomb site. This was a disaster, the like of which we had never seen and the people of Christchurch were numb with grief. Carolyn was so lucky. She had been in town shopping when the earthquake struck and she was thrown to the ground. Half an hour later, a woman in the shop with her went back to get her handbag and a second almighty tremor happened and the building came down on top of her. It must have been absolutely terrifying.

New Zealanders are used to feeling minor quakes, but when we lived in Christchurch we never even felt a tremor and I don't think anyone was prepared for a wholesale disaster like that. The scariest thing was all the liquefaction when the ground cracked and mud spread all over the place. James's school boarding houses had to be destroyed and some of his friends lost parents or relatives. Carolyn put up loads of kids who couldn't go home. The only good thing was that everyone pulled together; the children were amazing and went around helping people clean up their houses.

It was a horrible time. I felt terribly cut off and useless and guilty for carrying on as normal. There's my family under siege and I'm worrying about entering for some novice horse trials.

***

When I got back from skiing, it was time to plan the season. I was pleased to have mainly the same team again: Sydney Dufresne, a young French rider who is very talented and really good company, came back for another season; I still had Charlie as my excellent head girl, Becky as my ever-efficient and tolerant PA – she worked for William Fox-Pitt for 13 years, so knows what she's doing – and a new addition, Fay Briant, replacing Catherine, whom we were sad to lose when she went to university. Katherine Robinson and Joe Ugolotti had moved their horses, but they were still living in a flat at the stud.

The horses were all going really well on the flat, much of which was due to Charlotte Dujardin. At the end of 2009, I wanted someone to keep Gandalf and Riley ticking over and Carl Hester, whom I've trained with on and off for years, suggested that I use Charlotte. I have always trusted his judgement and I knew that anyone trained by him would be good and on the same wavelength, and I was really pleased with what she achieved. Both she and Carl ride so sympathetically

– never forcing horses into shapes – and yet with such a sense of fun, so it was a fantastic result and hugely deserved when the pair of them were part of Britain's first dressage gold medal team in the summer of 2011.

During my time away, I'd got into a few bad habits with my flatwork and all riders need someone to tell you if you need more angle on the half-pass, or to be more engaged, or simply: 'Don't just sit there – do something.' I needed someone on the ground and, although Charlotte is years younger than me, she's not afraid to speak her mind, and I like that about her. If I say: 'Well, you get on and do it,' she will. I'm not so big-headed as to think I can do it all, and if a horse is having difficulty, as Riley was with his flying changes, I'm happy for her to get on and sort it out. I just hope that she will be able to find a bit of time to help me before the London Olympics, as she'll have a lot on with her own preparation.

The spring season of 2011 was a good one. It started at Isleham in Cambridgeshire where Milo did the test of his life – to my astonishment he scored 23.2 – and Campino and Regent Lad had scores in the twenties as well. Milo and Regent Lad went on to be second and third behind Oli Townend who went faster than me across country. Campino inexplicably pulled himself up at the coffin, but I put it down to being cast in his box that week and feeling slightly under the weather.

Then came Tweseldown, where Leonidas, a new purchase from Germany, won a novice section on his first time out with me, and Land Vision (Ben) and Riley were second and sixth in open intermediate sections. At Lincolnshire, Regent Lad and Ben won their sections; Campino was second and Riley third. Campino then did his first CIC, at Somerley Park, and led the dressage by a ridiculously large margin, about 15 marks. He show jumped clear and all I had to do to win was stay on across country. Peter and Pam Vela had come over to watch and we were all set up to see their promising young horse win his first international competition.

Unfortunately, he tripped and fell in the water, the exact fence where, of course, Peter and Pam had stationed themselves. Having deposited me, Campino jumped the string and galloped merrily back to the lorry, leaving me to stagger back, soaked to the skin.

Belton was rather more satisfactory, with Regent Lad and Ben fourth and fifth in the three-star CIC. I had hardly had a single show jump or cross-country fault all spring, bar the dunking at Somerley, and it all seemed slightly too good to be true.

Regent Lad kept up the good work at the two-star three-day event in Compiègne, France. Although he was qualified to do three-star level, he's a chunky horse that hadn't learned to gallop properly and I wanted to give him a bit more mileage at a lower level. He did a very good dressage and was only beaten by Michael Jung and River of Joy, who went on to win.

Jules put in a new all-weather gallop that spring, which was great and meant that we were preparing horses solely off the property instead of having to travel. Previously, I had used the Baldings' gallops in Kingsclere, the next village, or gone over to Marcus Tregoning at Lambourn. It takes a while with a new gallop to assess how much work you should be doing and, in hindsight, I realised that I probably hadn't done enough to get the four-star horses properly fit that spring.

***

I was quietly optimistic of a good Badminton because I knew that if Ben went as well as he was capable of on the flat, he would be competitive. I knew he was a good cross-country horse, albeit slightly unproven at that distance and difficulty, and that he could show jump well. I rated him as one of the best I'd ever ridden, even though he hadn't yet hit the heights – it all just needed to happen. I must have exuded confidence without realising it as, following a dinner party at the Lloyd Webbers, Lady Carolyn Warren, wife of John, told me afterwards that she regretted not backing me. 'You tipped yourself without knowing it,' she told me.

At Badminton, I parked the lorry in my usual spot in the field beside the vicarage. The year before, I had invited the vicar and his wife, Christopher and Mary Mulholland, for a drink and Christopher started apologising that the grass was so long. I flippantly asked if he had a lawn mower and at 7.30am the next morning, I heard him outside delivering it. I mowed around my lorry and, next thing, Zara Phillips had stuck her head out and asked if I could do hers as well. Then Alice Fox-Pitt appeared in her pyjamas wanting to know what the din was, so I did the area around William's lorry which was parked next door to mine, and then around the 'passion wagon' of Mary King's owner Gilly Robinson. This year, the vicar lent the mower without prompting, and it's become a tradition. Gilly took a photo of me mowing and stuck up a poster saying: 'Lawn mower, competitive rates, no job too small' and stuck it on my lorry.

Milo was to be my warm-up act. I had thought of taking him to Kentucky, but his dressage seemed to have gone downhill and I couldn't see the point of going all the way to America if he wasn't going to do a good test. I was keen to have a crack at getting points in the HSBC Classics series, which is worth quite a bit of money to the five most successful riders across the world's four-stars, so Riley would be going to Kentucky instead. He was packed off in good time and, as I thought it was a bit much to ask of Fay, as she had only just joined us, I employed Nicky Fleming, a former Badminton rider and ex-employee of Heather Holgate, so that I felt he would be in good hands. Charlie would still be at Badminton with those horses.

Milo, somewhat predictably, earned a rather dismal 64 for his dressage test but he did try, bless him. He was so uptight that it was a bit of a 'sit and pray' job and when he gets nervous, he doesn't have the best canter.

Ben, who was last to go on Saturday afternoon, scored 36.8 to be fourth, behind three British girls who are all brilliant in the dressage arena: Ruth Edge, Piggy French and Laura Collett, who was only 21 and hadn't even been born when I won my first Badminton. Ben got a bit tight, which spoilt the test a little, but he compensated by looking so attractive and moving so well. His lateral work – half-passes, flying changes, and so on – are so good that he picks up marks all the way through the test and you are really able to ride him.

The current four-star dressage tests are not nice to ride. There is too much counter-canter, which seems to me to be such negative training, and they don't flow that well. I've told Chris Bartle who designed them that I don't like the tests, but he points out that the Germans can do them!

The general impression of the cross-country course was that very little had changed from the year before, except that it was in the reverse direction, which was disappointing. No rider ever likes to be caught muttering about the Badminton course in case they look silly afterwards – I once opined on the BBC that I thought Frank Weldon's coffin was kinder that year only to find myself upside down in it twice – but we all know that this is the richest event in the world and a lot of us felt that a bit more thought and effort should have been put into making it interesting.

Milo is a real cross-country machine and gave me a good feel of the course. I was a bit surprised, though, that by the time we came away from the Lake, at around seven minutes, he wasn't as full of running as he should have been. I couldn't understand it, as he is normally such a galloping machine. I got eight time-faults on him, partly because he'd jumped into the Lake so exuberantly that I had to take a long route, but it was slightly worrying that he felt tired at the end and that perhaps the horses weren't as fit as they should be. However, in between my two rides, I was asked to do some commentating for the BBC, and I noticed that quite a few horses looked tired, both after the Lake and especially after Huntsman's Close, so perhaps it was a general thing. Even Andrew's horse Nereo looked a little jaded, and he is a class galloper.

The gap between two rides at a three-day can feel like a very long time to fill. I often go to sleep or meet friends, but I also find it interesting to watch the competition. However, the important thing when watching is to be aware of whom you're looking at. If you watch a stream of inexperienced riders, you can get a completely different picture and start wondering if you should change your plan, which isn't always wise. By the time I set out for my second ride, Ruth had had a refusal in Huntsman's Close on Two Thyme, and Laura and Piggy had incurred a few time-faults. Ingrid Klimke, who was also in close contention, had had a fall, as had Oli Townend on Ashdale Cruise Master at the Quarry, and the course was held while Elizabeth (Izab) Power of Ireland was taken to Frenchay Hospital at Bristol after being knocked unconscious.

I knew Ben was capable of all the direct routes, and that if I could get round with just a few time-faults, I would still be right up there. I was having a really smooth ride, and he was feeling confident and full of energy. The only slightly dodgy moment I had in the first half of the course was at the fence over the Vicarage Ditch where I just felt his concentration wander and had to jam my leg on. I gave him a slap behind the saddle to say 'Oi, wake up', and he jumped the next fence, the Dewpond, really well.

I was tempted to take the direct route at the double of open corners, having done so successfully on Milo, but because most people had taken the long route and it wasn't that expensive on time, I decided to play safe and do the same. Ben also had a bit of a look at the second flower-bed fence at the Hollow and broke a bit of timber off.

He had been lobbing along easily with his lovely long stride, but when we got to the Lake, I had a bit of difficulty manoeuvring him on the turn to the direct route. It occurred to me that he wasn't feeling as fresh as I'd like, and there were about four minutes to go. I took the pressure off for a bit on the mild but steady uphill pull from the Wadsworth Barrels fence after the Lake to Huntsman's Close. By this stage, Ben was definitely feeling tired but we were still on time and he jumped the accuracy fences through the wood well.

Then we turned for the pull up to the Quarry fence and Ben started to labour, so much so that I began to debate whether I should pull him up. The log into the Quarry is a big fence with a significant drop and I started wondering about the long route. I was in a quandary because if I took the long one, I'd be chucking the competition. These thoughts were all whizzing around in my head in those few hundred yards but eventually I decided that as I'd got that far, I'd got to give it a go, and I felt I hadn't pressurised him too much.

I let him take his time and, as I turned to the log, I gave him a couple of slaps down his shoulder to wake him up. Thankfully I managed to see a decent stride, and he pricked his ears and picked up. It seemed easier to keep going on the quick route, but I really was hoping and praying because it's impossible to see a stride to the log at the bottom of the slope in the Quarry – you just have to let it come to you. Ben wasn't on the best of strides, but he managed to chip in a tiny shuffle, got his front end over and dragged the rest of himself over it. All I could think was 'I've got to get you going and out of here as soon as possible.'

On instinct, I picked up my whip and gave him three slaps behind the saddle. I'm always aware that this doesn't look good, and when I saw the replay I did think that I'd used my stick a bit, but what was encouraging was that Ben responded and picked up really willingly. There were just three more fences to jump, and they were on a slightly downhill run, so I just let him freewheel and gave him another slap down the shoulder nearing the next fence. His ears were still flicking back and forth, listening to me, so although he was tired he wasn't out of it. With the end in sight, he pricked his ears and jumped the last three fences to finish, amazingly only with 6.8 time-faults.

Charlie grabbed Ben to wash him down and cool him. After a few minutes I could see that he was fine and looking brighter, but there was no time for a post-mortem because, as I was last on course, I was whisked off to a press conference. I was lying in second place, just behind Germany's Marina Köhncke, who is a lovely girl and also recently returned to this level of competition. Funnily enough, the last time she'd been at Badminton, in 1994 when I won on Horton Point, she led me after the dressage and then fell at the second Luckington Lane crossing with Sundance Kid.

I wasn't disappointed at not being in the lead because I was just thrilled to get the horse back in one piece and be second, but during the press conference it was announced that there had been a miscalculation of Marina's time-penalties – she had been held on course, which often leads to discrepancies – and I was actually in the lead. However, I couldn't be too celebratory, not only because Marina was pretty cheesed off but also because my lead was so slender. In an extraordinary result, there were 12 of us within a rail of winning, a statistic I have never heard of before.

Although Andrew Hoy won Kentucky in 2006 from eighth place after cross-country because there were so many dramas in the show jumping, that is an extremely unusual result. The winner most usually comes from the first three riders – but here it could be any one of 12, and the first of them to jump a clear round would be in the driving seat and putting pressure on everyone else, including me.

Winning was obviously far from a given – I had a tired horse and there were some good jumpers breathing down my neck, not just Marina, but also Piggy, Laura, Andrew Nicholson, Mary King on Imperial Cavalier, Nicola Wilson on her rubber-ball of a horse Opposition Buzz, and the Swedish rider Niklas Lindback on a beautiful horse called Mister Pooh. Yet, without being over-confident, I somehow had a feeling that it was going to go my way.

It's a funny thing, but every time I've won Badminton, it's been a bit of a story. The first time, in 1980, I was a complete unknown and the first foreigner to win for 15 years. Then, in 1994, it was the Horton Point story – a horse I'd never ridden before and the possibility of life-changing prize-money for his owners, Lynne and Ros Bevan. And the third time, in 1996, was the culmination of the Bertie Blunt saga when I wondered if I would ever gain the win this horse deserved and his owners expected. Now, here I was coming back out of an eight-year retirement to ride at Badminton, and I couldn't help thinking: 'This would make a really good story.'

It wasn't impossible. Ben is a good jumper and, although no horse is guaranteed to jump clear, he hadn't had a rail down all spring. When I got back to the stables, I met Charlie, who had looked after him immaculately. She told me that by the time she took him back to his stable, he was on his toes and dragged her the whole way. This in itself encouraged me that the horse was fine.

Brendan Corscadden was over for Badminton and was due to be going back to Ireland that night, but there was some consternation in the Irish camp about Izab's fall – fortunately she had come round by that stage – and he was umming and aahing about what to do. I told him: 'You'll kick yourself if you're not here and I win.' Frances Stanley, Cassie Neville's sister-in-law, was there as well, also debating about whether to go home, plus Jo Preston and Peter Vela, so we cracked open some champagne – I'm usually superstitious about doing this before the end of the competition, but Peter likes it. I ended up cooking supper – steaks on the barbecue and salad – and it was a really nice relaxed evening.

All I could focus on was the next day's show jumping. I warned Peter: 'It's just so close,' and he reminded me: 'Well, you're in the best position – they've all got to get past you.' It was true – they could only win if I lost it. Somehow I managed to have a good night's sleep and, next day, Ben was as lively as a box of birds and not at all stiff. The team physio, Leigh Miller, had a look but he was in good shape and trotted up well at the horse inspection. He'd had fluids overnight, which had aided his muscle recovery, and I felt that we'd done everything we could.

It's a long day when you're in the lead, but it does go quickly. You're half longing for your round to happen and half dreading it. I just had to take the attitude if it's meant to be, it's meant to be. I knew I would do everything I could to ride well enough to have a clear round, I knew the horse was a good jumper, and I knew I was used to jumping under pressure and that I could handle it. Still, it was considerably more pressure than I'd been used to for more than a decade!

Luis Alvarez-Cervera, a Spaniard who used to show jump

and turned his hand to eventing in the 1990s, is now our team jumping coach and he was busy warming up Andrew, but I didn't want to do too much on Ben, as he was jumping well, despite his exertions the day before. By the time I went into the arena, I knew that Marina had had fences down and a time-fault, but Piggy went clear on Jakata, so I had no leeway for error and had to jump clear to win. I can't really remember how I felt at that stage, but I knew it was important to stay totally focused, relax and breathe normally.

I was almost too relaxed coming to the first fence and Ben just clipped the rail with his hind legs but, happily, it stayed in place. That woke us both up and, while I wouldn't have said I produced the most classic show jumping round ever, it never really felt in doubt. Rather like my round at the Sydney Olympics on Eye Spy 11 years ago, I was aware that I was perhaps being a little over-cautious, but Ben was so focused that I didn't want to break his rhythm by speeding him up. The last fence had caught out a few and I knew I had to stay totally focused to the end. He jumped the last fence really well and I galloped for the finish, but I was almost reluctant to celebrate in case I'd incurred time-faults.

Winning felt surreal. It was an achievement that shouldn't have been possible. As I cantered around the arena, with all those thousands of people getting to their feet and cheering, I actually picked out Peter Vela, who was with Lucy Sangster, among all the faces in the stands. And as I came out of the arena, Lucinda Green, a mate for so long, rushed up to congratulate me but all I could do was shrug. I simply couldn't think of anything to say because I couldn't really take in how it had happened.

I had imagined that I'd get a bit emotional and, ironically, my biggest worry had been that if I won, I wouldn't able to speak and would look a blithering idiot. I was determined not to do a Nicolas Touzaint – when he won in 2008, he flung himself all over the place in a fit of Gallic emotion – and, for me, I was amazingly composed. I have got worse about this as I've got older, as the more you do, the more you realise how difficult it is to win major events. When I first won Badminton in 1980, I didn't entirely take in the enormity of the achievement.

One of the nicest things was how genuinely pleased everyone seemed. It was heart-warming and quite humbling. I have always got on well with the British public and the media, who gave me great coverage, but it would only be natural that they want Brits to win their major event. Piggy, who finished second, was gutted, but she is a hugely talented rider destined to be the next big thing in British eventing. She's also got more than 20 years on me!

Straight away, Jules got into gear and sprang a barbecue back at the yard. As it was the Easter weekend, some friends had stayed away and gone to Eddy Stibbe's place, where he had organised a lavish lunch party with a big screen to watch all the action on both cross-country and show jumping days. Rodney Powell, Alex Franklin and Jackie Green were there and as soon as they realised I might win, they got ready to leap in their cars to come over to Headley. The Baldings and Lloyd Webbers came over too, and, as it was a freezing evening, everyone crowded round the flaming braziers that Jules seemed to have magicked out of nowhere.

Unfortunately for me, the timing was terrible as I was due to leave the house at 5am for Kentucky, so I didn't manage to get to my own party until about 9pm. I also wanted a bit of time to myself. I drove home from Badminton on my own, which was nice because I wanted to absorb the whole thing quietly. When I got home, I suddenly felt knackered and all I wanted to do was watch the tape of my round and examine the results. When you're in the heat of the moment, you're so focused that you have no idea what everyone else has done, or even what you've done yourself. You're so stunned, that it's nice to have a little while to sit back and reflect.

* * *

No high can last for ever, and I did come down to earth quite quickly. Next morning, bleary-eyed, I met up at the airport with Mary King, who had finished third at Badminton, William, Oli and Yogi Briesner, the British team's Swedish performance manager.

We flew to Cincinnati where there was a long wait for the connecting flight, by tiny plane, to Lexington, so we decided we'd go for a beer and a pizza. We were having a great time, chatting away, when something made me ask what time it was. We thought we had sited ourselves just outside the gate for the flight, but, to our horror, it was the wrong one. So we ran like hell through the airport to find they'd shut the flight. The plane was still there so we ran up and tapped on the window to get the attendants' attention and, miraculously, they let us on.

Yogi kindly let me travel in the British team car and, as we were all staying at the same hotel, the Marriott, I joined forces with them. We went to see the horses and discovered they had all been moved to the indoor school as there had been a tornado warning. The Americans seem to be able to predict weather conditions rather more accurately than the rest of us and there was indeed a tornado on its way. Next morning, we woke up to be told that we weren't allowed out of the hotel. There were announcements that we should all leave our rooms and go downstairs, where we just sat listening to the wind howling and watching on television the extraordinary destruction in the area.

Fortunately, the tornado went off course and eventually it

passed, but there was an incredible amount of rain and the cross-country course was virtually under water. The coffin fence had turned into a raging torrent – you couldn't even see the lines of the ditch. We did wonder how on earth the event would be run, but the water got pumped out.

Realistically, I knew I wasn't going to win Kentucky – or, at least, that Riley wouldn't be an obvious winner – but the idea was to try and get a reasonable placing and some HSBC Classics points to add to the 15 for winning Badminton. Riley did a reasonable dressage, though not as good as at the previous year's World Equestrian Games, to score 51. However, the cross-country is usually influential at Kentucky, so I was hopeful.

If anything, I thought the course was at least as difficult as it had been for the Games and quite tough. Derek di Grazia, who took over from Mike Etherington-Smith, seemed to have made maximum use of the hills, but I was happy with it. It was another true four-star course, the same double of brushes at the end and this time I was determined to take the short route.

I wasn't due to run until the second half of the day, by which time the course had caused quite a lot of trouble. Riley didn't feel quite as fluent as I'd hoped now he had more mileage under his belt, but we were on time at the minute markers. Then, in the same way as Ben had begun to struggle at Badminton, I felt Riley tiring at around the eight-minute marker. We got to the infamous double brushes, three from home, and I did wonder about taking the long option but I told myself not to be stupid – he'll be fine, he's jumping well. Unfortunately, he ran out at the first part of the complex, jumping to the side and across the ditch. I felt cross with him and with myself. I couldn't believe I'd travelled all that way just to stuff up – we'd have been third without the run-out – but you've got to compose yourself and get to the end.

Things went downhill after that. Riley is not the greatest at trotting up at the best of times, as he has a tendency to shuffle, but he usually finishes the cross-country totally sound. However, he didn't look quite right that evening. Next morning, I lunged him on the all-weather arena and he passed the trot-up, but I thought I had detected a bit of heat in a front leg, so I asked Tim Randle, a British vet, to run the scanner over it. Sure enough, there was a tiny hole in the tendon. No wonder he stopped; he must have been starting to feel his leg, because it was so out of character for him to refuse.

I withdrew him from the competition, which was a major disappointment after the high of Badminton. However, the rest of my group had a good competition, especially Mary who finished first and second on Kings Temptress, a horse she had bred herself, and Fernhill Urco. Like Andrew, Mary has been around for most of my career and, like him, she works incredibly hard, and I always feel heartened by the fact although there are so many talented young riders around, the senior riders are still holding their own.

* * *

As a precaution, I had Ben scanned two weeks later and he was fine. I gave him a few weeks off, the idea being to take him to Aachen for the three-star CIC team competition and then to Burghley. His first run back was a quiet one, an open intermediate class at Little Downham in June. We led the dressage, show jumped clear and went quietly round the cross-country for ten time-faults and fourth place.

Soon after, I was doing some cantering work with him when he pulled up feeling a little bit lame. There was nothing obvious to see, and after a week, I got my vet Buffy Shirley-Beavan to look at him. She scanned him and found a small hole in the tendon, which was a major blow. To cap it all, Regent Lad

didn't feel right either, and it transpired that he had some liga-
ments that needed tidying in his fetlock. The operation effec-
tively put him out for the rest of the season as well. So my
best three horses were now all off the road. Nightmare. But
the good news, if there could be said to be any, was that all
their injuries had been caught early enough and I was told they
should all be recovered well in time for the London Olympics.
The bad news was that only Ben, thanks to his Badminton
win, was qualified, owing to the FEI's draconian qualifying
rules. How a horse can win a medal at a world championships,
as Riley did, and not retain that qualification for two years for
the Olympics seems over the top.

The rest of the season was going to be all down to Campino
and Milo. I took the former to Saumur in the spring, where he
was second in the two-star CIC behind Nicolas Touzaint who
was riding his 2008 Badminton winner, Hildago d'Ile, a somewhat exasperating result. However, I liked Campino enough
to consider him a long shot for the Olympics and to give him
a chance to get there.

It seemed ideal to give him a practice run at the long-awaited
Olympic test event at Greenwich Park in July. There has probably been more written and said about Greenwich as an
equestrian Olympic site than there was about either Atlanta or
Hong Kong, two other controversial sites. However, because
the 2012 Olympics weren't remotely on my radar when it was
announced in 2005 that Greenwich would be the venue, much
of the discussion has gone over my head and I didn't have any
preconceived ideas. It sounded both a nightmare venue, and
yet very exciting.

Greenwich was chosen because of its proximity to the main
stadium and press centre, a condition of the original bid. The
idea was to create iconic pictures of horses and riders against a
backdrop of the Queen's House, the Thames and Canary Wharf,

in much the same way that the arcing high-diver became the image of the Barcelona Olympics. This has certainly worked, but there are obvious severe space restrictions, not to mention furious local opposition and the dismay of some of the horse world who expected the Olympic equestrian events to have been at an established venue like Hickstead or Badminton.

Certainly, I can't see why they didn't opt for Windsor: it would more or less count as a London venue, and there is plenty of space, plus the striking backdrop. Repairing the ground there would only have been a fraction of the cost of what has been spent on Greenwich, but LOCOG (the London Organising Committee for the Olympic Games) have stuck to their guns. Whatever problem has been thrown at them, they've just paid out to solve it.

Strangely enough, riders were, for once, probably the least vocal and I think many of us are excited about being, for the first time in history, in the centre of everything. I think it will be a great competition; people will just have to adjust to the idea that it's not going to be a Badminton or a Burghley. It will suit the riders and horses that can adapt the best.

The New Zealand team – nations had been invited to bring up to three riders – was to be me on Campino, Andrew on Nicky Salmon's young horse Viscount George and Clarke on Incognito. We had the full raft of officials, and Jock and Caroline were there to watch, so it was another good bonding exercise.

The whole thing was a brilliant feat of organisation. The directions to the first check-in station were good and we found it easily and unloaded the horses. Our gear was put into a van and we were escorted onto the compound; by the time we got there, our kit was already unloaded. The stables were fantastic; they were raised above the ground so all the horse pee could be drained away and not damage the grass – one of the many strict conditions placed on the organisers by Greenwich Council – and they were airy and cool. We were really impressed.

We then went to explore. The first thing we noticed was the steepness of the hill, and the second was a pub, the Greenwich Tavern, right outside the park gates. The whole of the eventing community was in there in no time, and it was a fantastic atmosphere but I hope they get in more staff this year!

We were staying in a hotel only 10 minutes away, and it was all rather a novelty. We checked out the night spots of Greenwich; it was all great fun. The night after cross-country I went to a fund-raiser for the Christchurch earthquake victims. There were quite a few New Zealand legends there – All Blacks including Sean Fitzpatrick and Anton Oliver, plus Brendan Cole from *Strictly Come Dancing*.

The dressage took place on an extraordinary arena, which was built up on a platform in front of the Inigo Jones-designed Queen's House and the Maritime Museum. We were all happy with the all-weather surface, but the show jumpers, who had their test event after us, found it dead and rather like porridge – it took a further six months for the FEI to sign-off an improved recipe.

I thought Campino could go really well. I had him in a double bridle to get him up together more and he's an easy horse that doesn't take much working in. However, I think I must have overdone it, and the combination of that and the very hot weather, exacerbated by being on a sand surface which tends to give out more heat, seemed to take the edge off him. He felt lacklustre and instead of the double bridle lifting him up, he curled over and leant on it in a tired sort of way, so we didn't get a very good mark. I was annoyed with myself for over-cooking him and now he has a maximum of 20 minutes warm-up.

We were all dying to walk the cross-country, not so much for the fences, which we knew would be small portables brought in for the competition, but for the terrain. The fences were irrelevant really, and most people had clear rounds anyway, it was the twisting and steepness that was the test. Riding it was a hectic five minutes – the real thing will be nearly twice as long – which felt like being on a speedway track.

As I was well down the order after the dressage, I wasn't going to go all out. I went reasonably quickly, but comfortably, and ended up with 10 time-faults. I was really pleased with Campino, and he show jumped clear in both rounds.

The crowds, which included a lot of excited, squealing schoolchildren who had been given free tickets, seemed quite close to the strings, but it all added to the atmosphere and I think most of us were pleasantly surprised by how well the course rode and the work that had been done on the ground. It was hot and, being in a river basin, there wasn't much breeze, but the cooling facilities provided were excellent.

The most depressing thing, after such a well-organised day, was when I was walking back to the stables after the cross-country and a smartly dressed local woman with a refined voice said to me: 'Please go home. I like the horses and the sport, but you are not welcome here.' It felt like quite a rejection.

There was a bit of a local protest, with a few placard holders outside the gate each day. They were somewhat intimidated when Piggy's father, the very tall Wally French, towered over them and jokingly pointed out that he thought the 'Piggy go home' placard was a bit personal. I can't help thinking that if this was Auckland, people would be thrilled to have an Olympic competition in their back yard. It makes me cross that they can't just get into the spirit of it a bit. The pub was getting masses of custom – more in three days than they'd had all year, probably – and yet we heard one of the grumpy bar staff say:

'I can't wait until this lot leaves.' If they could change their attitude, they might really enjoy it.

The test event was a bizarre competition. It had a big event feel, and yet you knew it was really nothing except a practice. The Brits won, with the individual 'medals' going to Piggy French (gold), Michael Jung (silver) and Pippa Funnell (bronze), but we were quite happy with that. Who wants to win the dress rehearsal!

There was a lot of talk about the type of horse needed for the cross-country – quick and rideable – but I still think the dressage will be really important. Nowadays, the top horses are good at all three phases, so it's no good thinking you can just catch up afterwards, as everyone found to their cost in Hong Kong. Certainly the only way to beat Michael Jung will be in the dressage, but I think that is possible. I just hope that we have some fair judging – everyone gets away with murder at times, and when you get to the top of the sport you sort of earn a little leniency, but it's important that there is no ludicrous scoring that distorts the competition.

***

The next big excitement was Zara Phillips's and Mike Tindall's wedding in Edinburgh. I was thrilled to receive an invitation, and it turned into a great outing. Bettina Hoy, who had been staying with me on and off in the summer, organised the hotel and a large group of us flew up, including Rodney, Alex, Oli, Izab, and Dan and Tanya. Zara and I are both godparents to Jazz, Dan and Tanya's daughter, and she was a bridesmaid. There were also several from the racing world, including the champion jockey AP McCoy.

Despite all the security and the tight arrangements – we had to be at the church a long time in advance – it just felt like a lovely, normal family wedding, even if it was one where the Queen was sitting a couple of pews away.

After that, we were straight into Gatcombe, where Milo played a blinder and came fourth in the British Open. Admittedly, the best British horses were absent in preparation for the European Championships, but that didn't lessen the satisfaction of a Kiwi monopoly – just like old times. Andrew was first and second on Nereo and Avebury and Jock was third on Clifton Lush. The *Horse & Hound* report said: 'The final line-up in the British Open was like a throwback to the 1990s when the brilliant horsemen from New Zealand ruled the world.'

Burghley was another good Kiwi result: Andrew was second on Nereo and eighth on Avebury, Caroline was fourth on the amazing Lenamore, who we all hope will still be enjoying the game come the Olympics, when he will be 19, and Jock was fifth on Clifton Lush. Dear old Milo did not disgrace himself with 14th place with a double clear – he moved up 32 places after dressage!

William Fox-Pitt won for the sixth time, overtaking our joint record with Ginny Elliot of five wins, so that has now provided me with another ambition. I would love a Burghley win to complete this second part of my career.

I can't take any credit for it, as I wasn't in the team, but the next weekend New Zealand scored a satisfying win in the Olympic qualifier for the Pan-Asian nations at Blenheim, beating Japan and Australia. It didn't really matter what happened, as we were already qualified after our bronze medal in Kentucky, but Andrew, Wayne, Jock and Lucy Jackson all finished in the top 20 and it was another occasion when we all got on well together and looked like a proper professional team outfit.

Campino came into his own in the autumn and earned his Olympic credentials at Boekelo. He had an annoying run-out in the young horse CIC at Blenheim when lying second behind William Fox-Pitt and Oslo in the dressage. Luckily, though, he was still qualified to go Boekelo, and he did another really good dressage test there to be equal first with Dutchman Raf Kooremans.

Just as I was getting ready for the cross-country, the heavens opened, turning the ground into a slushy, slippery mess which meant you had to be careful on the turns. Campino had been getting quite strong, but Bettina lent me a drop noseband; it had a chain, in a soft leather cover, which went under the nose, and it made a huge difference as the horse didn't argue with me as much.

I was worried about the seventh fence, which had been influential – Zara was eliminated there. It was in a clearing and was approached off a left turn with two strides to a tall, skinny brush. Horses had to be really honest and, having had the problem at Blenheim at a triple brush which was much wider than this, I was a bit concerned. However, Campino locked onto the fence and jumped it without a moment's hesitation and, two fences later, he was brilliant at another skinny fence at the water. I had a fantastic ride all the way and finished with only 2.4 time-faults, good enough to put me in the lead for the second year running.

I had a fence in hand over the German rider Andreas Dibowski – Raf Kooremans had dropped out of contention with time-faults – but I had a feeling this wouldn't be enough. Campino hadn't jumped clear recently and he had had a long and busy season. Unfortunately, he used up his one life right at the first fence, but I told myself not to panic. He was jumping really well after that, but there was a combination which faced into the crowd which took his attention, so he had a rail down there. He jumped the rest beautifully and we ended up third, behind Andreas and Irish rider Camilla Speirs.

It was disappointing to have another Boekelo win slip away, but if anyone had told me beforehand that I was going to be third, I'd have been delighted. Campino secured his all-important Olympic qualification, and I think he could be a major contender, along with Ben who is, thankfully, now back in work.

And what of the medal prospects for London 2012? Last year there was a lot of discussion about the sort of horse that could best adapt to Greenwich, but while it will not be ideal to ride a strong-puller, the emphasis will be on riders that are able to keep up the pace and ride the course fast.

The team medals will be fought out between Britain, Germany, New Zealand and Australia – anything outside of those four would be a turn-up for the books – and the individuals will most likely come from these countries too. Having said that, Stefano Brecciaroli of Italy has a wonderful partnership with Apollo Van De Wendi Kurt Hoeve – they finished fifth and best of the non-Germans at the 2011 European Championships. Mister Pooh, the ride of Niklas Lindback of Sweden, is a horse I really like, though we haven't seen anything of him since he won the World Cup qualifier in Malmö last August.

Britain will, as usual, start favourite. William Fox-Pitt has an abundance of talent in his string at the moment and the choice of several horses, and Mary King and Piggy French would be other favourites for the podium.

Germany, defending their 2008 gold, could again field a strong team though they seem to have sold a couple of horses and their better medal chance will be in the individual with the stand-out champion Michael Jung – the course should really suit his sharp little La Biosthetique Sam. Germany improved significantly during my time out of the sport under the management of Chris Bartle, though any trainer is only as good as the team he has got and Chris took over when a new breed of rider was coming through, such as Andreas Dibowski and Dirk Schrade. These guys have embraced the modern sport, and short format has helped them; Germany quickly cottoned-on to what was needed and bred a lot more really nice Thoroughbred-type horses, and now a lot of people want to buy from Germany, rather than Germany buying from us.

Australia, bizarrely, did not get a team through during the 2011 qualification process but should still be able to make one up out of its qualifying individuals. They have been in this underdog position before and have an uncanny knack of being able to bounce back to where they need to be at an Olympic Games. Stuart Tinney, Christopher Burton and Sam Griffiths should all have a live chance of making the cut this time.

I'd expect two former Australians, Philip Dutton and Boyd Martin, to lead the US effort. From a personal perspective it would be great if Jules Stiller can get on the team; she has worked very hard and I am pleased to have been able to help her consistently improve her results. In a further unashamed bias, I would be delighted to see my stable jockey Sydney Dufresne on the French squad for the first time. He is remaining in France this season and we will miss him at Headley Stud.

We have the basis of a strong New Zealand team and Andrew and myself have individual chances. A lot has been written about Blyth Tait's 'comeback', although when he resumed competitive riding last spring he did not set himself the same deadline-driven schedule as I did, and only planned to ride a couple of horses when he first arrived in the UK. He was disappointed about early progress and, at the time of writing, wasn't qualified for the Olympics but he has a four-star horse, is very determined, and was aiming to go to Badminton where a top five placing would put him right back in contention. You can never discount riders of his class.

Anything can happen between now and London 2012.

Greenwich is a new venue for everyone and there are three very different days to get through – that variety is what makes our sport so great.

People talk about this Olympics as a watershed, and I know some people will be expecting me to retire – again. The original deal with New Zealand Bloodstock was to sell the horses after London, but I am keeping an open mind. The lure of top competition and the competitive instinct doesn't seem to be lessening with age. I am as excited about 2012 as I was about the ill-fated 1980 Games, and the whole thing still means as much to me as it ever did.

I'm still loving the sport; I have lovely horses to ride and a brilliant and generous sponsor; I still have my fitness, touch wood, even if I have to take it much more seriously than I did 30 years ago; I have loads of friends around me and the support of my family. I know I'm a lucky man. I honestly have no idea what the future holds after the Olympics – except that it will be something to do with a horse.

ACKNOWLEDGEMENTS

WHEN I RETIRED from eventing in 2000 after the Sydney Olympics I thought my life would take on a much quieter aspect. How wrong could I have been? From becoming a full-time racehorse trainer and breeder in the North Island of NZ, then a move to the quieter South Island, the breakdown of my marriage and then a return to top-level international eventing, my life in the last twelve years has been anything but quiet.

When Susan Lamb approached me about doing another book, my initial reaction was a definite no! But Susan is very persuasive and eventually talked me round so it is with thanks to her that this book came about.

It would also not have been possible without good friend Kate Green who gently bullied me into telling this story and made sense of it. There were many long evenings, a lot of laughs and a few glasses of wine to get this finished. Also thanks to Pippa Cuckson who proofread this and made valuable contributions.

The team at Orion have been very helpful and encouraging and special thanks must go to Alex Hippisley-Cox and Lucinda McNeile, the patient editor, in bringing this to life.

A special thanks must go to all the people who have worked for me over the years to make my life with horses possible, and especially at the moment head girl Charlie Gardiner and my PA Becky Elvin who between them make sure that things run smoothly.

This story would not have happened without the friendship and support of Peter and Phillip Vela and NZ Bloodstock who supported me when I was training racehorses and backed me without hesitation in my endeavour to get back to top-level eventing. I will always be grateful to them.

And finally to my family, Lauren and James, ex-wife and dearest friend Carolyn, who have had to put up with me gallivanting round the world, but always backed me with my dreams, and to my dear parents Norman and Lenore who have been a support from day one.

It has been a hell of a ride.

PICTURE CREDITS

21. Photograph by kind permission of © Horse & Hound/ IPC+ Syndication.
22. Photograph by kind permission of Mike Capps, Kappa Photography.
23. Photograph by kind permission of © Horse & Hound/ IPC+ Syndication.
24. Photograph by Trevor Meeks, by kind permission of © Horse & Hound / IPC+ Syndication.
25. Photograph by Trevor Meeks, by kind permission of © Horse & Hound / IPC+ Syndication.
26. Photograph by Trevor Meeks, by kind permission of © Horse & Hound / IPC+ Syndication.
27. Photograph author's own.
28. Photograph author's own.
29. Photograph author's own.
30. Photograph by Trevor Meeks, by kind permission of © Horse & Hound / IPC+ Syndication.
31. Photograph by Trevor Meeks, by kind permission of © Horse & Hound / IPC+ Syndication.
32. Photograph by Trevor Meeks, by kind permission of © Horse & Hound / IPC+ Syndication.
33. Photograph by Trevor Meeks, by kind permission of © Horse & Hound / IPC+ Syndication.
34. Photograph by Trevor Meeks, by kind permission of © Horse & Hound / IPC+ Syndication.
35. Photograph by kind permission of Race Images (New Zealand).
36. Photograph by kind permission of Race Images (New Zealand).
37. Photograph by kind permission of Race Images (New Zealand).
38. Photograph by kind permission of Race Images (New Zealand).

39. Photograph author's own.
40. Photograph by kind permission of Al Crook
    Photography.
41. Photograph by kind permission of Libby Law
    Photography (New Zealand).
42. Photograph author's own.
43. Photograph by kind permission of Kit Houghton.
44. Photograph by kind permission of Nico Morgan
    Photography.

INDEX

Delta 90, 91–2
Derby, Lady 20
Derby (formerly Hamilton), Mary 10, 14, 30, 38, 40, 41, 165, 167
father 11
di Grazia, Derek 12, 236
Diamond Hall Red 124, 125, 126, 127, 130, 131
Dibowski, Andreas 170–1, 200, 211, 244, 245
Dick, Daisy 200
Disco 140, 146
Dixon (formerly Straker), Karen 65, 67, 77, 90, 126
Dobson, Keith and Martin 52
Doddington Park 72
Donckers, Karin 138, 190
Done For Fun 60, 73, 74, 76
dope tests 121–2
Double Take 69, 82, 84, 85, 150
Double Trigger 75–6
Douglas, Sheryl 33
Drummond-Hay, Anneli 1, 119
Duff (formerly O'Brien), Mel 46, 50, 53, 58, 63, 221
Duff, Mick 58, 59, 63, 221
Dufresne, Sydney 223, 246
Dujardin, Charlotte 210, 223–4, 227
Dunwoody, Richard 63
Durand, Pierre 69–70
Duroy, Marie-Christine 99
Dusky Moon 171, 172
Dutch, the 91
Dutton, Phillip 110, 170, 190, 246
Duvander, Erik 39, 49, 164, 206
Dynes Hall 51, 73

Edgar, Ted 42
Edge, Ruth 227, 228
Elizabeth II, HRH Queen 26, 119, 243
Elliot (formerly Holgate; Leng), Ginny 26–7, 28–9, 31, 34, 38, 41, 42, 45, 46, 48, 54, 55, 65, 67, 72, 77, 87, 126, 165, 176–7, 203, 243

Elsworth, David 59
Elvin, Becky 221, 223
Emerson, Denny 12
Empire Rose 135
Enterprise 76
Enzed 130, 131
ERA (Event Riders Association) 119
Erhorn, Claus 54, 65
Ethereal 153
Etherington-Smith, Mike 130, 176, 210, 236
European Championships, 1987 61
European Championships, 1993 94
European Open Championships, 1995 98–9
European Open Championships, 1997 108–11
Event Riders Association (ERA) 119
Eventing 116, 129, 139
eventing in 1970s 19
Eye Spy 117, 124, 127, 131–2, 233

Face the Music 78, 80–1
Fair Lady 54
Fairbanks Bounce fence 40
Farrier see Nicholls, Andrew
Federation Equestre Internationale (FEI) 76, 118–20, 121, 129, 165, 177, 238, 240
scoring system 119–20, 121
Feld, Wolfgang 82–3
Felday Farmer 15
Felix Too 30, 32
Fenicio 155, 156, 157
Fernhill Urco 237
Ferry, Bryan 58–9
Fife, Nicoli 6, 10, 14
Finvarra 48, 54
Fitzpatrick, Sean 240
Fleishman (formerly Watkins), Torrance 12, 30, 46, 48, 54
Fleming, Nicky 226–7
Fletcher, Graham 50
Flint Curtis 192
Fontainebleau 27–8, 29
Foster, David 27, 111, 124

Mandiba 213
Manton racehorse training centre 174
Maoris 135
Marbella 57
Marcroix 70
Marius 171
Mark Todd Collection 183
Market Harborough 181
Martin, Boyd 246
Master Craftsman 29, 65, 72
May, Mimi 30, 32, 45, 128, 155
May, Tom 30, 45, 128, 155
Mayhill 70
Meade, Richard 13, 15, 18, 21, 23, 49
Meeks, Trevor 109, 139
Meggelen, Frans van 215
Mer du Sud 137
Merchant, Ismail 58–9
Mere, Wiltshire 49
Merely-a-Monarch 1
Merganser 24, 25
Merrill Lynch 55–6
Messiah 75, 76, 82, 83–4
Meyer, Joe 174, 175, 177
Michaelmas 132
Michaelmas Day (Mick) 49, 50, 75
Michelet, Pierre 171
Might Tango 14
Miller, Leigh 195, 232
Milo see Major Milestone
Milton 47, 84
Milton Tyson 30
Miners Frolic 191
Mister Pooh 231, 245
Mitchenor, Cindy 52
Monty see Southern Comfort
Moore, Owen 98, 203
Moreton-in-Marsh 87, 133
Mortanges, Charles Ferdinand Pahud
    de 70
Moscow Olympics, 1980 27, 247
Moss, Michael and Karen 160
Mossman 53
Mossman, Jan 12, 16
Mouse 194, 200, 202
Mr Maxwell 81

Mr Papagopolous 7
Mr Pete (pony) 135
Mr Smiffy 129
Mr Todd 61, 62, 63
Mt Maungnamui 58
Mulholland, Rev Christopher and
    Mary 226
Murdoch 9
Murdoch, David 33
Murphy Himself 71, 89
Murray River 53
Myross 55
Mystery Creek polo club 139, 140

Necarne, Northern Ireland, two-star
    event 74
Neiderer, Wally 38, 82, 110, 206
Nereo 210, 211, 228, 243
Never Dwell 14
Neville, Bobby 20, 59
Neville, Cassie and Hetty 20, 30
Neville, Penny 20
Neville family 28, 30
New Flavour 103
New York (city) 217–20
New York (horse) 129, 138
New York Marathon 208, 218–19,
    220
New York Marathon Club 217
New Zealand, South Island 159–60,
    161, 162
New Zealand Bloodstock 140, 153,
    166–7, 182, 195, 199, 247
    Royal Stakes 145
New Zealand European Open Cham-
    pionships team, 1997 108, 109,
    110
New Zealand Eventing 167
New Zealand Federation 10
New Zealand Horse Society 32, 61
New Zealand in 1960s 1, 2–7
New Zealand Olympic equestrian
    team
    1984 35, 38, 39, 40–1, 42, 43
    1988 61, 62, 64, 65–6, 67, 68
    1992 82, 83–4, 85